Awakening
the Heart

John Welwood

AWAKENING THE HEART

East/West Approaches
to Psychotherapy
and the Healing Relationship

NEW SCIENCE LIBRARY

Shambhala *Boston & London* 1985

NEW SCIENCE LIBRARY
An imprint of Shambhala Publications, Inc.
Horticultural Hall
300 Massachusetts Avenue
Boston, Massachusetts 02115

Library of Congress Cataloging in Publication Data
Main entry under title:
Awakening the heart.
   Bibliography: p.
   Includes index.
   1. Psychotherapist and patient. 2. Psychotherapy.
3. Psychotherapists—Mental health. 4. Meditation—
Therapeutic use. 5. East and West. I. Welwood,
John, 1943–
RC480.8.A9   1983   616,89'14   83-42807
ISBN 0-87773-237-X (pbk.)
ISBN 0-394-72182-9 (Random House: pbk.)

This book is dedicated to the great lineages of bodhisattvas, whose tireless efforts in behalf of all sentient beings are the inspiration for this work.

Contents

Introduction

The Eastern traditions and disciplines steadily taking root in our culture during the past few decades have finally begun to influence the practice of psychotherapy. This has happened as more and more health professionals are practicing meditation and applying their experience with it to their work with others.

The growing attraction of the Eastern teachings grows out of a widespread perception that Western psychology and medicine are incomplete both in their understanding of human nature and in their ability to promote health and well-being. What Western psychology has done well is to describe and analyze neurotic behavior—primarily in terms of childhood conditioning and family dynamics—and to develop therapeutic methods to help free people from bondage to their past. What Western therapists know much less about, however, is how the mind actually works, and how people can either perpetuate or heal their neurosis from within. Our general ignorance about the sources of health inside us has contributed to the crisis of modern health care (so that hospitals are usually too sterile to provide a truly healing environment, the major form of therapy for psychiatric patients is drug maintenance, many health providers suffer from burn-out, and the suicide rate among psychiatrists is notoriously one of the highest of all professions).

This book presents new perspectives on health and the healing relationship growing out of the cross-fertilization between Eastern meditative disciplines and Western psychological practice. The chapters are primarily practical and personal, rather than theoretical or technical. And this is as it should be. For the major orientation of the book is to explore the healing relationship as an intimate encounter that can awaken the heart—of both therapist and client. This perspective, which developed for me out of my own attempt to bring what I have learned from meditation and Eastern teachings to bear on therapy may not be shared by all the authors in this book; yet the writings assembled here were chosen in light of how they contribute to understanding this kind of approach.

But what does it mean to "awaken the heart"? No doubt this phrase may sound strange to those reared in traditional Western psychology, which speaks of the goals of therapy in much more technical terms, such as "ego strength," "reality testing," or "impulse control." The word "heart" has a rather sentimental ring in our culture—it seems to belong in love lyrics and Hollywood movies, but hardly in the context of psychotherapy, which has been striving since its beginnings to achieve a certain technical expertise and scientific respectability. In our culture, "heart" is considered to be something quite distinct from "mind," the latter usually referring to our rational, thinking capacity. In the Eastern traditions, however, the word "heart" does not mean emotions or sentimental feelings. In Buddhism, the words "heart" and "mind" are part of the same reality (*citta* in Sanskrit). In fact, when Buddhists refer to mind, they point not to the head, but to the chest. The mind that the Eastern traditions are most interested in is not the thinking capacity, but rather what the Zen master Suzuki Roshi called "big mind": a fundamental openness and clarity which resonates directly with the world around us. This big mind is not created or possessed by anyone's ego; rather, it is a universal wakefulness that any human being can tap into. The rational thinking apparatus we know so well in the West is, in this perspective, a "small mind." The mind which is one with the heart is a much larger kind of awareness that surrounds the normally narrow focus of our attention.

We could define heart here as that "part" of us where we can be touched—by the world and other people. Letting ourselves be touched in the heart gives rise to expansive feelings of appreciation for others. Here is where heart connects with big mind. For we can only appreciate others if we can first of all see them clearly as they are, in all their humanness, apart from our ideas and preconceptions about them. In seeing and letting ourselves be touched by the humanness in others, we come to realize that we are not so different from them (at heart). This gives rise to real compassion, considered by many Eastern traditions to be the noblest of human feelings. Awakening the heart, then, involves a double movement: both letting others into us, which allows us to appreciate their humanness, and going out to meet them more fully. (As we say: "I took her into my heart," or "My heart went out to him.") Heart is not only the open, receptive dimension of our being, but also an active, expansive opening out to the world.

How then can the encounter between therapist and client help awaken the heart? How can client and therapist keep waking each other up, sparking and inspiring each other to open up more fully?

First of all, it is important to recognize that the therapeutic encounter, like any intimate relationship, is full of mystery, surprise, and unpredictable turns. No matter how well trained therapists are in psychological theory and therapeutic techinque, the encounter with another human being who seeks relief from suffering invariably challenges them in ways that their clinical training has not prepared them for. Most therapists will admit, at least privately, that they often do not know just what is going on for their clients, that they are often uncertain and at a loss about how to help their clients. If a therapist perceives this uncertainty as a threat to his expertise, then he might treat it as a sign of failure or defeat. But when healing is seen as a mutual opportunity for real opening, a therapist can approach these moments of uncertainty in a different way. For they do challenge the therapist to put aside his theories and beliefs for the moment, and to pay closer attention both to the client and to his own responses in order to get a better sense for what is happening.

These moments of uncertainty, when the therapist has to let go of his mental agenda, may force him into a more direct relationship with the client. At these times, a new quality of sharpened perception and "being with" the client can emerge if the therapist does not fall back on theory and technique when he does not know what to do next. As the therapist's need to be in control relaxes, he can be present with more heart.

In supervising student therapists, I have found that they usually have an inordinate fear of these moments of uncertainty. The one essential ingredient that most graduate schools neglect to train is the therapist's ability to draw on his intuition in responding to the client. So, when therapists suddenly find that they do not know what to do or say next, they tend to search around in their bag of techniques, or else shift the client's attention to safer and more familiar ground—thereby leaving the present moment with all its threatening uncertainties far behind. In so doing, however, they miss the very real creative possibilities that lie here. Not knowing what to do forces us to slow down, become more attentive, and wait—which allows space for a larger intelligence in us to take over.

Much has been written about overcoming the client's resistances to therapy, but more could be said about the therapist's own resistances to greater openness. The fact is that both therapists and clients often get into more than they bargained for or feel comfortable with in their encounter. The most effective healing seems to occur when the therapist opens to the client just as much as the client opens to the therapeutic work. The client's pain and distress are an appeal to the therapist to drop the attachment to being an expert and instead dig in and share the client's world.

Of course, this can feel quite threatening, in that the client's fears, anxieties, and problems may often mirror unresolved areas in the therapist's own life. Since few therapists have conquered all their fears and frailties, letting the client's reality into him may often force the therapist to face and deal further with his own "unfinished business." Yet, though this kind of engagement with the client may be threatening, it can also be quite enriching. In working with a client's fear, I find that I also have an opportunity to work further with my own fear. If I am helping someone explore an empty feeling of loneliness underlying even his most intimate relationships, I am also getting a chance to check in and come to terms with that part of myself as well. My experience has been that there really is only one mind. Although this may sound strange and mystical to some, I mean it in a very practical sense: the client's awareness and mine are two ends of one continuum in our moments of real contact. And mind works in certain regular ways and patterns, although perhaps at different intensities of confusion in psychotic, neurotic, and "normal" forms. Fear is essentially fear, self-doubt is essentially self-doubt, blocked desire is essentially blocked desire—though they may of course take a multitude of different forms. Realizing that I share one mind with the people I work with keeps opening my heart despite all my attempts to pull back and assume a more distant position.

I have found that if I can work with my own resistances to this kind of engagement with a client, it opens up new joy and delight in this work. I cannot count the times I have had occasion to feel grateful to clients for waking me up from my dreams and preoccupations through the genuineness of their pain and searching. Unfortunately, many health professionals buy into the attitude widespread in our culture that helping others is a duty, rather than a source of joy. We often do not allow ourselves or know how to enjoy and appreciate what we learn and get from working with our clients. This is of course a sure-fire prescription for burn-out. What the therapist receives from this intimate encounter is the opportunity to open up in new ways, to expand his repertoire of how to feel and express his own humanness.

In short, I have found that I most enjoy my work and am most helpful to others when I let them affect me. This does not mean that I should identify with their problems or get caught up in their neuroses. There are ways that clients try to draw the therapist into their world in a manipulative way which should, in fact, be resisted. Yet the therapist can still leave himself open to seeing what that pull or manipulation feels like, for this will provide essential clues to guide him in responding more helpfully to such a person. What I am speaking of here is not losing my boundaries, but letting myself experience what the other person's reality feels like.

If I can hear another person's words, not from a place of clinical distance, but as they touch me and resonate inside me, then I can bring a fully alive, human presence to bear on the other's experience, which is much more likely to create an environment in which healing can occur. Many other factors also determine the outcome of therapy, but without this kind of authentic presence on the part of the therapist, real change is unlikely to occur. Authentic presence is sparked in therapists when they let themselves be touched by the client, when they can really feel what it is like to be in the client's world so they can respond from a place of true empathy and compassion.

As humans we have two kinds of awareness available to us at any given moment: we are focused on personal problems, needs, and feelings, while also having access to a larger awareness that allows us, if only briefly, to step out of those problems, take a larger perspective on them, and experience some freedom from their entanglement. Real change and growth happen in therapy when both these levels of awareness are addressed, namely: (1) when we first of all respect our needs and feelings, face them directly, and see what they are telling us, rather than belittling or avoiding them; and (2) when we can bring our larger awareness to bear on these personal issues, so that we can begin to see how what we are is always wider and deeper than all the problems we carry around.

Most Western therapies focus on personal needs and feelings; most Eastern traditions emphasize the big mind that surrounds our personal world. An East/West approach to therapy would include both kinds of awareness. In going to the core of what touches a person most deeply in his life situations, both therapist and client are reminded of what it is to be human. It is in being called on to span and connect these two halves of our nature—the personal and the more-than-personal—that the heart begins to stir and awaken.

When the therapist can receptively let in the client's world, expansively go out to meet the client, and provide a larger perspective on the client's problems—this can help awaken the client's heart as well. What often affects clients most is knowing that the therapist is really letting their reality in *and* feeling the therapist's presence as providing a larger space in which they can explore, unravel, and resolve their problems. The client can more readily move through a problem when the therapist allows himself to be "in it"—to share the real feeling of the problem—but not "of it"—to bring a larger awareness to bear on the problem, without getting caught in it.

The client's experience always contains elements of both confusion and clarity. For the therapist to be "in the confusion" means being willing to hear out and accept the tangles of the client's most intimate thoughts and feelings, even to let himself become confused if necessary. Yet to avoid being "of the confusion," the therapist must also stay attuned to the client's inherent intelligence and positive life directions underneath all the neurosis and confusion. When a therapist can maintain a larger awareness of the client's inherent goodness and well-being, while allowing him to go through whatever he needs to go through to arrive at this awareness himself, this provides a model for how a client can begin to trust himself. In discovering his own greater heart and mind, a client begins to connect with his own wisdom, which helps him see that he is much larger than the stories—good or bad—he tells about himself.

Yet for the client to make these discoveries, it is essential that the therapist have this kind of trust himself, not as an article of belief, but as a living experience. Here is precisely where the practice of meditation can be of particular value for the psychotherapist or health professional. Meditation provides a very direct, practical way to discover the larger awareness and aliveness in us and to learn to trust its natural direction toward well-being. Meditation also trains attention in both the ways we have spoken of here as essential for therapeutic change. It helps us cultivate a friendly attitude toward all the phenomena of the mind—so that the inner struggle and conflict of trying to get rid of neurotic patterns can be replaced by what in Buddhism is called *maitri*—unconditional friendliness toward oneself. At the same time, it allows a person to tap into a larger awareness in which ordinary emotional entanglements are seen in a different perspective—as clouds in the sky, rather than as the whole sky itself. Meditation, then, provides a basic practice for awakening the heart—which includes both developing warmth and compassion toward all our fears, insecurities, and emotional entanglements, as well as discovering our basic openness and goodness underneath them.

When I studied Rogerian therapy in graduate school, I felt frustrated because I was never taught *how* to develop "unconditional positive regard" for the client. I was told that this was essential, and it sounded good to me, but it was just assumed that I should be able to feel this way toward anyone who walked into my office. What I discovered many years later was that meditation provided a concrete operational method for developing just those ingredients of acceptance and unconditional friendliness that are most essential for successful therapy. A therapist who sits through the subtle, complex twists and turns of his own thoughts and feelings is unlikely to find many of his clients' problems all that alien, shocking, or unfamiliar. The more a therapist trusts his own basic goodness underneath his confusion, the more he can help clients find their way between these two aspects of themselves. And the more he can face his own fear, the more fearlessly he can approach his clients' problems as well, which may help them develop greater self-confidence themselves. Meditation is a direct experience of how change is more dependent on how we *be* with ourselves than anything we *do* to try to improve ourselves. In these ways, the traditional meditation practices of the East provide an immediate and comprehensive way of studying thought and emotion, and developing compassion toward everything that arises in the mind.

Just how far can psychotherapy go in awakening the heart and liberating us from the distortions of the confused mind? The first section of the book takes up this issue in greater depth, exploring both the contributions and limitations of psychotherapy as a path of liberation. The second section of the book explores working with oneself as the necessary basis for working with others. Here the questions of how to relate to self and to emotions become paramount. The third section addresses the main concern of this book: how the openness of heart that arises out of meditation practice can influence working with others.

All the contributors to this book have practiced one kind of meditation or another, and most of them are or have been psychotherapists as well. They have been trained in a wide range of different Western and Eastern disciplines, representing such diverse approaches as psychoanalysis, Gestalt, Christian contemplation, Aikido, Hindu devotional practices, and various Buddhist styles of meditation. What is particularly interesting is how well practitioners from such different traditions can agree or complement each other's understanding on so many important aspects of working with oneself and working with others.

When I put together my first book, *The Meeting of the Ways: Explorations in East/West Psychology,* very little had been written on the therapeutic implications of this field. It is testimony to how rapidly this area has blossomed that only five years later there were many more articles available than there was room for here. There is now at least one accredited doctoral program in the field, and several institutes where a person can learn to apply contemplative disciplines to the practice of psychotherapy.

This is the first book to concretely explore how meditative and contemplative practices can inform and provide a larger context for the healing relationship. The essays in it present a very human picture of psychotherapy, one which is not often found in the traditional therapeutic literature. In exploring the interface between psyche and spirit, between our individual, personal lives and the larger dimensions of our being, this book should prove useful not only for therapists, students of therapy, and other health professionals, but also to all those who are interested in knowing more about themselves, their relationships, and the fathomless quality of human experience.

I

BASIC QUESTIONS: PSYCHOTHERAPY AND SPIRITUALITY

Introduction

More and more Western psychologists are beginning to realize what the world's great contemplative traditions have pointed out for thousands of years—that there are two different arcs in human development, corresponding to two different tendencies in human nature. On the one hand, we want to realize our own individual nature; on the other hand, we also want to connect with or be part of something larger than ourselves. Our very posture in this world—with our feet planted firmly on the ground and our heads thrust upward toward the open sky—perfectly expresses our twofold nature. Our vision sees far beyond what is immediately in front of us, allowing us to move out beyond ourselves, give ourselves to others, and open ourselves to new possibilities. Yet, in that our feet root us to this earth, we cannot escape from our karma—our personal needs, feelings, and habitual patterns—as well as our drive to find our own way in this world.

Western psychology is concerned with the self, Eastern psychology focuses on transcendence of the self. One of the first questions we face in bringing West and East together is how personal development and fulfillment fit with the contemplative journey of discovering a larger awareness and being in us, beyond our purely personal concerns.

In his book, *Turning East,* the theologian Harvey Cox warned of the danger of confusion that could arise from psychologists and scientists trying to appropriate ideas and practices from the Eastern traditions which they do not fully understand:

1

> Western psychology still continues to concentrate on the *self* . . . with only peripheral interest directed toward the integral enmeshment of the self in its society, its cosmos, and the immense traceries in which it lives . . . The result is that some psychologists, including a growing number of clinicians, are beginning to feel that they have reached a dead end: . . . It should come as no surprise, therefore to discover that Western psychology today is [looking] . . . to the Orient for a fresh transfusion.
>
> [Yet] Western psychology's present love affair with the Orient seems to me . . . dangerous. The danger lies in the enormous power psychological ways of thinking now wield in our culture, a power so vast that the current psychologizing of Eastern contemplative disciplines—unless it is preceded by a thorough revolution in Western psychology itself—could rob these disciplines of their spiritual substance. It could pervert them into Western mental-health gimmicks and thereby prevent them from introducing the sharply alternative vision of life they are capable of bringing to us.[1]

In order to avoid robbing the contemplative disciplines of their power to help us see beyond ourselves, we need to be clear about the different functions of psychotherapy and meditation before we can begin to see how these two paths might overlap or complement each other. Sorting out these two paths and disciplines is the focus of the first section of this book.

In the opening chapter, Jacob Needleman raises important questions as he distinguishes between the search for personal fulfillment and the search for transformation. Needleman's article clearly sets up the basic opposition: the therapeutic task is to build a stable personal identity, while the contemplative path shows us how the energy we put into maintaining a consistent identity diverts us from a larger kind of wholeness.

Robin Skynner goes a long way toward addressing many of Needleman's concerns about the confusion between these two paths. He clearly spells out the real merits of psychotherapy, exploring the overlap between personal growth and contemplative practice, as well as the real differences between them. Then, in a surprising dialectical turnaround, Skynner questions the possibility of finding simple answers in this area and reminds us that the challenge of being human is to keep facing the ambiguity of living in two different worlds.

These same issues are taken up in a different way in the next chapter by three men who all have extensive training in both Western psychology and Eastern meditation. The discussion focuses on where psychological growth leaves off and spiritual practice begins.

In the final chapter in this section, I examine more concretely the experiential process in both psychotherapy and meditation. This brings to light real differences between them, as well as their central common concern with developing friendliness toward our own experience.

NOTES

1. Cox (1977), p. 75.

=1=

Psychiatry and the Sacred

Jacob Needleman

Modern psychiatry arose out of the vision that man must change himself and not depend for help upon an imaginary God. Over half a century ago, mainly through the insights of Freud and through the energies of those he influenced, the human psyche was wrested from the faltering hands of organized religion and was situated in the world of nature as a subject for scientific study. The cultural shock waves were enormous and long lasting. But equal to them was the sense of hope that gradually took root throughout the Western world. To everyone, including those who offered countertheories to psychoanalysis, the main vision seemed indomitable: science, which had brought undreamt-of power over external nature, could now turn to explaining and controlling the inner world of man.

The era of psychology was born. By the end of the Second World War, many of the best minds of the new generation were magnetized by a belief in this new science of the psyche. Under the conviction that a way was now open to assuage the confusion and suffering of mankind, the study of the mind became a standard course of work in American universities. The ranks of psychiatry swelled, and its message was carried to the public through the changing forms of literature, art, and educational theory. Against this juggernaut of new hope, organized religion was helpless. The concepts of human nature which had guided the Judaeo-Christian tradition for two thousand years had now to be altered and corrected just as three hundred years earlier the Christian scheme of the cosmos retreated against the onslaught of the scientific revolution.

But although psychiatry in its many forms pervades our present culture, the hope it once contained has slowly ebbed away. The once charismatic psychoanalyst has become encapsulated within the workaday medical establishment, itself the object of growing public cynicism. The behaviorist who once stunned the world by defining man as a bundle of manageable reactions finds himself reduced to mere philosophizing and to the practice of piecemeal psychological cosmetics. In the burgeoning field of psychophysiology, the cries of "breakthrough" echo without real conviction before the awesome and mysterious structure of the human brain. And as for experimental psychology, it has become mute; masses of data accumulated over decades of research with animals remain unrelated and seemingly unrelatable to the suffering, fear, and frustration of every-day human life.

The growing feeling of helplessness among psychiatrists and the cries for help from the masses of modern people operate in perverse contrast to the constant psychologizing of the media. Amid the "answers" provided by publications ranging in sophistication from *Reader's Digest* to *Psychology Today,* millions seem quite simply to have accepted that their lives have no great direction and ask only for help to get them through the night. The once magical promise of a transformation of the mind through psychiatry has quietly disappeared.

Of course, questions about the meaning of life and death and one's relationship to the universe may still tear at a person's insides. But now neither psychiatry nor the Church is able to respond even from the same gut level at which such questions can arise—far less from a level of universal knowledge and intuitive relationship which perceives certain cries for help as the seed of the desire for self-transformation.

No one suffers from this lack more than the psychiatrists themselves, more and more of whom despair over their inability to help other human beings in the fundamental way they once dreamed possible. Faced with the accelerating pressure of technology upon the normal patterns of human life, faced with the widespread effects of modern man's twisted relationship to nature, and yearning for a coherent purpose in living, they have come to see themselves as being in the same situation as their patients and the rest of us.

Such, in brief, is the background of a new question that is now arising concerning the hidden structure and distortions of man's inner life. Over the past decade, there has taken place in our culture a widespread attraction to ideas and spiritual methods rooted in the ancient traditions of Asia and the Middle East. Starting in California, this movement initially had all the earmarks of a fad, a youthful reaction against the excesses of scientism and technocracy. This "spiritual revolution" still retains many characteristics of naïve enthusiasm. But the tendency to mobilize scattered fragments of ancient religious teachings has spread far beyond the borders of what has been called "Californialand" and is now having its effect within the very realm that scarcely a generation ago banished religion under the label of neurosis. A large and growing number of psychotherapists are now convinced that the Eastern religions offer an understanding of the mind far more complete than anything yet envisaged by Western science. At the same time, the leaders of the new religions themselves—the numerous gurus and spiritual teachers now in the West—are reformulating and adapting the traditional systems according to the language and atmosphere of modern psychology.

For example, in Berkeley, during the summers of 1973 and 1974, the Tibetan lama Tarthang Tulku led a six-week seminar in meditation exercises and Buddhist philosophy especially designed for professional psychologists. "What I mainly learned there," remarked one participant, "was how limited my concept of therapy had been. Ninety percent of what we are concerned with would be a joke to Rinpoche."* Another, a Freudian analyst from New York, left convinced that Tibetan Buddhism can reverse the "hardening of the arteries" which has afflicted the practice of psychoanalysis.

Yet another Tibetan teacher, Chögyam Trungpa, Rinpoche, is working on an even larger scale in this direction and has established a psychology program where anicent Tibetan methods are mingled with modern psychotherapeutic techniques.

Taking his inspiration from elements of the Sufi tradition (the mystical core of the Islamic religion), psychologist Robert Ornstein writes:

> For Western students of psychology and science, it is time to begin a new synthesis, to "translate" some of the concepts and ideas of traditional psychologies into modern psychological terms, to regain a balance lost. To do this, we must first extend the boundaries of inquiry of modern science, *extend our concept of what is possible for man.*[1]

*Tibetan term meaning 'precious one", a respectful address for a teacher.

Space does not permit the mention of more than a fragment of all the activity and theorizing now taking place among psychiatrists and psychologists attracted to Zen and Tibetan Buddhism, Sufism, Hinduism in its numerous forms and, lately, even the practices of early monastic and Eastern Christianity, as well as certain surviving remnants of the mystical Judaic tradition—Kabbalah and Hasidism. There is also the work of the humanistic and existentialist schools of psychology, pioneered by the researches of A. H. Maslow, which are converging their energies on the mystical, or, as they call it, "transpersonal," dimension of psychology. Studies of states of consciousness, peak experiences, biofeedback, the psychophysiology of yoga, and "mind-expanding" drugs are more often than not set within the context of ideas and systems that hark back to the ancient integrative sciences of man. Finally, there is the acceleration of interest in the teachings of Carl Jung, who from the very beginning moved away from the scientism of his mentor, Freud, and toward the symbols and metaphysical concepts of the esoteric and occult.

With all these disparate movements, it is no wonder that thousands of troubled men and women throughout America no longer know whether they need psychological or spiritual help. The line is blurred that divides the therapist from the spiritual guide. As one observer, speaking only half facetiously, put it: "The shrinks are beginning to sound like gurus, and the gurus are beginning to sound like shrinks."

But is it so easy to distinguish between the search for happiness and the search for transformation? Are psychotherapy and spiritual tradition simply two different approaches to the same goal, two different conceptions of what is necessary for well-being, peace of mind, and personal fulfillment? Or are they two quite separate directions that human life can take? What is the real difference between sacred tradition and psychotherapy?

Consider this fragment of an old Scottish fairy tale attributed to the pre-Christian Celts. It tells of two brothers meeting on the side of an enchanted mountain. One is climbing the mountain and the other is descending. One is being led upward by a miraculous crane, to which he is attached by a long golden thread. The other is led downward by a snarling black dog straining at an iron chain. They stop to speak about their journey and compare their difficulties. Each describes the same sorts of dangers and obstacles—precipices, huge sheer boulders, wild animals—and the same pleasures—wondrous vistas, beautiful, fragrant flowers. They agree to continue their journey together, but immediately the crane pulls the first brother upward and the dog drags the second downward. The first youth cuts the golden thread and seeks to guide himself upward solely by what he has heard from the other. But although all the obstacles are exactly as the second brother has indicated, he finds them unexpectedly guarded by evil spirits, and without the crane to guide him, he is constantly driven back and is himself eventually transformed into a spirit who must eternally stand guard inside a gaping crevasse.

The larger context of this tale is not known, but it may serve very well to open the question of the relationship between psychiatry and the sacred. Of all the numerous legends, fairy tales, and myths that concern what are called "the two paths of life" (sometimes designated "the path of the fall" and "the path of the return"), this particular fragment uniquely focuses on a neglected point about the differences between the obstacles to awakening and the obstacles of happiness. The tale is saying that however similar the obstacles of these two aims might appear, in actuality they are very different. And woe to him who fails to take into account both possible movements of the inner life of man. Woe to him who does not attend to both the divinity and the animal in himself. He will never move either toward "earthly happiness" *or* toward self-trans-formation.

This tale almost seems specifically designed to expose our present uncertainty about so-called "spiritual psychology." Consider the ideas emanating from ancient Eastern traditions, that are now entering into the stream of modern psychological langauge: ideas about "states of consciousness," "enlightenment," "meditation," "freedom from the ego," "self-realization"—to name only a few. Is it possible that each of these terms can be understood from two different angles of vision? For example, does one meditate in order to resolve the problems of life or to become conscious of the automatic movement of forces in oneself?

Our question concerns psychiatry considered as a means to an end, as the removal of obstacles that stand in the way of happiness. (I choose the word *happiness* only for the sake of brevity; we could equally well speak of the goal of psychiatry as useful living, the ability to stand on one's own feet, or adjustment to society.) These obstacles to happiness—our fears, unfulfilled desires, violent emotions, frustrations, maladaptive behavior—are the "sins" of our modern psychiatric "religion." But now we are asked to understand that there exist teachings about the universe and about man under whose guidance the psychological obstacles, these "sins against happiness," may be accepted and studied as material for the development of the force of consciousness.

Perhaps at this point it would be helpful to pause briefly and reflect upon the general idea of the transmutation of consciousness. The word *consciousness* is used nowadays in so many different senses that it is tempting to single out one or another aspect of consciousness as its primary characteristic. The difficulty is compounded by the fact that our attitude toward knowledge about ourselves is like our attitude toward new discoveries about the external world. We so easily lose our balance when something extraordinary is discovered in science or when we come upon an exciting new explanatory concept: immediately the whole machinery of systematic thought comes into play. Enthusiasm sets in, accompanied by a proliferation of utilitarian explanations, which then stand in the way of direct encounters with the real, moving world.

In a like manner, a new experience of the self tempts us to believe we have discovered the sole direction for the development of consciousness, aliveness, or—as it is sometimes called—presence. The same machinery of explanatory thought comes into play, accompanied by pragmatic programs for "action." It is not only followers of the new religions who may fall victim to this tendency, taking fragments of traditional teachings which have brought them a new experience of themselves and building a religion around them. This tendency in ourselves also accounts for much of the fragmentation of modern psychology, just as it accounts for fragmentation in the natural sciences.

In order to call attention to this tendency in ourselves, the traditional teachings—as in the Bhagavad Gita, for example—make a fundamental distinction between *consciousness* and the *contents of consciousness*. In the light of this distinction, everything we ordinarily take to be consciousness (or our real self) is actually identified as the *contents of consciousness:* our perceptions of things, our sense of personal identity, our emotions, and our thoughts in all their colors and gradations.

This ancient distinction has two crucial messages for us. On the one hand, it tells us that what we feel to be the best of ourselves as human beings is only part of a total structure containing layers of mind, feeling, and sensation far more active, subtle, and unifying than what we have settled for as our best. These layers are incredibly numerous and need to be peeled back, as it were, one by one along the path of inner growth (the "upward path" of our tale) until one touches in oneself the fundamental intelligent force in the cosmos.

At the same time, this distinction also communicates that the awakening of consciousness requires a constant effort. It is telling us that anything in ourselves, no matter how subtle, fine, or intelligent, no matter how close to reality or virtuous, no matter how still or violent—any action, any thought, any intuition or experience—immediately devours our attention and becomes automatically transformed into *contents,* around which gather all the opinions, feelings, and distorted sensations that are the supports of our secondhand sense of identity. Seen in this light, there are no concentric layers of human awareness that need to be peeled back like the skins of an onion, but only one skin, one veil, that is constantly forming regardless of the quality of the psychic field at any given moment.

From this perspective, the main requirement for understanding the nature of consciousness is the repeated *effort* to be aware of whatever is taking place in the whole of ourselves at any given moment. All definitions or systematic explanations, no matter how profound, are secondary. Thus teachings about consciousness, both of the ancient masters and of modern psychologists, can be a distraction if they are presented to us in a way that does not support the effort to be aware of the totality of ourselves in the present moment.

In traditional cultures, special terms surround this quality of self-knowledge, connecting it to the direct human participation in a higher, all-encompassing reality. The existence of these special terms, such as *satori* (Zen Buddhism), *fana* (Islam), *pneuma* (Christianity), and many others, may serve for us as a sign that this effort of total awareness was always set apart from the normal, everyday goods of organized social life. And while the traditional teachings tell us that any human being may engage in the search for this quality of presence, it is ultimately recognized that only very few will actually wish to do so, for it is a struggle that in the last analysis is undertaken solely for its own sake, without recognizable psychological motivation. And so, imbedded within every traditional culture there is said to be an "esoteric" or inner path discoverable only by those who yearn for something inexplicably beyond the duties and satisfactions of religious, intellectual, moral, and social life.

What we can recognize as psychiatric methods in traditional cultures must surely be understood in this light. Psychosis and neurosis were obviously known to the ancient world just as they are known in the few remaining traditional societies that still exist today in scattered pockets throughout the world. In a traditional culture, then, the challenge of what we would call psychotherapy consisted of bringing a person back to a normal life without stamping out the nascent impulse toward transformation in the process of treatment. To do this, a practitioner would have had to recognize the difference in a man between thwarted normal psychological functioning and the unsatisfied yearning ("that comes from nowhere," as one Sufi teacher has described it) for the evolution of consciousness. Certainly, that is one reason why traditionally the "psychotic" was treated by the priest. It is probably also why what we would call "neurosis" was handled within the once-intact family structure, permeated as this structure was by the religious teachings of the culture.

It has been observed that modern psychiatry could have assumed its current place only after the breakdown of the patriarchal family structure that dates back to the beginnings of recorded history. But the modern psychiatrist faces a tremendously difficult task as a surrogate parent even beyond the problems that have been so thoroughly described under the psychoanalytic concept of transference. For there may be something far deeper, subtler, and more intensely human, something that echoes of a "cosmic dimension," hidden behind the difficulties and therapeutic opportunities of the classical psychoanalytic transference situation. We have already given this hidden "something" a name: the desire for self-transformation. In the ancient patriarchal family structure (as I am told it still exists, for example, among the Brahmin families of India) the problems of living a normal, fulfilled life are never separated from the sense of a higher dimension of human existence. What we might recognize as therapeutic counseling is given by family members or friends, but in such a way that a troubled individual will never confuse the two possible directions that his life can take. He is helped to see that the obstacles to happiness are not necessarily the obstacles to "spiritual realization," as it is called in such traditions. A great many of what we take to be intolerable restrictions—such as predetermined marriage partners or vocations—are connected to this spiritual factor in the make-up of the traditional patterns of family life.

Can the modern psychiatrist duplicate this aspect of family influence? Almost certainly, he cannot. For one thing, he himself probably did not grow up in such a family milieu; almost none of us in the modern world have. Therefore, the task he faces is even more demanding than most of us realize. He may recognize that religion has become a destructive influence in people's lives because the path of transformation offered by the traditions has become covered over by ideas and doctrines we have neither understood nor experienced. He may even see that this same process of getting lost in undigested spiritual ideas and methods is taking place among many followers of the new religions. But at the same time, perhaps he sees that there can exist in people—be they neurotic or normal—this hidden desire for inner evolution. How can the patient be led to a normal, happy life without crushing this other, hidden impulse that can bring human life into a radically different dimension—whether or not a person ever becomes happy or self-sufficient or adjusted in the usual sense of these words? For the development of consciousness in man may not necessarily entail the development of what would be called a "normal," "well-adjusted," or "self-sufficient" personality.

Let us now look more closely at the process of modern psychotherapeutic healing against the background of the ancient, traditional understanding of human nature.

Both the spiritual guide and the therapist come upon the individual existing in a state of hidden fragmentation and dispersal. A man cannot be what he wishes to be. His behavior, his feelings, his very thoughts bring him pain or, what is even worse, an endless round of empty satisfactions and unconfronted terrors. As it is said, "he does not know who he is." The sense of identity that society and his upbringing have thrust upon him does not square with what he feels to be his instincts, his gut-level needs, and his deepest aspirations.

Beneath the fragile sense of personal identity, the individual is actually an innumerable swarm of disconnected impulses, thoughts, reactions, opinions, and sensations, which are triggered into activity by causes of which he is totally unaware. Yet at each moment, the individual identifies himself with whichever of this swarm of impulses and reactions happens to be active, automatically affirming each as "himself," and then taking a stand either for or against this "self," depending on the particular pressures that the social environment has brought to bear upon him since his childhood.

The traditions identify this affirming-and-denying process as the real source of human misery and the chief obstacle to the development of man's inherent possibilities. Through this affirmation and denial a form is constructed around each of the passing impulses originating in the different parts of the human organism. And this continuous, unconscious affirmation of identity traps a definite amount of precious psychic energy in a kind of encysting process that is as much chemical-biological as it is psychological. The very nerves and muscles of the body are called to defend and support the affirmation of "I" around each of the countless groups of impulses and reactions as they are activated.

Several years ago, when I was moderating a seminar of psychiatrists and clinicians, the real dimensions of this affirmation process were brought home in a very simple and powerful way. We were discussing the use of hypnosis in therapy. At some point during the discussion, one of the participants began to speak in a manner that riveted everyone's attention. He was a psychoanalyst, the oldest and most respected member present.

"Only once in my life," he said, "did I ever use hypnosis with a patient. It was in the Second World War, when I was in the Swiss Army. There was this poor soldier in front of me, and for some reason I decided to test whether or not he would be susceptible to posthypnotic suggestion. I easily brought him into a trance and, simply by way of experiment, I suggested to him that after he awoke he would stamp his foot three times whenever I snapped my fingers. All perfectly standard procedure. After I brought him out of the trance state and we spoke for a while, I dismissed him, and just as he was leaving the room I snapped my fingers. He immediately responded and stamped his foot according to the suggestion. 'Wait a minute,' I shouted. 'Tell me, why did you stamp your foot?' His face suddenly turned beet red. 'Damn it all,' he said, 'I've got something in my shoe.' "

The speaker slowly puffed on his pipe and his face became extremely serious. The rest of us could not understand why he seemed to be making so much of this well-known phenomenon of posthypnotic fabrication. But he maintained his silence, staring somberly down the length of his pipe. No one else said a word—it was obvious that he was trying to formulate something that he took to be quite important. Then, with his face suddenly as open as a child's, he looked up at me, and said: "Do you think the whole of our psychic life is like that?"

A strange and rather awkward silence followed. Some of the company obviously felt that this man, whom everyone acknowledged as a great practitioner, was having a temporary intellectual lapse. But the others, myself included, were struck by the extraordinary feeling he had put into this simple question, as though he were at that very moment internally revising everything he had ever understood about the mind.

Everyone was looking at me, waiting for me to reply. And, in fact, what he was driving at had already dawned on me. But before I could speak, he went on in exactly the same way except that his face now registered not only amazement, but something akin to horror:

"Do you think," he said, "that every movement we make, every word we say, every thought we have is like that? Could it be that we are always 'fabricating' in a sort of low-grade posthypnotic haze? Because there's one thing I am sure of, though only now do I see its importance: the moment I asked that soldier why he had stamped his foot, there was a split second when he realized that *he* had not *done* anything at all. A moment when he realzied that the fact was simply that his foot stamped the ground 'all by itself.' By asking him why he had stamped his foot, I was in effect suggesting to his mind that *he* had *done* something. In short, I was still hypnotizing him—or, rather, I was playing into the general process of hypnosis that is going on all the time with all of us from the cradle to the grave. The contradiction made him blush, and the true facts about the foot-stamping were blotted out of awareness."

I was totally fascinated with where the thought of this speaker was taking him. He went on for quite a while, weaving his speculations around the possibility that the whole of man's psychic life is the product of suggestions coming from different sources, some immediately external and others stored in the mechanisms of memory. And this whole process, he concluded, is constantly screened from our awareness by the belief, also conditioned into us, that we are acting, individual selves. Our so-called "freedom of the will" is only an *ex post facto* identification with processes that are taking place "all by themselves."

From earlier conversations with this psychiatrist, I knew he had never gone very deeply into the study of spiritual traditions, not even Western traditions. He knew nothing, for instance, about the Buddhist diagnosis of the human condition as permeated by the delusion of selfhood.

What, then, is the picture of human nature we see here?

Through social custom, through education, through the indoctrinations and influences of religion, art, and family, the individual is made to accept at a very early age that he is an integral whole, persisting through time, possessing a real identity and a definite psychic structure. Yet as an adult, he is actually a thousand loosely connected psychophysical "cysts." As he leaves childhood and affirms this socially conditioned identity, he is actually leaving behind the possible growth of his inner being. The evolution of a true psychic integrity comes to a halt, requiring, as it does, the very energy that is now diverted and consumed in upholding the sense of "I." The individual becomes a lie, a lie that is now ingrained in the very neural pathways of the organism. He habitually, automatically pretends he is one and whole—it is demanded of him and he demands it of himself. Yet in fact he is scattered and multiple.

But he cannot help himself now. It is useless to throw moral imperatives at him. For there is no "ruling principle" within him and thus nothing that could change the course of his inner condition. The sensitive current of feeling that is meant to permeate the entire being as an indispensable organ of knowledge and will is now channeled instead into the "emotions" of the ego—such as fear, self-satisfaction, self-pity, and competitiveness. Blended with the extremely volatile and combinative energies of sex, these emotions become so pervasive that they are accepted as the real nature of man, as his "unconscious" or his "animal nature," the reality behind the appearances. In the ancient teachings, the real unconscious is the hidden psychic integrity, which has been forgotten and left behind in childhood, and which requires for its development not egoistic satisfactions, not "recognition from others," not sexual or libidinal pleasure, not even physical security, food, and shelter. This "original face" of man requires only the energy of truth—that is to say, the real impressions of the external and internal world carried to the embryonic essence of man by means of the faculty of free attention. Thus, according to tradition, there is something potentially divine within man, which is born when his physical body is born but which needs for its growth an entirely different sustenance from what is needed by the physical body or the social self.

In the great traditions, the term *self-knowledge* has an extraordinary meaning. It is neither the acquisition of information about oneself nor a deeply felt insight nor moments of recognition against the ground of psychological theory. It is the principal means by which the evolving part of man can be nourished with an energy that is as real, or more so, as the energy delivered to the physical organism by the food we eat. Thus it is not a question of acquiring strength, independence, self-esteem, security, "meaningful relationships," or any of the other goods upon which the social order is based and which have been identified as the components of psychological health. It is solely a matter of digesting deep impressions of myself as I actually am from moment to moment: a disconnected, helpless collection of impulses and reactions, a being of disharmonized mind, feeling, and instinct.

At the heart of the great traditions is the idea that the search for truth is undertaken for its own sake ultimately. These traditional teachings propose to show man the nature of this search and the laws behind it—laws which, as I have suggested, too often get lost in our enthusiasm for ideas and explanations that we have not deeply absorbed in the fire of living with all its suffering and confusion. Psychotherapy, on the other hand, is surely a *means* to an end. Unlike the way offered by tradition, therapy is never an end in itself, never a way of life, but is motivated toward goals that the therapist often sees more clearly than his patient. The therapist may even experiment with invented methods to achieve certain goals and often succeeds. But is it recognized that two kinds of success are possible in the process of therapy? On the one hand, the successful result may be a patient in whom the wish for evolution has been stamped out through the deliberate arousal in himself of the very quality of egoistic emotion which the traditions seek to break down and dissolve. But another kind of success may be possible in certain cases—a patient who now has within him an even greater sensitivity and hunger for deeper contact with himself. To the outside observer, such a person may seem to have developed a certain "inner-directedness," but in actuality he is precisely the sort of person who may desperately need what the traditions seek to communicate. The effort of contemporary teachers from the East to bring their message to such people in terms that are neither freighted with dead antiquity nor compromised by modern psychologisms constitutes the real spiritual drama of the present age.

I suspect that psychiatrists sense there can be these two different kinds of success in the process of psychotherapy. But the second class of patients probably leave the therapist before the treatment is far advanced, while the first class of patients stay in treatment as long as they can. Therefore, this second type of patient is probably not consciously or officially recognized by the profession of psychiatry.

So the question comes to this: in the personal crisis of my life, what sort of help do I seek? Which of you, spiritual guides and psychotherapists, can address both sides of my nature, these two sides that we are told are created in man to struggle with each other so that out of this struggle a new being, a real *I*, can be born. For the "third brother"—so the traditions tells us—can only come into being and move forward out of the struggle between the other two.

I see, therefore, that in the last analysis the names "spiritual guide" and "psychotherapist" are not the essential thing. I see that even the ideas and methods offered me by a spiritual teacher can be taken over by my egoistic "inner guide" and used to take me only toward the lesser unities of social happiness and independence. And what of the help offered me under the name of psychotherapy? Among you therapists, do there exist people who feel the two sides of human nature and are sensitive to their simultaneous claims, the possible struggle between them, the emergence within man of that middle world between heaven and earth in which—classically speaking, and using the ancient langauge of alchemy—good and evil, active and passive, masculine and feminine engage in a warfare that can discover the moment of internal love, an inner exchange of substance leading to the birth of a new kind of human being?

Spiritual guides and psychotherapists, what do your names mean? How should we accept what you call yourselves? Behind these names, which of you are the real spiritual guides and which the real psychotherapists? We need to know. I need to know.

NOTES

1. Ornstein (1972).

Psychotherapy
and Spiritual Tradition

A.C. Robin Skynner

I hope you will not mind if I speak rather personally. I am not a scholar—to my regret—but a craftsman of sorts, and I find even in the course of my professional teaching I communicate best when I speak from my own experience. It soon became clear to me that this was the only position from which I could approach the question I am examining here, and that I could only seek to live with the question more intensely than before, bringing it into contact with as much of my daily experience as possible and remaining attentive and open to the information it brought me. I have been made aware once again that this questioning attitude, and the immediate, receptive, and sensitive responsiveness to my life which it brings about, is perhaps the only useful answer to our question, if the idea of an "answer" is even appropriate at all. I therefore bring this attitude here and hope that some of you will share it with me.

This being so, perhaps I should begin by giving you some information about the path that has led me here so that you can better judge how much or how little you can trust what I have to say. Professor Needleman, in the previous chapter, spoke of a Celtic fable in which two brothers pass each other on a mountain; one is being dragged down by a black dog to which he is attached by an iron chain, the other is being drawn up by a golden thread attached to a mysterious crane somewhere above. The story has enchanted and preoccupied me since, perhaps because I am a Celt myself—and Celtic dogs of this particular breed are perhaps bigger, blacker, and more difficult to manage than most.

Certainly I was attracted to the study of psychiatry by a need to find a way of dealing with my own problems. And my present interest in training mental-health professionals leads me to believe that this is not only the usual motivation for taking up such work, consciously or unconsciously, but also the best one, provided it leads the professional to a real, direct, and systematic study of himself rather than a vicarious one through the study of his patients.

Without doubt, the knowledge I gained from my studies of psychotherapy provided some help in finding a different relationship to this unruly animal. Even before my own group analysis began, an attempt at self-analysis during my student days, based at first on the ideas of some of your so-called "neo-Freudians," particularly Horney, Fromm, and Sullivan, led the dog to begin a strange series of changes that have continued ever since. I mention this because ideas that can produce such effects must have some validity, and I feel it is important to add that these consequences seemed connected with a perception of the truth of many of the basic Freudian conceptions, particularly infantile sexuality and the Oedipus Complex, which led to a simple acceptance and enjoyment of ordinary sexuality not only in bed but also as this subtle energy pervades all relationships. I remember too the wonderful recognition that a strain of violence that had permeated my family history could be welcomed rather than escaped from, like a fearsome, untamed animal that could be a source of energy if one could find the right relationship to it.

At this time I was agnostic, indeed, a quite militant atheist writing regularly for the *Rationalist Annual*. But while still undergoing psychiatric training, I took part with other students as a research subject in an investigation into the effects of LSD, which had just then become available in England. Some of my fellow students had fearful paranoid hallucinations that haunted them for some time afterward, but my own experience was more fortunate—a perception of successive, ascending levels of reality and consciousness, and of the interconnectedness and meaningfulness of everything, all of which I retained as a certainty afterward and which exactly coincided with descriptions of mystical experience and religious ecstasy I had previously brushed aside as fantasy. I saw that this was what I had been searching for all along. And though I realized that drugs could do no more than enable one to glimpse such possibilities, and therefore did not use this approach again, the experience led me to a deep and increasing interest in the relevance of sacred tradition.

My own analysis—a combination of group and individual—took place some time after this interest had developed, so that I had the experience—perhaps rather unusual—of being under the influence of sacred tradition and psychotherapy simultaneously. And I have been working as a psychotherapist with individuals, groups, families, and institutions ever since, while also continuing this guided search for the deeper, spiritual significance of my life.

Now what does a psychotherapist do? Certainly I am constantly made aware, especially by acquaintances following one or another of the traditional paths, that though they accept that we might be able to relieve discomfort by drugs and soothing falsehoods, we could not possibly achieve much in the way of reliably facilitating change in those who come to see us. This is nonsense, of course, as untrue as the obverse assumption that we can change the world.

The kind of change that often happens in psychotherapy can be illustrated by a postcard I received from one former patient, a young married woman lacking any secure sense of identity and so unable to control her intense negative feelings that I had found it difficult to be in the same room with her and would not have taken her on for therapy myself had she not been so persistent in seeking it. As so often happens with such cases, she worked hard and did unusually well over her year of attendance. I will quote the card she sent me because it conveys so well what the psychotherapeutic process meant to her:

> I guess the most important thing to say is that what I gained from being with you all is extremely supportive during a period of enormous adjustment. I truly carry you all around with me—and am able to accept the ups and downs with much more equanimity and lack of self-doubt than before. It is possible now to be more open and honest, without being consumed and defeated by self-doubt. I think I will never lead a conventional life, but I am better able now to contain that reality and not be so frightened and disturbed by it [I think this is a reference to her bisexuality], even to enjoy its good side. I send you all much love and all best wishes for continued progress and support—the same which enabled me to take hold of my own life and not feel so helpless in doing so.

The typical psychotherapy patient has failed to develop an adequate sense of identity (in Erikson's sense), having failed to internalize in their early family environments adequate "models" of behavior and relationship, which could subsequently serve as reliable guides to action. Change appeared to take place through increased awareness of the existing, inappropriate "models", accompanied by learning of new ones from the therapist or other group members—a kind of second, corrective family experience. This is made very clear by the note from the patient mentioned above, when she says, "I truly carry you all around with me. . . ."

Now this patient did not display during her therapy any real interest in the deeper meaning of her life on this planet, orbiting our sun within its galaxy in this universe, at this time in its history. Usually I am given early on a clear indication from those patients who will later seek out a spiritual path. They are in some way more open and vulnerable, more aware of themselves as part of mankind, part of the universe, "leaves on a tree." They are more troubled about and interested in the meaning of their existence as a whole rather than the meaning of what happened to them yesterday or in their childhood, or in the hopes and fears of what will happen to them tomorrow. They behave as if they have at some time been given a view from higher up the mountain, which they dimly remember and which leads them thereafter to seek again what they once glimpsed. Such patients are more widely interested and more interesting to treat, not least because they are more directly challenging both to me as a person and to my practice as a psychotherapist. To work with them is a shared endeavor in which I am more in question and receive more of myself in consequence.

At some point, often late in therapy, they usually express their impression that I am holding something back from them, that I have another kind of understanding, which is implicit in all I do and say but not directly communicated. (This never happens with the other patients.) At this point I may become more explicit, though always in the context of the therapy, which remains my central concern, and within the context also of what they already understand. Some, previously members of established churches, may eventually return again to their faith with a more mature relationship to it, often after an earlier period in the therapy when they have rejected religion, or rather rejected the childish, magical attitude toward it with which they came. Others find their way to the Eastern teachings, which have emerged in England as here—some, for example, without any suggestion from me went to a Tibetan Buddhist monastery in Scotland.

This is not to say that other patients, or at least those whose treatment is successful, do not develop a deeper sense of themselves as part of something larger. Such a loss of egocentricity is, as Alfred Adler insisted, an inevitable accompaniment of any improvement, perhaps the most fundamental change of all. But there has always been for me a clear distinction between these patients and those who cannot forget that they have once perceived this other meaning of life, who behave as if they are in some way "children of God."

Now why is it that these two kinds of inquiry are confused at all? Perhaps we could look first at features that *appear* similar between them, which might lead to some confusion.

First of all, there is in both psychotherapy and tradition the idea that man's perception is clouded and distorted—that he does not see things as they are but as he wants to see them. In the spiritual teachings, there are the ideas of samsara, the false world of appearances, the shadows in Plato's cave; in psychotherapy we have the defenses of denial, projection, idealization, and withdrawal into fantasy.

Second, in both, man is seen as being divided. His problems and suffering are believed to stem from this fragmentation, this failure to become whole and to take responsibility for himself.

Third, self-knowledge, whereby he can find the lost parts of himself and become whole again, is seen as the key to the rediscovery of his integrity, so that he may become no longer divided into "I" and "not-I"—identifying himself with some parts of his being and rejecting others, which then become projected and perceived in negative fashion in those around him.

Fourth, this rediscovery and reacceptance is in both processes expected to be painful but regarded as bitter medicine that can ultimately heal and lead to growth. In individual and group psychotherapy, in encounter techniques, and in the challenging confrontations of family and marital therapy, we find a systematic exposure of associations of thought, or of spontaneous emotional responses, or of actions, in a situation where, though it is supportive and containing, escape is prevented, and the truth has sooner or later to be acknowledged. In the "confession of sins," in the acceptance of whatever internal manifestations arise during the stillness of meditation, in the openness to the inner voice of conscience, which is sought during the concentration of prayer, similar processes appear to be occurring. The unconscious is made conscious, the self is expanded as denial and projection are reduced and dissociated parts return; the lost sheep is found, the prodigal returns and is welcomed. In both spiritual traditions and in psychotherapy, a clearer perception of the world and a greater capacity to understand, accept, and relate to others can be seen to follow from this greater self-acceptance and objectivity.

Fifth, both see man as possessing hidden resources, which cannot become available without this greater self-knowledge and integration, even though the scale of this hidden potential is differently perceived in different schools of psychotherapy and, of course, even more so between psychotherapy generally and the spiritual traditions.

Sixth, as a corollary, much of man's suffering and pain is in both regarded as unnecessary, a product of ignorance and blindness, of confusion and complexity resulting from the inner division and the deceit and subterfuge necessary to preserve some illusion of coherence: intellectualization, fantasy, Jung's "persona" the "ego," in the ordinary sense, Horney's "ideal image," and what Krishnamurti calls "thought." It is expected, therefore (and it is the case), that negative feelings, suffering, and pain (or at least those which serve no useful purpose) gradually diminish and disappear in the course both of competent psychotherapy and the following of a sacred tradition.

And finally, seventh, both require that the searcher shall be in personal, regular contact with a teacher, guide, guru, analyst, or leader who has already been through the same experiences; has seen, understood, and accepted at least some aspects of himself; has escaped from some of his own fragmentation, delusions, and distorted perceptions; and so can, through being able to perceive the searcher more objectively, help him in turn to become more objective about himself.

There is, as we see, much *apparent* overlap, and I think we may be forgiven if we experience some confusion, at least initially, between these different kinds of exploration. My personal experience leads me to believe, however, that these two paths lie, if not in opposite directions, at least in quite different dimensions, and that we need to look for a much more subtle relationship between them. The fable of the two brothers, the golden thread, and the black dog, and the idea of the third brother arising from the relation between them, hints at this. Having looked at some similarities between these two paths, let us now summarize some of the differences, which I believe are not only greater but incommensurately greater.

First, all sacred traditions begin from the idea of an ordered, intelligent universe, where the idea of *hierarchy* is central and where each level is related to others in reciprocal dependence. Man appears very low down on this scale of being, though he has a definite place and serves purposes beyond himself necessary to the total structure.

Second, in the sacred traditions, man is perceived as having a choice of two purposes he may serve in this grand design—God or Caesar; the ordinary world of appearances or a more real world behind it; his natural appetites and desires or an inner voice or conscience, which comes into conflict with these; the black dog, perhaps, or the golden thread. The traditions tell us that we all serve nature, in our ordinary state of development, as unconsciously as the grass feeds the cow and its manure in turn feeds the grass again; and that our illusion of power and freedom, and our fantasies about ourselves and mankind ensure that we do this, just as the beast of burden walking endlessly in a circle to drive the primitive pump is kept at its job by the pole attached to its back and the blindfold that prevents it from seeing its true plight. But the traditions tell us that it is also possible, in the scheme of things, for some men to awaken to the situation and to perceive another possibility, another task they can fulfill, another influence that, if they can submit to it, will free them in some measure from the blindness and slavery of their ordinary existence. Though they must still live on earth, a connection begins to be made with heaven. For the person who is awakened to this other realm, a higher energy, a more subtle intelligence becomes available and begins to change the whole purpose and meaning of ordinary life, though the latter continues as before and may show little change of a kind discernible to those still circling the treadmill and absorbed in their dreams. Caesar must still be served, but the service of God transforms this totally and causes life to become an endlessly rich source of knowledge and experience to feed the new life growing like a child within the person called to this new service.

Now this kind of idea is not part of ordinary psychology, whether "scientific" or "humanistic." Though the latter might recognize and show more serious interest in some of the *experiences* previously called "religious" or "mystical" man is still perceived as being at the center of things; his ordinary desires, ambitions, hopes, and plans, whether selfish or altruistic, are taken at face value and used as a basis for action, for planning utopias and eupsychias. There is no concept of the second purpose to which man can give himself, and because of this, no real questioning whether the first could be illusory. Ordinary psychology then becomes another elaboration of the delusion itself, providing more blindfolds, another ring through the nose, more "hope" to keep us turning the treadmill.

Third, and following on from this, the possibility of recognizing and beginning to understand the significance of the sacred traditions begins from a disillusionment with ordinary life, with one's ordinary self, with ordinary knowledge. Only after the blindfold is removed and we see we are going in a circle all the time have we the hope of choosing another direction. We have to see that life is not going anywhere in the way we formerly imagined, that it never has and never will. Having faced this, we may realize that no escape is possible from the repetition of our ordinary level without help from another. Coming to disbelieve in our ordinary thought and emotion, and so becoming still enough and open enough to reach a deeper and more fundamental part of ourselves where another energy, a different possibility of consciousness exists, a connection may be made, since we are for a moment available for it. Thus we have to begin from the point of failure, to relinquish our valuation of our ordinary selves and to let this be replaced gradually by something which at first does not seem to be ourselves at all. Having awakened, we have to die in order to be reborn.

Now does not ordinary psychology rather lead to an *increase* of our ordinary self, more efficient, more fruitful, more enjoyable, and less conflicted perhaps, but still the same thing writ larger, the same ambitions fulfilled instead of unfulfilled, the same desires satisfied instead of frustrated? Ordinary psychology surely seeks to *improve* the self, according to the ideas *of* the ordinary self; it scarcely seeks to destroy it.

Fourth, sacred traditions are by definition, if they are anything at all, a manifestation of the higher level about which they tell us, a point at which the levels actually touch each other. And, perhaps because they can only touch *within* man himself, they have been transmitted by a chain of individuals who actually manifest, with part of their being (rather than simply know about), the possibility with which these traditions are concerned. From this follow two further differences between the paths. One is the idea that the traditions have always existed, from the beginning of recorded time, and are simply spread into the world from the human chain that transmits them, the influence widening or contracting from one period to another and the means of expression being adapted to the prevailing forms of thought and current ordinary knowledge, though always conveying the same essential truth. If anything, the understanding *deteriorates* as it spreads wider from the teachers, like ripples on a pond. This is totally different from ordinary psychology, where knowledge is seen as a progressive development beginning perhaps from Mesmer and the nineteenth-century hypnotists, and leading through the pioneering work of Janet, Freud, Adler, and Jung to the achievements of the present day. For ordinary psychology, the present time is one of unusual enlightenment and progress; for the sacred traditions, it is more likely to be seen as a dark age.

A fifth difference, which also follows from what was just said, concerns the relationship between teacher and pupil. The ordinary psychotherapist would certainly recognize a difference in authority between himself and his patient based on age, experience, knowledge, and skill, but this would be expected to change in the course of treatment. As the patient matures, it is hoped that the "transference" is dissipated, and, while some regard and gratitude may remain, persistent dependency and acceptance of the analyst's authority are taken correctly to indicate incomplete treatment. In the sacred traditions, by contrast, the teacher is in some part of his being an actual manifestation of a higher level, and so a sharply hierarchical pupil/teacher relationship is not only appropriate but, since the human chain continues presumably all the way up the mountain, the authority of the guide, or of the next man above on the rope, may appropriately continue indefinitely. (I am less sure about this difference than about the others. Though essentially true, I think analogous developmental processes must nevertheless occur in both kinds of change.)

I will mention other differences more briefly. The most important is the different view of consciousness, expressed by Professor Needleman. Following what one might call an "archaeological" concept of consciousness, our ordinary Western psychology tends to assume that we already possess the light of consciousness but that some parts of ourselves have been buried and need to be found and brought into this light again, after which they will remain at least potentially accessible. The light is assumed to be burning already, at least while we are out of bed and moving about, and its brightness and continuity are not very much questioned. By contrast, the great traditions maintain explicitly or implicitly the idea that man's consciousness is much more limited, fluctuating, and illusory than he usually realizes, and that an extraordinary amount of persistent effort is needed even to maintain it more steadily, let alone increase it. For the traditions, consciousness is more like the light powered by a dynamo, driven by the wheel of a bicycle, where we have to pedal constantly if it is to remain alight and pedal harder to make it brighter. It is true, of course, that the idea that attention and conscious-ness require effort and work, as well as the idea of finer levels of energy generated by the effort of more sustained attention, and the further idea that the two can lead automatically to the reintegration of dissociated psychic elements, are all present in the ideas of Janet, the Frenchman who in so many ways anticipated Freud. But then Janet was a religious man, and his eclipse by Freud was no doubt another consequence of the attitudes current in this epoch.

If we are to accept these differences as valid, it seems to me that they lead us to a view of psychotherapy and of sacred tradition as different dimensions at right angles to each other, with fundamental aims that cannot in their nature coincide at all. Psychotherapy is about ordinary life, the development of man along the horizontal line of time from birth to death. Just as the physician is concerned with countering threats to life and obstacles to physical growth, and remedying deficiencies and deviations in the development of the body, so the function of the psychotherapist (which developed originally, and is still based most firmly, within the role of the physician) can be seen as averting threats to psychological stability, relieving obstacles and inhibitions in the process of growth from the dependency of the child to the relative responsibility and autonomy of the adult. To do so the psychotherapist seeks to supply those experiences that have been lacking in the patient's history, particularly those that were missing or distorted in the early family environment.

The sacred traditions begin from the horizontal line of time but are concerned with a quite different, vertical line of development: man's increasing awareness of, connection with, and service to the chain of reciprocal transformation and exchange among levels of excellence, which the cosmic design appears to need some of mankind to fulfill. There is an analogy here with the physical sphere, where man is obliged to move about on the horizontal, two-dimensional surface of the earth if he is to survive at all but is not obliged to fly and exist in the three-dimensional atmosphere, though he can do so if he wishes and may find that this has consequences for his ordinary existence.

If these two endeavors are in fact quite distinct, then forms of psychotherapy that confuse them could be much more harmful to the possibility of spiritual development than those that do not recognize the existence of the traditions at all. Thus, I believe that the ideas offered by such people as Maslow, Fromm, Rogers, and many leaders of the encounter movement may as easily hinder as help people toward a recognition of their actual position. It is true that these approaches may indeed stimulate a desire for the kind of understanding that only the traditions can supply, and I am grateful for the way in which they have all personally assisted me. But because they mix the levels, they stand in danger of offering a half-truth sufficiently like the real thing to satisfy this deeper hunger without leading to anything more real and even of simply increasing the attachment to the ordinary self. Jung, too, though so much admired by people of a religious persuasion, in contrast to that terrible Sigmund Freud, seems to me to offer a particularly subtle temptation, precisely because of the depth and quality of his personal understanding, together with his fundamental confusion of psychology and sacred traditions, psyche and spirit.

This is why when I cannot find a good eclectic psychotherapist (in the sense of someone who seeks to integrate the best of the different schools), I tend to refer patients to competent Freudian analysts, provided they are agnostic rather than militantly atheistic and demonstrate by the quality of their lives that they are decent and responsible people. For I find that the better Freudians at least have their feet on the ground rather than their heads in the clouds, a good beginning if one wishes to travel reliably along the surface of the earth. Being concerned first and foremost with the development of ordinary competence in making a living, forming responsible relationships, enjoying sexuality and other natural appetites, raising a family, and generally coping adequately with life, they help to establish a firm base from which an interest in deeper meaning can develop.

The differences now seem clear enough, and it is hard to see how we could ever confuse these two different kinds of development. At this point we can all feel satisfied. Followers of sacred traditions can reassure themselves that, after all, they did not really need to have that analysis which seemed so much to improve the life of their neighbor. The psychotherapist can also feel relieved, finally satisfied that people who follow a traditional path are not really living in the real world and are best left to their delusions. I can comfort myself that I have answered in some measure the question Professor Needleman set us in the previous chapter. Had I been wiser, I would have arranged matters so that I could stop here and be well on my way home before the cracks appear and the whole edifice falls to pieces.

But if we go on, I fear that the simplicity disappears. Even though I believe that what I have said is correct as far as it goes, we begin to see that the important issue for us is the relationship that exists at the meeting point of these two dimensions: that cross, within each man, of the line of time and the line of eternity, level, or scale. In approaching this, I find I have to reconcile a number of facts, or at least a number of observations that I can no longer doubt.

The first is that many who follow a sacred tradition change profoundly as regards their ordinary life adjustment, whereby many of the problems that might otherwise take them to a psychotherapist simply melt away— like ice in the sun, disappearing without any systematic attempt to change—under the influence of some subtler, finer influence that begins to permeate and alter the whole organism.

Second, I have noticed that others who follow such traditions appear to become more closed, narrow, and intolerant both of others and of their own hidden aspects. Of those I see professionally, this group is the most intractable and untreatable of all, for the knowledge derived from a religious tradition has been put to the service of perceptual defenses, of complacency, of narcissistic self-satisfaction, of comfort and security.

Third, the difficulties of working with such individuals are only equaled by those encountered with people who have misused the ideas and techniques of psychotherapy in a similar fashion. Excepting only the group that I have just mentioned, no patients are as difficult to treat as psychoanalysts, particularly those who believe they have had a "full analysis" (what a marvelous expression!) already.

And fourth, others in psychotherapy, particularly those in psychotherapy groups—and in encounter groups in the early stages, before they become a new game—can reach a point of simple openness, of awareness of themselves as part of mankind and of the universe, and of direct communion with others, more intensely than many following a traditional teaching, at least as far as one can judge from the statements and external behavior of each. It does not last, of course, and cannot be pursued systematically, but in the psychotherapeutic experience, it is often there, sometimes in an awe-inspiring fashion, and we have to make a place for this in our ideas.

For some time after writing this I was uncomfortable with it and could take it no further, till I saw that I had assumed, for want of any real question to myself, that I might belong to the first or fourth groups, and that the second and third were made up of other people. But a moment's reflection showed that I was a member of all four, and that the principal obstacles to my own development were precisely those that stemmed from the misuse of such professional or religious understanding as I possessed, in order to preserve and enhance my ordinary image of myself. And this, I see, applies to us all; it is in the nature of things.

Whether in my ordinary life or in my search for its hidden significance, I am most alive, closest to the source and meaning of my existence, when I am open to my immediate experience, receptive to what it can teach me and vulnerable to its power to change my being. In this moment, when I am sure of nothing, I am yet most deeply confident of the possibility of understanding. My actions spring most truly from myself, yet I have no idea beforehand what I will manifest. Like water welling up from a spring, I am new every moment, appearing miraculously from some source hidden deep within the ground of my being.

The next instant I have lost this movement, this freedom, this life constantly renewed and am once again trying to be right, to be good, to know, to change, to be normal, to be successful—or alternatively to be bad, rebellious, a tragic failure, a pathetic victim—but one way or another always seeking to preserve some experience, like a butterfly gassed in a bottle and pinned to a board, losing in the process everything that made me wish to capture it in the first place. Seeking security, certainty, and beliefs to buoy me up, I cling to my experience in order to preserve it but find myself holding only the dead residue of a living process that has already changed and moved elsewhere. Small wonder that I find my life colorless, dull, flat, and boring, needing ever-increasing artificial stimulation to restore me to some feeling of alertness.

Perceiving this, I realize that I must live nearer the source of this inner spring, somehow maintaining myself at the point where this "living water" gushes forth into the visible world. I may see that I am constantly carried by the current into the more superficial manifestations to which this energy gives rise as it flows away from the source. Once I see this, I may begin to swim against the current, struggling to remain closer to the source, where my life is constantly renewed, no longer trying to hold on to things for fear of sinking, and realizing that the formlessness and endless change from which I shrink is a condition of real life itself.

If I can only realize my true situation and thereby loosen my attachment to the forms my life energy takes as it moves further from its origin, I may find that I *remember* the source, and that this memory brings a desire to find it again. Now I find myself swimming against the current to regain it, from love and delight. I need only free myself from my hypnosis long enough to remember what I have lost.

Then I am in the middle, between the hidden source of my life and its manifestations in this world, and I must then struggle not to deny either. If I forget the source, I drift downstream toward increasing repetition; or if I forget the nature of the stream itself and its constant downward pull, then I begin to dream I am already at the source, rather than to experience it and to swim toward it, and so I drift downstream again. Only when I realize my nature as a creature of two worlds do I discover the full potential of my life, which must be lived everlastingly between them.

Now this immediate experience of my living energy can be brought about by many kinds of events. Vivid and profound emotional experience can produce it, such as death of a loved one, the birth of a child, sometimes sexual love, great beauty, pain, an event on a world scale. Drugs like LSD and mescaline can give a taste of such experience by their capacity to destroy defenses and release emotion, and so can psychotherapy, particularly perhaps encounter techniques and the gestalt approaches that seek to release the most primitive and childlike emotions.

But without deeper knowledge, we drift downstream imagining we still live at this zenith, while the experience in fact becomes degraded, copied and repeated, fantasized. Then we need larger doses, stronger stimuli, bigger groups, new techniques to startle us out of our dreams again. If this is in fact the case, it would at least explain why those undergoing analysis appear for a time more real and open, only to become more closed than others sometimes, when the analytic process is over, particularly if there is a professional vested interest in demonstrating a good result. Many will recognize exactly the same process among followers of the sacred traditions—a marvelous openness and simplicity in younger people just beginning, deteriorating gradually toward complacency, rigidity, and parroting of formulas in those who begin to "know" and, in doing so, cease to live.

It is here, perhaps, that the place of the family and community as a "middle zone" and the need for ordinary effort and work, become vital factors, as Needleman has emphasized. For our natural tendency to drift with the streaming of our life energy into increasingly dead and ritualized manifestation—or to put it another way, our predisposition to convert real experience into fantasy and then repeat it, so that our lives not only become B-movies but even the same old B-movie over and over again—is so great that we need the discipline of *effort* to convince us, through our constantly experienced inability to swim against *any* current, that we are always drifting. And for this we need also the discipline of a group of intimates who know us well and love us enough to make demands on us for ordinary effort, who remind us when we drift too far from our more real selves and begin to live in dreams and selfish fantasies, and who demand of us that we be not less than ordinary men and women, fulfilling our ordinary responsibilities. For if we are not at least this, how can we hope to be more? Here, I believe, psychotherapy has its proper place, above all in the facilitation of this function of the family and the outer discipline and support it provides, or the provision of substitute group experience where this is missing. Given this ground, the sacred traditions have some possibility to guide us back to the source of our lives.

Psychological Adjustment is not Liberation

A SYMPOSIUM

Jack Kornfield · Ram Dass · Mokusen Miyuki

MODERATOR: The question we would like to present to the panel this evening is whether psychological growth can be considered to be the same thing as spiritual growth.

KORNFIELD: I'd like to start from the perspective of the *Abhidharma*, the Buddhist tradition of analytic understanding, which describes the spiritual process as a transformation of certain mental factors, or qualities of mind. The *Abhidharma* model is rather simple in its major components. It describes our world or experience in three parts. First, there is consciousness or that quality of mind which knows different objects. Second, the sense perceptions of sight, sound, taste, smell, bodily feelings and the perception of mind, which the *Abhidharma* also classifies as a sense organ. The third component is the whole category of qualities called mental factors, which determine how each moment of consciousness relates to the experiences of sights and sounds and so on. In Buddhist psychology, spiritual practice consists of techniques for altering the predominance of these mental factors from attachment, aversion and ignorance, to the qualities of mindfulness or awareness, compassion, loving kindness, generosity and equanimity. This alteration of mental factors begins to change the way we relate to experience from moment to moment. Seen from this point of view, there really is no difference between psychological and spiritual growth. Our different kinds of experiences are determined by the different qualities present in the mind, which arise in relation to our experience. From this perspective all the different traditions of religion and psychology can be judged by their ability to produce those factors of mind which are more wholesome or skillful and which allow for a clearer seeing and understanding of how things really are.

MIYUKI: If you talk about Buddhist tradition in terms of psychological theory, you probably get some interesting pictures to play with. You can externalize those inner realities and mental factors and analyze their wholesome and unwholesome natures, and then consider how to transform these unwholesome ones into wholesome mental factors. But those are, by and large, games for the extroverted and do not grapple with the question of the self or ego-consciousness. I feel it is more important to ask where is the individual in this investigation and transformation? More specifically, where am I? From that angle, psychological growth in the Western sense may not be applicable to the Buddhist tradition, though spiritual growth may be. Spiritual growth may contain all the phases of life: the rational, irrational, the feeling sensations, and will power. They are all included in a continuum of the various phases of life. In that sense spiritual growth is much more important and is much wider in scope than psychological growth.

RAM DASS: Thus far the answers reflect some confusion concerning what the word "psychological" refers to and what "spiritual" refers to. Jack clearly interpreted psychology in the most literal sense of the study of the mind and is correct in saying that it is not antithetical to spiritual growth. In the contemporary Western cultural framework, however, psychological growth is something very different. Psychotherapy, as defined and practiced by people like Erikson, Maslow, Perls, Rogers, the neo-Freudians, or the neo-Jungians does not in the ultimate sense transcend the nature of ego structure. They really seem to be focused on developing a functional ego structure with which you can cope effectively and adequately with the existing culture. They have very little to say about how deeply identified you are with the ego structure.

Spiritual growth, however, concerns the identification with the ego structure, and on that issue there is quite a gap between what is known as the psychological growth movement in America and the spiritual movement. The psychological world is primarily interested in worldly adjustment, happiness and pleasure. Psychology treats unhappiness as a negative state and happiness as a positive state, while Buddha started out with the proposition that it's all suffering.

KORNFIELD: Part of the confusion between spiritual and western psychological traditions may arise because of seeming similarity in teaching methods. The way that certain methods or tools are employed in western psychology can help bring people to balance, but, unfortunately, they don't have the depth that is common to spiritual practice. In Western psychology, from what I can see, there is a predominant emphasis on the qualities known in the Abhidharma as analysis and investigation. This is true even in the best awareness traditions, like gestalt, where people pay very close attention in a mindful way to their inner process. Still there is a real neglect for the cutting power of *samadhi,* the stillness of the mind in meditation, through deep focus and inner contemplation. Thus a lot of psychological tools which are similar to spiritual techniques achieve different results because they do not penetrate the surface of mind. They lack these other important aspects: concentration and tranquility and equanimity, which empower the awareness to cut neurotic speed. Buddha compared phenomena to movie frames that go by so fast that you need acutely developed attention in order to perceive that it's just one little blip after another on the screen. Western psychology hasn't developed this kind of depth and penetration in investigation. Instead, it's concerned with adjustment of personality. It is as if you climb the mountain a little way, and you have a very small view of the fields and trees but don't have the power to see the whole landscape, that is, who you are in relation to everything else.

MODERATOR: On the other hand isn't it true that often this very quality of *samadhi,* that separates psychological methods from spiritual practice, becomes over-developed in relation to the analytic faculty among western meditators who haven't experienced much quietness in their ordinary life? It becomes a great new toy and a way of circumventing the issue of personality. When *samadhi* is very strong, there really is no personality. That experience is a wonderful escape from the struggle of personality in the world. Is there anything in the type of spiritual practice that is being taught in America that returns the meditator to his personality in order to undo the knots that were simply avoided?

KORNFIELD: That's exactly what a good teacher does. You develop *samadhi,* and when you come to him, anything that you're holding onto or avoiding is brought to light in the circumstances of the teacher-pupil relationship. Fundamentally your question points to the need for balance. Just as in the West there's been too much emphasis on the analytic process and not enough on depth of mind, in the East the greatest danger of Buddhist practice has been getting caught in tranquility or in states which are blissful or composed but do not have a great deal of penetrating wisdom and investigation. We really need both.

MIYUKI: In Zen Buddhist practice, you are encouraged to do all your daily activities, cooking, cleaning, working, etc., with the mind of *samadhi. Samadhi* is never separate from the person.

Concerning the examination of the personality, I believe that you also need some special mind. Now is this special mind attained only by *samadhi* practice in meditation, or is it possible to attain it through some other method? I would like to maintain it is possible in other ways as well. This has been my experience with Jungian analysis which works from the belief in the universality of human life and the human mind.

KORNFIELD: There are several avenues to approach this question from. In terms of the absolute perspective of Buddhism, all problems arise from a mistaken notion of the self, from not being able to penetrate through the illusion of self. But much of what I've heard tonight is from a much more relative level. On that level I feel we need to approach many of these problems more practically. I send quite a few of the people who come to my meditation retreats to therapists who I know are good and also have some spiritual understanding and perspective. At the same time, I think there is a flip side of this question. There has been such an interchange between spiritual practice and psychological growth and human potential movements that there is a prevalent notion, at least in the psychological world, that western psychology can actually get you to the same place as spiritual practice. I think this is really quite a dangerous assumption. From my observation of how psychological techniques work, I see that although they can lead to some very useful growth and transformation, they do not develop the penetrating insight that helps one cut through the deeper layers of illusion and hallucinations about individual separateness. They also do not create the space for what we might call a mystical appreciation of the world. They are useful techniques but their limitations have to be explicitly stated, or people can get caught in them as a dead-end.

RAM DASS: I would like to reinforce what Jack said, concerning psychological systems taking over and preempting spiritual terminologies. By turning them toward worldly ends, they close the door conceptually to a lot of people who could go further spiritually but would have to go into much deeper practices. Instead they are given labels like "enlightenment," and phrases like "I'm free," and "I've got It." I say "It's not it." It* has nothing to do with it. I think we have to deal with these issues sooner or later; we have to keep some perspective on the gap between these two different ends.

MODERATOR: Ram Dass, what about a character like your own teacher Maharajji. As you have often described him, he is not particularly sane by any western model of sanity. It seems the western psychological notions of adjustment and sanity are very secular definitions. This goes to the heart of that equivalence that psychological movements make with spiritual movements. Perhaps their objectives are fundamentally different?

RAM DASS: Very much so. I don't think spiritual movements care that deeply about psychological health. They see it as a passing show. Most of the high spiritual beings are at least neurotic if not completely off their rockers. You go see the teacher Munindra in India and he is wearing funny looking ear flaps, and Maharajji's pants were always falling off. Their whole thing is absolutely weird from a psychological point of view. Read about the recent saint Ramana Maharshi who sat around with ants walking all over him. Imagine a psychiatrist watching that. It seems to me that from the spiritual point of view, "nuts" just means to be holding on to something. It is the clinging mind that is crazy. That's very different from the western notion of sanity.

MIYUKI: Anthropologists these days are extremely aware that how we judge others really depends on our cultural context. If you become a *sanyasin,* a wandering mendicant, in India, you are respected. Here you will have trouble with the authorities. In Japan too, the attitude toward people in mental hospitals is somewhat different from your attitude. There mental illness is understood in terms of *ki,* the energy flow in a person. We say original *ki,* the *ki,* of Aikido. Ki is both the macro and micro cosmic force, undifferentiated. It can be spiritual, can be mental, and can be physical. Mental illness is simply a coagulation of *ki.* So when I judge others I step back and say, "ah, my *ki* and his *ki* do not come to be united in the place where I would like to be with him," that's all.

---

*A reference to the EST training, where participants are told that getting the point of the training—getting "It" is enlightenment.

MODERATOR: Perhaps the participants are sidestepping the more difficult issue by pointing to the very easy black and white contrast of sanity and insanity. What about that grey area of neurosis where most of us spend our time? In other words, is it possible to meditate if you're fixated on mother?

KORNFIELD: I don't really know what my mother would say about that. I see, as Ram Dass has stated so clearly, limitations in this spiritual practice. Many people are getting caught up in their own neurosis. However, in the course of spiritual practice, I have also observed what we would call psychological transformations, in which people become increasingly aware of different motivation patterns, different kinds of attachment, and different images or relationships in the most profound ways. Through practice, and through a sitting meditation discipline which is most central in Buddhism, I have observed many people going through the kind of growth that would also happen in psychotherapy. It's a by-product, but it's a useable by-product.

RAM DASS: Perhaps problems that would be psychologically maladaptive might eventually become irrelevent for a person who is on a spiritual path. A lot of the spiritual people I know have what might be diagnosed as maladapted neurotic patterns from a worldly point of view, but they don't seem to care much because that really isn't what their life is about.

I really think that there are even certain self-selecting, neurotic patterns which lead people to begin spiritual journeys. I don't think it's a random thing. I don't think this group here tonight is a healthy normal population. If we give them a standard psychological test, the results are going to be off the edge. That's fine from my point of view, because normal patterns really aren't interesting anymore.

In the late 60s a lot of what passed for the spiritual movement was really psychological in nature. As a result when the psychological needs of the whole group of participants changed, a lot of these people fell away and are now good solid, middle Americans. They're nice people, and they have great scrap books and great memories. The percentage of people who are actually drawn by spiritual pulls is very small. I am quite sure those few serious practitioners have very neurotic patterns from a cultural point of view.

MIYUKI: This brings to my mind the Jungian distinction between the psychological problems of middle age and youth. In their youth most people are busy establishing their egos and attaching themselves to the external environment: getting through their education, developing a profession, marrying and having a family. The problems of this period of life differ from the middle-age crisis which is a very different kind of neurosis. The middle-age crisis is more centered on the discovery of the unsatisfactory nature of human life, the discovery of human mortality. The Jungian expression of this is not so different from the Buddha's first Noble Truth, that all is suffering. The deep questions of the meaning of life are different from ordinary neurosis. In such a case a neurotic problem is really spiritual. Often Jung's patients expressed their gratitude for having such neurosis, because these neurotic symptoms were not necessarily symptoms of disease but rather manifestations of a functional person who now questions seriously the nature of life. It is clear that differing types of neurosis can produce very different effects. The mother complex should be differentiated from the neurosis that concerns the suffering over the meaning of life.

KORNFIELD: I appreciate your clarification of the modes of neurosis. I think it is important in the West to establish models which give people the faith and the inspiration to work with inner turmoil, beyond the point of becoming satisfied that they're comfortable. There really are two levels of practice. On one level of practice in any spiritual tradition people are working in order to become comfortable. That is, in a sense, the psychological level of practice, which aims, for example, at establishing a harmonious community where you can chant before meals and keep enough precepts of conduct to allow people to live together without exploitation. There is another level of practice, however, which is really inspired by the greatest teachers and saints. It comes from the most profound kind of archetypal possibility for human development. This level of practice requires a very deep transformation, a death of who you think you are. It requires working with all the things that bring comfort and then being willing to go far beyond that comfort through realms of different kinds of neurosis, through despair, through crisis. I think it is a very important thing that in the West that kind of possibility for transformation be kept alive and not become confused with other goals.

MODERATOR: Professor Miyuki, at one point in our discussion the other night, you came out with the statement, "It can be dangerous for Westerners to do meditation." As I interpreted that, you were saying that a Westerner, trying to sit down and do *zazen,* has something very different in his mind than someone from Japan. Could you perhaps elaborate on that?

MIYUKI: What I tried to say was that the individual ego structure is different in the East and West. I think the religious man in the West faces God at a distance all the time. You are ready to be judged by God. You take it quite personally. You are an individual here. You can even sue your parents in America. In Japan, if you sue your parents, you're really nuts. Before your parents will be judged, you'll be judged as crazy. In Japan your ego is very much tied to the family ego, and there is a strong identification with the collective ego. They are conscious of a greater social and spiritual totality. The Western ego, however, is very clearly separated and independent from the unconscious, as Jung would describe it. Whatever you do not see in the West doesn't exist. That is very clear for you. But for the Japanese it is not so clearly separated. The Japanese ego manifests in terms of operating harmoniously with the collective conscious and unconscious. Thus, family structure is very important. So is the community structure.

RAM DASS: And how does this relate to the dangers of meditation?

MIYUKI: When you meditate, and this is also, in part, Jung's interpretation, you take all the ego energy and are drawn to some inner place which then stimulates the unconscious. In other words, states beyond the ego suddenly arise. If the individual ego is the only form of reality you have experienced prior to that, you could be psychologically disturbed. The ego has to continue to function, and if you suddenly absorb the energy that has been invested in the ego, and then activate the content within, you really could go crazy. But if the ego has always been close to a communal ego, then there is less danger when these deeper states arise.

KORNFIELD: I'd like to put in a plug for my company in response to warnings by Dr. Miyuki about the dangers of meditation. I think what you say is true, that the ability to function in the world must be maintained in practice. Otherwise, there has to be some institution, as there is in India, which can cover for people during the time they go through a transformation that does not allow them to be functional. But I do not think this dysfunction should be viewed as an automatic stage of practice. In all the Buddhist traditions, the mental training emphasizes first and foremost the factor of mindfulness that arises in relation to mental feelings, and experiences, without getting caught by them. As that mindfulness grows, it also has the function of deepening *samadhi,* which is not just the *samadhi* of withdrawal but the *samadhi* of being very present in daily life moment to moment. If mindfulness or awareness is cultivated first, then the mind becomes prepared in a natural way for more difficult exposure to the unconscious, as well as the extremes in feelings and emotion that will inevitably come up in practice. In a sense, the balanced ego is strengthened to deal with those phenomena and still remain functional.

I'd like to comment on the importance we are giving to different ego structures that have developed in Japanese or American or Indian cultures. The basic question in spiritual practice is not the particular structure of the individual or collective ego, which is actually in the realm of content of mind. Spiritual practice really focuses on the nature of the activity of mind. The work in practice is to come to a balance of two perspectives. One is a mystical or absolute perspective which transcends all kinds of ego structure, which sees through the self as any kind of solid entity and transcends any sense of duality. At the same time that must be balanced with an ongoing ability to function in the world. I see the spiritual practice of Buddhism transcending the cultural differences of Buddhism. I do agree, however, that it is essential to either remain functional within the world, or find a protected environment; otherwise, practice can be dangerous.

RAM DASS: I disagree with Jack. I think Professor Miyuki has raised an extremely profound point in differentiating between the types of ego structures. The narrow ego, identified with a very separate individual, immediately creates that kind of cliff-hanging quality that results when most Westerners start to do any kind of intensive meditation practice. I see a decrease in disciplined, intensive practice in West these days because our ego structure cannot handle the more severe kinds of discipline or the deeper level of commitment needed. There are very few people prepared to delve deeply into this kind of practice. For one thing, Westerners do not have the depth of resource that other cultures have provided their spiritual seekers. In India the practitioners are coming out of a culture steeped in the understanding of rebirth and karma. There is a social system to support their practice. All of this is so deep in their beings from the beginning that they have a greater understanding of what spiritual practice requires than we do.

The Western ego has thus far reasserted itself and said, "We will take from the spiritual movement the psychological systems which keep the ego very strong, systems that encourage us to say we're enlightened." In a way, the West has done one of the worst things it could do to the Eastern traditions, though I do see people who are aware of this problem. They are struggling deeply and delving into their ego attachments. There are people who are willing to stay on that edge and have gone way beyond their cultural wagon train. Ultimately, the traditions imported from Asia will find only a few to carry them forward. If we are talking about mass phenomena of change, or larger numbers awakening, we are going to have to find new metaphors that are more suitable for our culture.

MODERATOR: Psychology has misappropriated a lot of spiritual terminology for its own sake. What about the other side of it? Do you think there are problems in translating and discussing Eastern spiritual practices using psychological jargon?

KORNFIELD: There can be an equivalent danger in that using the language and concepts from psychology to interpret or explain spiritual experience may cause their diminution by leaving out some vast areas of experience that are simply not covered by psychological terminology. However, I also see it as useful because it is a fact that psychology is a big part of our country's religion right now. Psychology and science both. I don't see that we have to abandon them, but just exercise a lot of care in our use of both psychological terms and the language of scientific technology.

MIYUKI: In a way I am doing that kind of thing in my work. I think this is a period of transmission of Buddhism, and it should appeal to some of the existing concepts in the culture. That was clearly done by the Chinese who introduced Buddhism from India. They used the language of Taoism and then several hundred years later they cleaned it up.

KORNFIELD: I'd like to say one more thing. I like to think of the transmission of Buddhism in a very long-range perspective. It took a long time for Buddhism to go from India to China, and I wonder if there were not similar problems in China when Buddhism arrived; whether it was coopted or whether Buddhism was initially misinterpreted and lessened in its value by people who didn't take it to its fullest depth. I don't know the answer to that, but I have certain faith that it will evolve in its own form in this country. There are a few people in each spiritual movement who will come to a deep enough understanding of Buddhist Dharma to keep it alive even after their teachers die. And that transmission, even among a very few at first, is enough to create the possibility that the Dharma will eventually blossom in its own way in this culture.

—4—

On Psychotherapy and Meditation

John Welwood

As Eastern psychologies and meditative practices have an increasing influence in our culture, questions about the relationship between psychotherapy and meditation frequently arise in people's minds. If a person is dissatisfied with the course of his life, where should he turn for guidance? Is psychotherapy or a meditative practice more likely to help him find his way? Do therapy and meditation cover the same territory, or are they oriented in quite different directions? How far can psychotherapy take a person, and at what point might meditation be a more appropriate vehicle for growth?

No clear consensus about the proper domain of meditation and psychotherapy exists today. My own perspective on these questions, which are not readily amenable to definitive answers, has kept changing over the years. Part of the difficulty in addressing these issues is that the terms "psychotherapy" and "meditation" are both used loosely to refer to a very diverse range of practices, so that discussions about them are often not very precise or meaningful. To go beyond loose generalizations, it is necessary to look more clearly at the specifics of change and development in these two different modalities. For this purpose, I will base my reflections here on my practice with experiential Focusing, within a context of existential therapy, and mindfulness meditation, within the context of Buddhist psychology.

THERAPEUTIC CHANGE AND UNFOLDING

According to one body of research,[1] what seems essential for change to occur in psychotherapy is that clients speak *from* their immediate experience, rather than from familiar thoughts, feelings, beliefs, or judgments *about* their experience. And yet it is not all that easy to speak from our immediate experience. For instance, if you ask yourself how you are feeling right now, the first sense you may have is "I don't know. I'm not quite sure." Since it is easy to give up looking further at this point, we have to learn how to follow and stay with what is still unclear in our felt experience, if we are to let it unfold and reveal itself to us. The research mentioned above suggests that therapy is successful when a person can attend to this fresh yet unclear edge in his experience, gently question it, and allow himself to sense and gradually unfold its meanings. Focusing developed as a way of teaching clients how to do this.[2]

With any given problem or situation, there are aspects of it that we know and understand, and other aspects that we are not aware of (these are the ones that usually give us the most trouble). But though we do not know all the ramifications of a situation and how it affects us, we usually have some kind of global *felt sense* of the situation. For instance, if you pick a problem in your life right now, and ask yourself how it feels to you as a whole (aside from all your familiar thoughts and feelings about it), the overall, perhaps fuzzy, feeling-texture it has for you is a "felt sense." A felt sense is a wider way our body holds or "knows" many aspects of a situation all at once—subverbally, holistically, intuitively. It is concretely *felt*—in the body—as a *sense*—something not yet cognitively clear or distinct. It is not yet clear because it contains many aspects of the situation—it needs to be "unpacked" or "unfolded." Contacting and unfolding the wider felt sense of a situation we are in often leads to important therapeutic changes.

Let me illustrate this by taking a somewhat simplified case example. A certain client comes in feeling angry, along with a familiar round of thoughts and emotional stories surrounding the anger. Instead of having him talk *about* the anger and try to figure it out, I ask him to sense how he is holding it in his body right now. "Something is sitting in my gut, weighing me down, eating at me from the inside," he says, describing a felt sense. The next step is to feel out this sense more fully. Resting with the unknown, waiting, and letting it take shape is one of the most important, though subtle and difficult, moments in therapy, which often takes patience and practice.

As he sits with his felt sense in this way, he is going underneath the familiar feelings and thoughts associated with anger to contact its *fresh* quality in *this* situation. He spends more time sighing and shifting around in his chair, but he is beginning to get in touch with where it gets to him right now: "It's frustrating living with her." Pause. "And disappointing . . . she let me down really badly this time." Another pregnant pause. "I've invested to much in her . . . for so many years I've wanted so badly to really communicate with her." There is a vitality to his words and tone of voice now that tells me he is moving further into new territory here. "But you know, it's not really her I'm angry at . . . I'm angry and disappointed in myself. That's what's got me right now." Another sigh, and a deep breath. I give him plenty of space to let that sink in, to let him feel out the ramifications of this new edge of the felt sense. "Things used to be so good between us, and now we don't even listen to each other." His voice is shaky, alerting me that he is still exploring new ground. His next words really crack it open: "I'm just now realizing I haven't let her know how much I care about her in a long time. That's what feels so heavy in my gut—I've sat on my love for the past six months. No wonder she is giving me such a hard time." A really deep breath this time, his head is nodding, and he sits up straight. By unfolding the meanings in the felt sense, he is released from its grip. In getting to the crux of his anger, the client has experienced a *felt shift.* He smiles at this point and talks about how much he really does care for her.

In going beneath his anger to feel out the unknown dimensions of it, he becomes a larger awareness that can question the anger and have it speak to him. When it has its say, its contraction in his stomach can release, and he can leave not only with a new resolve to relate to his wife in a new way, but also with a fresh sense of his aliveness. In this way, psychotherapy can often provide a glimpse of how we live in a larger way that is not entangled in problems. Insofar as it can tap into this larger sense of life when releasing a person from the grip of personal problems, psychotherapy can also serve as a bridge to meditation.

PSYCHOTHERAPY AND MEDITATION: DIFFERENCES

When I first discovered it in the mid-sixties, Focusing seemed to resemble what writers such as D.T. Suzuki and Alan Watts were describing in their books on Zen. I wondered whether the diffuse feeling of a felt sense was the same as what Zen referred to as *emptiness,* and how a felt shift might be akin to the famous *satori.* In those days, before I actually started meditating, I used to speculate that psychotherapy could be a Western equivalent of meditation and other Eastern paths of liberation. But after practicing meditation for many years, their similarities do not seem as great to me as the following major differences between the orientation of therapy and meditation.

Expanding Identity or Letting Go of Identity

The basic task of psychotherapy is to expand a person's sense of who he is by integrating the parts of himself that he treats as alien—what Freud described by saying, "Where there was id (it), there shall ego (I) be." This kind of work can help people develop personal stability, self-respect, and an expanded sense of what they can feel and do. Meditation practice, however, goes one step further. Instead of expanding or shoring up the "I," meditation is a way of inquiring into what this "I" consists of.

Before proceeding further, I should describe the practice of mindfulness meditation more fully. It involves sitting straight, following the breath, and letting thoughts come and go, without trying to control them or direct them in more pleasant directions. As soon as we give up control and let ourselves be in this way, the confusion of churning thoughts and feelings may become more noticeable. In observing our thoughts, which graphically portray what is driving us, we get a very intimate sense of the areas of our life where we are afraid, fixated, or grasping too tightly. Meditation provides an opportunity to let this confusion arise and be there, rather than, as therapy does, trying to sort out the confusion.

Gently bringing our attention back to the breath helps keep us from getting lost in the chaos of thoughts and feelings, so that we can let the confusion arise without identifying with it, and eventually go to its root. We begin to learn how to "keep our seat," how not to get thrown or carried away by the wild horse of the mind, but rather to stay alert and keep riding no matter where the mind may go. In so doing, the mind begins to slow down (the horse gets tired!), and we get glimpses of another way of being. Instead of being driven and carried away by our thoughts, we can begin to tap into a deeper, wider awareness, which is quite refreshing.

Meditation takes us directly to the root of confusion. It allows us to see how we are driven by fear, which arises from our uncertainty about who we are amidst the constantly changing flux of life. Meditation provides an opportunity to directly experience how we keep trying to manufacture and hold onto a fixed identity as a defense against the uncertainties surrounding our lives. The Tibetan word for ego-identity (*dagdzin*) literally means "holding on to oneself." We create this seemingly solid identity out of various stories we tell ourselves about who we are and what we like or don't like, as well as from unconscious scripts that we act out over and over again, which seem to imply that we are a predictable "somebody." In the Buddhist view, this attempt to maintain a solid identity is the root of certain universal tendencies that produce suffering, called the five *kleshas*: hatred, greed, envy, pride, and ignorance. Although psychotherapy works with the specific manifestations of these *kleshas* in a person's life, it does not provide a means of going to their source, which is our ingrained habit of trying to hold onto and shore up "I." And while therapy can help us let go of specific objects of hatred, envy, greed, and so on, meditation can teach us to let go of this "I-fixation" altogether. This is essential for coming to terms with the essential questions of human life, such as change and impermanence, aging, adversity, love and death.

The process of meditation reveals a deeper core of well-being beyond ego strength in the therapeutic sense of a well-adjusted, functioning personality structure. If psychotherapy can heal the self-defeating splits between different parts *within ourselves,* meditation allows us to go one step further, by starting to dissolve the fortress of "I," and heal *our split from life as a whole.* Then a wider way of perceiving life can arise, which is known in Buddhism as *vipassana. Vipassana* is a panoramic awareness that includes the surrounding environment and helps us see situations in a larger way, beyond how they just affirm or negate "I." This larger awareness is the basis for compassionate action and service to others, which is perhaps the ultimate orientation of meditation and spiritual practice in general.

Building Meaning-Structures or Dissolving Meaning-Structures

Psychotherapy focuses on and observes the personal world. It takes the question, "Who am I?" seriously, in order to untangle and straighten out the unconscious scripts that may be driving us to act in self-defeating ways. Then we can develop more positive meaning-structures that support an active, wholesome lifestyle. The therapeutic search is to find meaning in our experience where it was previously unclear or misunderstood. For example, the client mentioned above suffered digestive problems, which had no particular meaning for him until he focused on his anger and saw how he was blocking his caring about himself and his communication with his wife. Unfolding these meanings changed how he related to this situation, which not only cleared up his digestion, but also gave him new energy for working on his marriage. Yet although therapy can help free a person from emotional and personal entanglements, it does not generally provide a path for accessing or deepening the larger sense of freedom and aliveness that arises in a moment of shift and opening, when old scripts and story-lines fall away.

Meditation can provide such a path, taking us further into the larger sense of aliveness that opens up in moments of release and shift, because it focuses not on personal issues, but on the nature and process of mind as a whole. The question "Who am I?" from a meditative point of view has no answer. Since we are never able to pin down this "I," meditation helps dissolve fixation on "I" altogether. Then we may begin to experience pure, open moments of just being here, which feel very spacious because they are free of personal needs, meanings, and interpretations. Meditation can teach us how to contact this larger space or emptiness that lies beyond the constant search for personal meaning. This can effect a radical transformation in the way we live. As we begin to give up holding onto ourselves so tightly, this larger sense of aliveness starts permeating everything we do.

Goal Orientation or Letting Be

Psychotherapy is more goal-oriented than meditation. If there were no specific goals for therapy, termination of therapy would not be possible.

Mindfulness practice, on the other hand, does not have specific goals, but is open-ended. It could easily be practiced for a whole lifetime, for broadening and deepening awareness has no limit. Meditation does not have the aim of solving problems or making us feel better; rather it, provides a space in which we can let ourselves be, just as we are, and thus discover our basic nature (beyond all our stories and problems). As Suzuki Roshi once said, "As long as you think you are practicing meditation for the sake of something, that is not true practice. You may feel as if you are doing something special, but it is only the expression of your true nature."[3]

In letting oneself remain open toward whatever comes along in this way, considerable anxiety may arise. Yet in meditation this anxiety is not considered to be a particular problem. By not trying to find release from the anxiety that goes along with openness, but letting it be, facing it mindfully, the meditator strengthens the "muscles" that allow him to ride his mind and accept whatever arises in his life.

MAITRI: THE COMMON GROUND OF PSYCHOTHERAPY AND MEDITATION

If the differences between psychotherapy and meditation could always be so clearly demarcated, there would not be so much confusion about their relative effectiveness. But the fact is that the effects of these two practices overlap in certain important ways as well. Not only can therapy often help people tap into a larger transpersonal sense of aliveness, but meditation can also help ground people, so that their personal lives take a more satisfying direction.

Though therapy and meditation both may take a person through many stages of development, I see their major point of overlap as helping to develop what is known in Buddhism as *maitri,* or "unconditonal friendliness to oneself." Usually we are friendly with people (or parts of ourselves) because they are pleasant or praiseworthy in some way. *Maitri* is a kind of friendliness with ourselves that is not conditional in any way. It means being friendly toward our experience, not because we are necessarily enjoying it (in fact, it may be painful or unpleasant), but just because it is what we are experiencing. Instead of trying to get ourselves to live up to how we think we *should* be, *maitri* involves accepting ourselves unconditionally and allowing ourselves to be human. How do therapy and meditation at their best help develop this friendliness with ourselves, which is an important first step in awakening the heart?

First, both psychotherapy and meditation involve a certain disciplined attention. Although such a formal practice of inquiry into our experience may at first seem contrived or difficult, it is often necessary to help us break through the habitual thought patterns that prevent us from contacting our experience more fully. Unfortunately, many of us associate discipline with harsh or coercive measures, either using it to "whip ourselves into shape," or else rebelling against it. Yet there is a more natural kind of discipline that is an expression of caring for ourselves and the quality of our lives.

Secondly, therapy and meditation can teach us how to "make space" for whatever obstacles arise, instead of getting caught in struggling with them, judging them, or pushing them away. Fighting with our feelings only gives them a greater charge of energy, and thus more power over us. Making space for whatever feelings we have to be there, by contrast, allows us to become larger than them, not by "rising above them," but by stretching to include them. When we can include pain in our lives, then it no longer has such a hold over us.

One client of mine who was experiencing fear said, "I don't like this fear. I want to be strong." She was trying to get rid of her fear, keep it down, suppress it because it did not suit her image of herself. This was the opposite of *maitri*. So I said to her, "Can you make a space for your fear to be there? And then make another space for your dislike of the fear? They can both be there, and one does not have to negate the other." When she could let her fear be in this way, she found that it immediately lessened, as it no longer had to keep struggling to be recognized.

Mindfulness meditation works in a similar way, as the meditator neither suppresses nor indulges the thoughts and feelings that arise while sitting. It is important in both therapy and meditation to develop a "light touch"—the ability to contact our experience directly, but not get bogged down in any particular content.

Thirdly, both therapy and meditation can help us respect the unknown in our lives, out of which new ways of being can arise. To face and admit our uncertainties is a way of being kind to ourselves. Trying to fit an image of being "on top of things" can be aggressive and self-destructive, for it forces us to deny and manipulate what we are actually experiencing. Admitting uncertainty, rather than trying to fit our experience into preconceived ideas and images, allows natural, spontaneous directions and insights to emerge, which are likely to serve us better than our old concept and beliefs.

Being friendly with ourselves means living in our bodies in a more wholesome way as well. For example, in both Focusing and mindfulness meditation positive life directions emerge out of coming down to earth—grounding ourselves more fully in the body. A process such as Focusing undermines the tendency to explain or figure out experience "from the top (head) down" by letting experience speak to us "from the ground (body) up." In meditation, the posture itself is a *mudra* (symbolic gesture) expressing our connection with the earth and a willingness to slow down and face our experience directly. Rinzai Zen has a word—*kufu*—for the process of placing a *koan* or question in the abdomen and waiting for an answer to come from there. D.T. Suzuki describes *kufu* as "not just thinking with the head but the state when the whole body is involved in and applied to the solving of a problem."[4] This does not sound so very different from those crucial moments in therapy when we ask questions and wait for answers to emerge from a bodily felt sense.

In helping us overcome fear of our own experience in these ways, psychotherapy and meditation can point us toward a core of strength and well-being underneath all our problems and neurotic patterns. If a client can stay with and unfold his negative feelings, they will eventually yield or point to some more positive, wholesome direction underneath them. In meditation, the practice of being with parts of ourselves that we would rather not look at builds confidence as we realize that nothing inside is as bad as our avoidance or rejection of it. By not running away from our experience, but staying with ourselves through thick and thin, we begin to accept ourselves in a new way and appreciate the basic openness and sensitivity at the root of our being.

RECOGNIZING THE WHOLE RANGE OF HUMAN DEVELOPMENT

One of the most important contributions of the East to Western psychology has been in helping us extend our vision of the whole range of human development beyond the normal aims of psychological adjustment. The Eastern psychologies have helped many Western psychologists realize that there is another dimension of growth beyond merely finding fulfillment in achieving personal goals. Beyond the desire for self-actualization—the tendency to realize ourselves as individuals and live full and rich personal lives—we seem to have a need to go beyond ourselves, to step outside our familiar safe boundaries and taste life on a larger scale.[5] Important as personal fulfillment is, it does not prepare us for dealing with impermanence, death, aloneness, or the basic pain that is inherent in having an open heart, apart from any specific personal problems.

On the other side, the contribution or Western psychology to the East/West dialogue is in pointing out that we cannot begin to transcend self-centeredness if we do not first "have" a strong sense of self. The Eastern teachings about emptiness and selflessness can be confusing to people who may not yet know what it is to feel the fullness of life or have a self they can respect. And it is certainly true that many people take refuge in meditation or spiritual groups as a way of escaping from the normal developmental tasks of growing up. A certain kind of self-deception is common among such persons: exposure to the great ideas of the spiritual traditions may cause them to imagine themselves to be more detached and enlightened than they actually are. They may become inflated and carried away with themselves, or else emotionally flat, lacking color and personal warmth.

One person who came to me for counseling vividly illustrated this confusion of wrongly applying the Eastern teachings, which speak about the higher stages of human development, to her situation. She had difficulties with men, giving herself to them too soon, so that she always wound up being hurt and abandoned. This exacerbated her feelings of worthlessness and distrust of the opposite sex. She had read widely in Eastern literature, which led her to believe that she should give up self-importance, but the task facing her was clearly the opposite: to develop a sense of self-worth, to respect herself, and to start setting limits, drawing boundaries, learning to say no and to protect her own space. Like many others who use spiritual teachings to avoid normal developmental tasks, she tended to dismiss and belittle her own needs and feelings. In Buddhist terms, she was confusing absolute and relative truth. From an *absolute* point of view, no solid, permanent self exists; therefore distinctions between self and other are highly arbitrary and ultimately false. However, from a *relative* point of view, distinctions between self and other are quite real and functional. If self doesn't get out of the way of other's car, then there will be no one around to appreciate absolute truth. If distinctions between self and other are muddled or confused, as in psychosis, then they can never really be transcended in the larger panoramic awareness of big mind.

The kind of confusion exemplified by this client is familiar to many psychotherapists and meditation teachers. The Eastern teachings assume that a person already has a healthy self-structure. However, in modern society it may be dangerous to make such an assumption. The breakdown of family, tradition, and community has undermined the whole fabric of meaning and supports that help people develop a realistic sense of themselves, their possibilities and limitations. Especially if a person has not developed the ability to relate to others in a wholesome way or is unable to acknowledge and express feelings, psychotherapy may be the first treatment of choice before he can even begin to consider meditation. Psychotherapy helps people understand themselves in a very pragmatic way. To attempt to skip over this area of our development in favor of some spiritual bliss beyond is asking for trouble.

In short, therapy and meditation have their own proper domains, which should not be confused. People often ask me whether I teach my therapy clients to meditate. I generally do not try to mix these two paths, partly because my clients do not come to me for meditation, and in most cases do not seem ready for it. Since mindfulness is the most powerful method I know for dissolving the rigidity of ego-clinging, introducing it as a purely therapeutic technique for feeling better would be to risk treating it as a "mental health gimmick," as Harvey Cox warns against doing.[6] And as Robin Skynner points out in chapter two of this book, "the more powerful a technique is, the more dangerous it can be in preventing real change if it is misused." Moreover, for certain clients like the one mentioned above, mindfulness practice might even reinforce distance from feelings.

Some psychotherapists have introduced meditation into therapy as a way of helping clients to see through their egos, but this could be problematic. It is not so hard to help people see through ego-clinging—this can happen in many moments of crisis, intoxication, or altered perception. But helping a person live beyond ego in a genuine or lasting way takes an enormous commitment on the part of both a teacher and a student of meditation. This kind of commitment is inappropriate for the therapy relationship, which is limited by professional and monetary constraints. A teacher in one of the meditative traditions, moreover, has typically undergone lengthy, intensive training and discipline, and has been allowed to teach by one of his own teachers, who has carefully tested his realization. A psychotherapist who has not had such training or testing could run the danger of confusing the two roles and becoming inflated by pretensions to a level of spiritual understanding and authority he may not genuinely possess.

For these reasons, I prefer to maintain a clear distinction between psychotherapy and meditation in my work with clients, seeing them as complementary, sometimes overlapping paths that apply to different aspects of human development. Psychotherapy has different levels and functions to it, depending on the goals and the understanding of the client and the therapist. At the very least, it is an effective way of solving life problems and developing a functional sense of self. Beyond that, it can also help people deepen feelings and their sense of their inner life. Finally, it may help people begin to break through the protective shell that surrounds the heart, so that they can let the world in and go out to meet others more fully. In this way especially, psychotherapy can serve as a stepping stone to meditative practices, which can take the process of awakening the heart still further.

It is important not to blur the distinction between therapy and meditation, for this may lead to confusing self-integration and self-transcendence. This confusion could weaken the effectiveness of therapy to help us find ourselves—by trying to make it achieve something more than it is designed for. And it could dilute the power of meditation, distorting the larger reality it can reveal, thereby diminishing its unique potential to open our eyes to a radically fresh vision of who we are and what we are capable of.

NOTES

1. Walker, Rablen, & Rogers (1959); Tomlinson & Hart (1962).
2. Gendlin (1964, 1978): Gendlin et al. (1968).
3. S. Suzuki (1970), p. 40.
4. D.T. Suzuki (1959), p. 104n.
5. Two major Western psychologists who recognized these larger human needs were Abraham Maslow and Carl Jung, both of whom were influenced by Eastern thought. Maslow called this the need for self-transcendence. Jung saw this need as more appropriate to the second half of life.
6. Cox (1977).

II

WORKING
ON ONESELF

Introduction

Western theories of personality and mental health have mostly focused on the causes and symptoms of neurosis and psychosis, while rarely spelling out what healthy human functioning consists of. The Eastern traditions, on the other hand, have emphasized states of optimal health and expanded being, rather than focusing on disease or psychopathology. An East/West approach to psychotherapy needs to bring a larger understanding of human well-being into the healing process.

In accord with the ancient dictum, "Physician, heal thyself," it is essential for therapists and health professionals to know more about the nature of well-being from within, as it lives inside themselves, in order to better recognize and help awaken it in their clients and patients. What this section of the book explores is how self-knowledge—the way we relate to ourselves and our emotions—is central to psychological health.

In the opening chapter, Erich Fromm studies the nature of well-being, not just as normal functioning or adjustment, but rather as something greater: being fully born, overcoming narrow views of self, and being completely awake and responsive to the world we live in. Fromm recognizes that this is no easy task and points out how this greater awareness may go beyond the aims of psychotherapy. He offers important suggestions about how psychotherapy can be useful to students of spiritual traditions, as well as how meditation practice can take a person beyond where therapy leaves off.

In the following chapter, the Zen master Sasaki Roshi clearly and simply describes the twofold nature of humans as individual and universal beings. He points out how human nature is continually alternating between realizing individuality and letting go of individual identity to connect with a larger sense of being. Genuine well-being clearly requires awareness of and respect for these two movements of human consciousness.

Karl Sperber addresses the unhappy consequences of confusing these two kinds of awareness, of trying to claim personal ownership and credit for the growth and change that has come from a larger level of our being. His brief chapter sounds an important warning for those in the helping professions about how in the very process of trying to free ourselves and others we might imprison ourselves further.

In the next chapter, I take up the difficult question of the emotions and how to work with them in the context of both psychotherapy and meditation. This chapter distinguishes the useless ways we go around in emotional circles from feeling emotions more directly, and indicates how we can respect emotions, allowing them to connect us with the larger life stream coursing through us.

Adrian van Kaam goes into greater detail about how to work with the specific emotion of anger in the context of gentleness. Gentleness is one of the most important by-products of meditation practice and plays an important role in Eastern views of human growth. However, gentleness has rarely been mentioned in the literature of Western psychology, and van Kaam's unique phenomenological description of it is quite valuable. Especially useful is the way he shows how gentleness does not require the suppression of anger but is actually fostered when we can genuinely express anger as a form of communication rather than as a weapon to hurt others.

Finally, Roger Walsh concludes this section with an interesting account of his own personal journey away from conventional, inherited beliefs about reality toward a more inquisitive approach to life, primarily through his experience with mindfulness meditation. This chapter provides a fitting conclusion to this section, for it graphically illustrates the importance of working on oneself as a basis for working with others. And Walsh's humor and honesty give the reader a personal sense of what the journey of discovering well-being may entail.

5

The Nature of
Well-Being

Erich Fromm

At the beginning of this century, the people who came to the psychiatrist were mainly people who suffered from *symptoms*. They had a para-
lyzed arm, or an obsessional symptom like a washing compulsion, or
they suffered from obsessional thoughts which they could not get rid of.
In other words, they were sick in the sense in which the word "sickness"
is used in medicine; something prevented them from functioning socially
as the so-called normal person functions. If this was what they suffered
from, their concept of cure corresponded to the concept of sickness. They
wanted to get rid of the symptoms, and their concept of "wellness"
was—not to be sick. They wanted to be as well as the average person or,
as we also might put it, they wanted to be not more unhappy and
disturbed than the average person in our society is.

These people still come to the psychoanalyst to seek help, and for
them psychoanalysis is still a therapy which aims at the removal of their
symptoms, and at enabling them to function socially. But while they
once formed the majority of a psychoanalyst's clientele, they are the
minority today—perhaps because their number is relatively smaller in
comparison with the many new "patients" who come to the psychoanalyst without knowing what they really suffer from. They complain about
being depressed, having insomnia, being unhappy in their marriages, not
enjoying their work, and any number of similar troubles. They usually
believe that this or that particular symptom is their problem, and that if

they could get rid of this particular trouble, they would be well. However, these patients usually do not see that their problem is not that of depression, of insomnia, of their marriages, or of their jobs. These various complaints are only the conscious form in which our culture permits them to express something which lies much deeper and which is common to the various people who consciously believe that they suffer from this or that particular symptom. The common suffering is the alienation from oneself, from one's fellow man, and from nature; the awareness that life runs out of one's hand like sand, and that one will die without having lived; that one lives in the midst of plenty and yet is joyless.

What is the help which psychoanalysis can offer those who suffer from this "maladie du siècle"? This help is—and must be—different from the "cure" which consists in removing symptoms, offered to those who cannot function socially. For those who suffer from alienation, cure does not consist in the *absense of illness* but in the *presence of well-being*.

However, if we are to define well-being, we meet with considerable difficulties. If we stay within the Freudian system, well-being would have to be defined in terms of the libido theory, as the capacity for full genital functioning, or, from a different angle, as the awareness of the hidden Oedipal situation—definitions which, in my opinion, are only tangential to the real problem of human existence and the achievement of well-being by the total man. Any attempt to give a tentative answer to the problem of well-being must transcend the Freudian frame of reference and lead to a discussion, incomplete as it must be, of the basic concept of human existence, which underlies humanistic psychoanalysis. Only in this way can we lay the foundation for comparison between psychoanalysis and Zen Buddhist thought.

The first approach to a definition of well-being can be stated thus: *well-being is being in accord with the nature of man.* If we go beyond this formal statement, the question arises: What *is* being, in accordance with the conditions of human existence? What are these conditions?

Human existence poses a question. Man is thrown into this world without his volition and taken away from it again without his volition. In contrast to the animal, which in its instincts has a "built-in" mechanism of adaption to its environment, living completely within nature, man lacks this instinctive mechanism. *He has to live* his life, he *is not lived by* it. He is *in* nature, yet he *transcends* nature; he has awareness of himself, and this awareness of himself as a separate entity makes him feel unbearably alone, lost, powerless. The very fact of being born poses a problem. At the moment of birth, life asks man a question, and this question he must answer. He must answer it at every moment; not his mind, not his body, but *he,* the person who thinks and dreams, who sleeps and eats and cries and laughs—*the whole man*—must answer it. What is this question which life poses? The question is: How can we overcome the suffering, the imprisonment, the shame which the experience of separateness creates; how can we find union within ourselves, with our fellowman, with nature? Man has to answer this question in some way; and even in insanity an answer is given by striking out reality outside of ourselves, living completely within the shell of ourselves, and thus overcoming fright of separateness.

The *question* is always the same. However, there are *several answers,* or basically, there are only two answers. One is to overcome separateness and to find unity by *regression* to the state of unity which existed before awareness ever arose, that is, before man was born. The other answer is to be *fully born,* to develop one's awareness, one's reason, one's capacity to love, to such a point that one transcends one's own egocentric involvement, and arrives at a new harmony, at a new oneness with the world.

When we speak of birth, we usually refer to the act of physiological birth which takes place for the human infant about nine months after conception. But in many ways, the significance of his birth is overrated. In important aspects, the life of the infant one week after birth is more like intrauterine existence than like the existence of an adult man or woman. There is, however, a unique aspect of birth: the umbilical cord is severed, and the infant begins his first activity: breathing. Any severance of primary ties, from there on, is possible only to the extent to which this severance is accompanied by genuine activity.

Birth is not one act; it is a process. The aim of life is to be fully born, though its tragedy is that most of us die before we are thus born. To live is to be born every minute. Death occurs when birth stops. Physiologically, our celluar system is in a process of continual birth; psychologically, however, most of us cease to be born at a certain point. Some are completely stillborn; they go on living physiologically when mentally their longing is to return to the womb, to earth, darkness, death; they are insane, or nearly so. Many others proceed further on the path of life. Yet they can not cut the umbilical cord completely, as it were; they remain symbiotically attached to mother, father, family, race, state, status, money, gods, etc.; they never emerge fully as themselves and thus they never become fully born.

The regressive attempt to answer the problem of existence can assume different forms; what is common to all of them is that they necessarily fail and lead to suffering. Once man is torn away from the prehuman, paradisaical unity with nature, he can never go back to where he came from; two angels with fiery swords block his return. Only in death or in insanity can the return be accomplished—not in life and sanity.

The individual's emergence from regressive unity is accompanied by the gradual overcoming of narcissism. For the infant shortly after birth, there is not even awareness of reality existing outside of himself in the sense of sense-perception; he and mother's nipple and mother's breast are still one; he finds himself in a state *before* any subject-object differentiation takes place. After a while, the capacity for subject-object differentiation develops in every child—but only in the obvious sense of awareness of the difference between me and not-me. But in an *affective* sense, it takes the development of full maturity to overcome the narcissistic attitude of omniscience and omnipotence, provided this stage is ever reached. We observe this narcissistic attitude clearly in the behavior of children and of neurotic persons, except that with the former, it is usually conscious, with the latter, unconscious. The child does not accept reality as it is, but as he wants it to be. He lives in his wishes, and his view of reality is what he wants it to be. If his wish is not fulfilled, he gets furious, and the function of his fury is to force the world (through the medium of father and mother) to correspond to his wish. In the normal development of the child, this attitude slowly changes to the mature one of being aware of reality and accepting it, its laws, hence necessity. In the neurotic person, we find invariably that he has not arrived at this point, and has not given up the narcissistic interpretation of reality. He insists that reality must conform to his ideas, and when he recognizes that this is not so, he reacts either with the impulse to force reality to correspond to his wishes (that is, to do the impossible) or with a feeling of powerlessness because he can not perform the impossible. The notion of freedom which this person has is, whether he is aware of it or not, a notion of narcissistic omnipotence, while the notion of freedom of the fully developed person is that of recognizing reality and its laws and acting within the laws of necessity, by relating oneself to the world productively by grasping the world with one's own powers of thought and affect.

Returning now to the question of well-being, how are we going to define it in the light of what has been said thus far?

Well-being is the state of having arrived at the full development of reason: reason not in the sense of a merely intellectual judgment, but in that of grasping truth by "letting things be" (to use Heidegger's term) as they are. Well-being is possible only to the degree to which one has overcome one's narcissism; to the degree to which one is open, responsive, sensitive, awake, empty (in the Zen sense). Well-being means to be fully related to man and nature affectively, to overcome separateness and alienation, to arrive at the experience of oneness with all that exists—and yet to experience *myself* at the same time as the separate entity *I* am, as the in-dividual. Well-being means to be fully born, to become what one potentially is; it means to have the full capacity for joy and for sadness or, to put it still differently, to awake from the half-slumber the average man lives in, and to be fully awake. If it is all that, it means also to be creative; that is, to react and to respond to myself, to others, to everything that exists—to react and to respond as the real, total man I am to the reality of everybody and everything as he or it is. In this act of true response lies the area of creativity, of seeing the world as it is *and* experiencing it as *my* world, the world created and transformed by my creative grasp of it, so that the world ceases to be a strange world "over there" and becomes *my* world. Well-being means, finally, to drop one's ego, to give up greed, to cease chasing after the preservation and the aggrandizement of the ego, to be and to experience oneself in the act of being, not in having, preserving, coveting, using.

I have said that man is asked a question by the very fact of his existence, and that this is a question raised by the contradiction within himself—that of being in nature and at the same time of transcending nature by the fact that he is life aware of itself. Any man who listens to this question posed to him, and who makes it a matter of "ultimate concern" to answer this question, and to answer it as a whole man and not only by thoughts, is a "religious" man; and all systems that try to give, teach, and transmit such answers are "religious." On the other hand, any man—and any culture—that tries to be deaf to the existential question is irreligious. There is no better example that can be cited for men who are deaf to the question posed by existence than we ourselves, living in the twentieth century. We try to evade the question by concern with property, prestige, power, production, fun, and, ultimately, by trying to forget that we—that I—exist. No matter how often he *thinks* of God or goes to church, or how much he believes in religious ideas, if he, the whole man, is deaf to the question of existence, if he does not have an answer to it, he is marking time, and he lives and dies like one of the million things he produces.

What is common to Jewish-Christian and Zen Buddhist thinking is the awareness that I must give up my "will" (in the sense of my desire to force, direct, strangle the world outside of me and within me) in order to be completely open, responsive, awake, alive. In Zen terminology, this is often called "to make oneself empty"—which does not mean something negative, but means the openness to receive. In Christian terminology this is often called "to slay oneself and to accept the will of God." There seems to be little difference between the Christian experience and the Buddhist experience which lies behind the two different formulations. However, as far as the popular interpretation and experience is concerned, this formulation means that instead of making decisions himself, man leaves the decisions to an omniscient, omnipotent father, who watches over him and knows what is good for him. It is clear that in this experience, man does not become open and responsive, but obedient and submissive. To follow God's will in the sense of true surrender of egoism is best done if there is no concept of God. Paradoxically, I truly follow God's will if I forget about God. Zen's concept of emptiness implies the true meaning of giving up one's will, yet without the danger of regressing to the idolatrous concept of a helping father.

The average person, while he thinks he is awake, actually is half asleep. By "half asleep" I mean that his contact with reality is a very partial one; most of what he believes to be reality (outside or inside of himself) is a set of fictions which his mind constructs. He is aware of reality only to the degree to which his social functioning makes it necessary. He is aware of his fellowmen inasmuch as he needs to cooperate with them; he is aware of material and social reality inasmuch as he needs to be aware of it in order to manipulate it. *He is aware of reality to the extent to which the goal of survival makes such awareness necessary.* The average person's consciousness is mainly "false consciousness," consisting of fictions and illusion, while precisely what he is not aware of is reality. We can thus differentiate between what a person *is* conscious of, and what he *becomes* conscious of. He *is* conscious, mostly, of fictions; he can *become* conscious of the realities which lie underneath these fictions.

Inasmuch as consciousness represents only the small sector of socially patterned experience and unconsciousness represents the richness and depth of universal man, the state of repressedness results in the fact that I, the accidental, social person, am separated from me the whole human person. I am a stranger to myself, and to the same degree everybody else is a stranger to me. I am cut off from the vast area of experience which is human and remain a fragment of a man, a cripple who experiences only a small part of what is real to him and what is real to others.

Man in the state of repressedness does not see what exists, but he puts his thought image into things and sees them in the light of his thought images and fantasies, rather than in their reality. It is the thought image, the distorting veil, that creates his passions, his anxieties. Eventually, the repressed man, instead of experiencing things and persons, experiences by *cerebation.* He is under the illusion of being in touch with the *world,* while he is only in touch with *words.* Parataxic distortion, false consciousness, and cerebration are not strictly separate ways of unreality; they are, rather, different and yet overlapping aspects of the same phenomenon of unreality which exists as long as the universal man is separated from the social man. We only describe the same phenomenon in a different way by saying that the person who lives in the state of repressedness is the alienated person. He projects his own feelings and ideas on objects and then does not experience himself as the subject of his feelings, but is ruled by the objects which are charged with his feelings.

The opposite of the alienated, distorted, parataxic, false, cerebrated experience, is the immediate, direct, total grasp of the world which we see in the infant and child before the power of education changes this form of experience. For the newborn infant, there is as yet no separation between the me and the not-me. This separation gradually takes place, and the final achievement is expressed by the fact that the child can say "I." But still the child's grasp of the world remains relatively immediate and direct. When the child plays with a ball, it really sees the ball moving, it is fully *in* this experience, and that is why it is an experience which can be repeated without end and with a never-ceasing joy. The adult also believes that he sees the ball rolling. That is of course true, inasmuch as he sees that the object-ball is rolling on the object-floor. But he does not really *see* the rolling. He *thinks* the rolling ball on the surface. When he says "the ball rolls", he actually confirms only (a) his knowledge that the round object over there is called a ball and (b) his knowledge that round objects roll on a smooth surface when given a push. His eyes operate with the end of proving his knowledge and thus making him secure in the world.

The state of nonrepressedness is a state in which one acquires again the immediate, undistorted grasp of reality, the simpleness and spontaneity of the child; yet, *after* having gone through the process of alienation, of development of one's intellect, nonrepressedness is return to innocence on a higher level; this return to innocence is possible only after one has lost one's innocence.

What happens then in the process in which the unconscious becomes conscious? In answering this question, we had better reformulate it. There is no such thing as "the conscious" and no such thing as "the unconscious." There are degrees of consciousness-awareness and unconsciousness-unawareness. Our question then should rather be: What happens when I become aware of what I have not been aware of before? In line with what has been said before, the general answer to this question is that every step in this process is in the direction of understanding the fictitious, unreal character of our "normal" consciousness. To become conscious of what is unconscious and thus to enlarge one's consciousness means to get in touch with reality and—in this sense—with truth (intellectually and affectively). To enlarge consciousness means to wake up, to lift a veil, to leave the cave, to bring light into the darkness.

Could this be the same experience Zen Buddhists call "enlightenment" or *satori?* Satori is *not* an abnormal state of mind: it is *not* a trance in which reality disappears. It is not a narcissistic state of mind, as it can be seen in some religious manifestations. "If anything, it is a perfectly normal state of mind. . . ."[1] *Satori* has a peculiar effect on the person who experiences it. "All your mental activities will now be working in a different key, which will be more satisfying, more peaceful, more full of joy than anything you ever experienced before. The tone of life will be altered. There is something rejuvenating in the possession of Zen. The spring flower will look prettier, and the mountain stream runs cooler and more transparent."[2]

It is quite clear that *satori* is the true fulfillment of the state of well-being which Dr. Suzuki described in the passage quoted above. If we would try to express enlightenment in psychological terms, I would say that it is a state in which the person is completely tuned to the reality outside and inside of him, a state in which he is fully aware of it and fully grasps it. *He* is aware of it—that is, not his brain, nor any other part of his organism, but *he,* the whole man. He is aware of *it;* not as of an object over there which he grasps with his thought, but *it,* the flower, the dog, the man, in its, or his, full reality. He who awakes is open and responsive to the world, and he can be open and responsive because he has given up holding on to himself as a thing and thus has become empty and ready to receive. To be enlightened means "the full awakening of the total personality to reality."

This aim of the full recovery of unconsciousness by consciousness is quite obviously much more radical than the general psychoanalytic aim. The reasons for this are easy to see. To achieve this total aim requires an effort far beyond the effort most persons in the West are willing to make. But quite aside from this question of effort, even the visualization of this aim is possible only under certain conditions. First of all, this radical aim can be envisaged only from the point of view of a certain philosophical position. There is no need to describe this position in detail. Suffice it to say that it is one in which not the negative aim of the absence of sickness, but the positive one of the presence of well-being is aimed at, and that well-being is conceived in terms of full union, the immediate and uncontaminated grasp of the world.

But it would be a mistake to believe that the radical aim of the de-repression has no connection with a therapeutic aim. Just as one has recognized that the cure of a symptom and the prevention of future symptom formations is not possible without the analysis and change of the character, one must also recognize that the change of this or that neurotic character trait is not possible without pursuing the more radical aim of a complete transformation of the person.

What happens in the analytic process? A person senses for the first time that he is vain, that he is frightened, that he hates, while consciously he had believed himself to be modest, brave, and loving. The new insight may hurt him, but it opens a door; it permits him to stop projecting on others what he represses in himself. He proceeds; he experiences the infant, the child, the adolescent, the criminal, the insane, the saint, the artist, the male, *and* the female within himself; he gets more deeply in touch with humanity, with the universal man; he represses less, is freer, has less need to project, to cerebrate; then he may experience for the first time how he sees colors, how he sees a ball roll, how his ears are suddenly fully opened to music, when up to now he only listened *to* it; in sensing his oneness with others, he may have a first glimpse of the illusion that his separate individual ego is some*thing* to hold onto, to cultivate, to save; he will experience the futility of seeking the answer to life by *having* himself, rather than by being and becoming himself. All these are sudden, unexpected experiences with no intellectual content; yet afterwards the person feels freer, stronger, less anxious than he ever felt before. The authentic psychoanalytic insight arrives without being forced or even being premeditated. It starts not in our brain but, to use a Japanese image, in our belly. It can not be adequately formulated in words, and it eludes one if one tries to do so; yet it is real and conscious, and leaves the person who experiences it a changed person.

I have suggested that the method of uncovering the unconscious, if carried to its ultimate consequence, may be a step toward enlightenment, provided it is taken within the philosophical context which is most radically and realistically expressed in Zen. But only a great deal of further experience in applying this method will show how far it can lead. The view expressed here implies only a possibility and thus has the character of a hypothesis which is to be tested.

But what can be said with more certainty is that the knowledge of Zen, and a concern with it, can have a most fertile and clarifying influence on the theory and technique of psychoanalysis. Zen, different as it is in its method from psychoanalysis, can sharpen the focus, throw new light on the nature of insight, and heighten the sense of what it is to see, what it is to be creative, what it is to overcome the affective contaminations and false intellectualizations which are the necessary results of experience based on the subject-object split.

In its very radicalism with respect to intellectualization, authority, and the delusion of the ego, in its emphasis on the aim of well-being, Zen thought will deepen and widen the horizon of the psychoanalyst and help him to arrive at a more radical concept of the grasp of reality as the ultimate aim of full, conscious awareness.

If further speculation on the relation between Zen and psychoanalysis is permissible, one might think of the possibility that psychoanalysis may be significant to the student of Zen. I can visualize it as a help in avoiding the danger of a false enlightenment (which is, of course, no enlightenment), one which is purely subjective, based on psychotic or hysterical phenomena, or on a self-induced state of trance. Analytic clarification might help the Zen student to avoid illusions, the absence of which is the very condition of enlightenment.

Whatever the use is that Zen may make of psychoanalysis, from the standpoint of a Western psychoanalyst, I express my gratitude for this precious gift of the East. How could such understanding be possible, were it not for the fact that "Buddha nature is in all of us," that man and existence are universal categories, and that the immediate grasp of reality, waking up, and enlightenment are universal experiences.

NOTES

1. D.T. Suzuki (1949), p. 97.
2. Ibid., pp. 97-98.

=6=

Where is the Self?

Joshu Sasaki Roshi

As human beings, we are composed of two activities. The first is called *absolute self*, in which you forget or do not recognize yourself, as in the moment of truly embracing your lover. When a man and a woman embrace, does a woman think, "I am a woman," and does a man think, "I am a man?" Try it. Your lover would probably shove you away if you were thinking about something else while you embraced. It's only after embracing and separating that the man says to the woman, "You're the prettiest woman in the world," and the woman says to the man, "You're as strong as King Kong." The second activity is that of the *individual self*, which objectifies the world and self and deals with these problems. Both are necessary factors of life.

For instance, if you were to remain in your lover's embrace all the time, you could never lead a creative individual life. Man and woman must separate to do their work in this world. If two lovers spent all their time in bed, after three or four days, the sheets would start to smell. You have to get out of bed and leave your lover to go outside, get some fresh air, do your work, play, and then go back to bed again. Each of us lives by manifesting ourselves in two ways: as absolute self and as individual self. Human life is basically the endlessly repetitious cycle of forgetting the self and affirming the self.

When the self that has been lost in the embrace comes to life again and the two lovers separate, two belly buttons face each other. It is in this separation that you affirm the self. Then conflict arises as one praises and one criticizes the other's belly button. When you affirm yourself as "I," "me," "mine," you are affirming your center of gravity. Every person possesses what I call a center of gravity. It is also possessed by this table and this cup. When you affirm yourself as "I am," at the same time the bird is affirming itself and so is the pine tree, the mosquito, and the rock. Each being affirms itself. Each has its own belly button.

Each reality in the world has its own center of gravity. But the center of gravity is not an object you can point out. It is the integrative force, the function, that unifies you as yourself.

Buddhism says that you have to come to a realization of this function which constitutes your essential selfness: how you are put together and what puts you together. In more ordinary language, it means to know yourself. You may or may not understand this function of self. Even without understanding, though, you are already manifesting its function, just as in their natural state, the mosquito or the pine tree or the rock manifests a unifying, integrative function without their awareness.

A man has his own center of gravity, and a woman also has her own. While the pine tree or stone or bird may not have to think about the function of self, a human being is a thinking animal. When you affirm yourself and say "I am," or when you claim things for yourself, you are different from the stone or the pine tree which claims nothing. You have an individual self. Once you have this self, you have to be fully aware of this unifying integrative function of the center of gravity. A man, when he looks at woman, must reach the awareness that he is manifesting himself as a unifying integrative function together with that woman and must experience absolute self with that woman. Without dissolving the individual self, you cannot experience the absolute, and if you affirm yourself simply as "I am" without the absolute experience, then conflicts are bound to arise.

With an awareness of the nature of self, you have respect for yourself and you can respect others as well. Man has respect for woman and vice versa. If you do not have this kind of consciousness, then when you see a pretty flower, you pick it and smell it, and then you throw it away. There is a complete lack of respect for that flower which also has its own unifying integrative center by which it manifests as a flower. When you individually have the awareness of what you are, how you are put together and of the basic function of your being, you are properly human. With this awareness, interpersonal relationships, whether with other men or women, work smoothly because there is a basis of respect. From the Buddhist standpoint of life, you must learn to respect equally even the smallest thing, a stone as well as other humans, because each thing manifests the same unifying center of gravity as you do. This same consciousness which understands the nature of self is the basis of a respect for life.

Now when you embrace your lover or when you hold your pet dog, where does the self go? To where does the belly button dissappear? When I rub this table, feeling how smooth it is, how fine it is, where does my self go? There is no need to explain this, because clearly my center of gravity and the table's center of gravity have become one. My individual self is given up completely to the individual self of this table and I no longer need to affirm a separate self. When two people embrace, it is not that the self is lost. There is simply no need to assert the self. There is no need to argue the self. And this is what is meant by absolute self in Buddhism. I call this *absolute center of gravity*. True love is the realization of absolute center of gravity. When you love a flower, when you embrace your loved one, when you play with your pet dog, you are manifesting the absolute center of gravity. And yet you do not know it, you don't recognize it, because the individual self that knows it has dissolved.

I have been working with Americans for sixteen years, but somehow it seems that the reality behind such words as *absolute self* and *absolute center of gravity* is very difficult for them to grasp. You have been educated and trained to affirm the self as "I am," to see and think about life and the world from that assertion of self without even questioning its validity. Probably you have never been trained in the activity of absolute self. This is why, even though all of you are constantly manifesting absolute self, you lack the recognition of the function and the ability to revive it when it is appropriate in your life. However, even without any formal training in the activity of absolute self, there have been individuals in your history who have attained this awareness and reflected their experience of the absolute in works of love and truth and beauty. Buddhism teaches that to realize the absolute, you do not need any special gift.

Everyone talks about *satori*. Americans love this exotic animal called *satori*. Actually *satori* has two parts: to realize absolute self (in which there is no self left to experience), and then, when this unification breaks up, to realize the individual self which objectifies the absolute. It is the essential tragedy of modern education that you are taught only to affirm the self, to develop just this one aspect. By affirming the individual self without knowing absolute self, you are approaching the problems of the world as if they were external to yourself. However, from such a one-sided perspective of self, you will be forever seeking that which appears only as an object to yourself. Since you only experience the world as external to you and you are never unified with it, then you are forever seeking the world. You are enslaved by it, and you can never experience life in its true joy. *Satori* means, ultimately, that there is only one center of gravity in the universe, and you are sitting in the center of gravity. What you ordinarily call the absolute or ultimate reality must become your own experience. When you have such an experience of the absolute, then there is no need to go on seeking things outside of yourself. When you are really embracing your friend, you are not seeking your friend or yourself. This is absolute self.

Separating from that embrace, you now recognize the experience of fulfillment. Having experienced God or Buddha as none other than yourself, you separate and worship Buddha, you pray to God. Two lovers embracing each other experience absolute self, but when they separate, then respect for each other arises. There is nothing mystical about these two activities whose endless repetition is the basis of human life. All that is lacking is the true wisdom to realize this function.

Does the absolute, Buddha, or God have to eat? If Buddha or God is hungry, he is not "Absolute." In the world of the absolute, the world of *samadhi*, there are no restaurants, no restrooms. The poet Gary Snyder sitting over there, if he understands this, will probably write a poem, "No toilets in heaven, no restaurants in the pure land, and I sure don't want to live there." Poets sing praises of the world, of the flower, and of the mosquito, and of man and woman. As human beings, surely you prefer to live in this human world, with all its distinctions, and its variety of things. But as human beings, you are also capable of realizing this world as the absolute. After all, who speaks of God and who experiences enlightenment? It is none other than human beings. Man's deepest wisdom is to base his human life on the realization of the world, both as relative or individual and as absolute.

Desire is natural in the human activity of individual self. The culture of today, however, is based only on this one aspect of life, individual self, and so it only represents human desire. Thus, if we are to truly examine the problems of this society, we must begin by examining the nature of desire and the individual self on which this society is built.

Buddhism teaches that there is no constant entity such as "self." Self is like the present. Moment by moment, as present dissolves into past and future becomes present, there is no fixed entity that can be identified as "present." The present-creating-activity is ceaseless. We can understand the "self" in the same way. Self is not a constant thing. It arises in the limiting activity of the absolute. To attach to the self is actually impossible because the self has no fixed nature. Therefore, trying to satisfy the desires of self is also impossible. A culture based on providing this satisfaction cannot succeed. What is needed is the wisdom to realize the self-beyond-attachment and to create a culture with this wisdom as its base.

Once you experience this absolute self, you will clearly comprehend the repetitious function of life: the individual self dissolving in the realization of absolute self, followed by the breaking up of the absolute, as the individual self arises again to dissolve anew into the absolute. This repetitious function is described as *sunyata*, or emptiness. I call this the function of zero. The realization of zero is the true way of affirming self. Since this true self-affirmation does not rely on the satisfaction of desire, it is real freedom. Once you experience the absolute, the limiting of your own individual desires arises naturally, with joy.

This culture is only familiar with the activity of individual self. We talk about solving the world's problems, of saving our environment, but who is willing to give up their attachment to self and to manifest freely as zero? This endless self-reformation is the only life that is possible for us.

7

Psychotherapeutic Materialism

Karl Sperber

There have been times when, as a client in psychotherapy, I was just finishing work in a group session, expressing an outpouring of anger, stark and strong, and just a touch of the littleness, the hurt, and the helplessness that lie beneath it. Having finished, perhaps even before I finished, I felt split. A part of me looking on with great approval—proud. I swung around in a crouch and clutched with confident fingers at what had happened, claiming *I* had done it, and adding it to the collection of proofs that I am what I believe myself to be; what I need to be. I had been strong enough to face my pain, to risk and to "grow." I could see myself again as an open-minded and self-integrated person. My self-image had been confirmed.

But there are, of course, other times. Vague discomfort becomes no more clear for all the pushing, focusing, and deep breathing that I do. For all my trying, all my conscious effort, I feel closed, unsure of myself. I suspect all previous gains and growth experiences. They are threatened with invalidation by this present inability to turn this moment into one more confirmation of that self which I wish to be. I become self-critical to the point that my shoulders are stooped, my voice loses all energy, my words are carefully chosen and meaningless. I try. I push. I am aware of all eyes on me. I imagine all eyes judging. But of course, it is myself that judges most harshly. "Scared of his own feelings. Closed. Lacks self-awareness. No flow. Phoney. Boring. Stuck." I slink on through the group sessions, dejected and depressed, until that time comes when, again for reasons still unknown to me, I stop pushing, stop trying, stop doing, and something in me is allowed to surface.

It is the evaluation of self on the basis of such experiences, and their collection in an attempt to affirm one's chosen self-image that is psychothera-peutic materialism. Chögyam Trungpa describes the same phenomenon in the seeker of spiritual enlightenment: "The problem is that ego can convert anything to its own use, even spirituality"[1]—even growth experiences. "Our vast collection of knowledge and experience is just part of the ego's display, part of the grandiose quality of the ego. We display them to the world and in so doing reassure ourselves that we exist, safe and secure, as 'spiritual' people."[2] For me this can be accurately para-phrased to read: We display our accumulated growth experiences and self-understandings to the world, and in so doing reassure ourselves that we exist, safe and secure and full of worth, as "self-actualizing" people.

But, of course, such self-affirmation does not last. There always enters doubt, not only from encountering others who seem to be further along the way than we, but also because this is an identity that requires constant reaffirmation. Since growth is a process and not an end state, in order to maintain an identity as a growing, self-integrating person, one cannot go too long without a growthful experience before one begins to feel its lack and begins to desire it, to need it. To be without the confirmation of that self-image which we have chosen as our unique identity threatens that self with invalidation, with death. And, just as in the pursuit of spirituality, this need for growthful experiences simply gets in the way of its own gratification. All such striving is a function of the ego, dissatisfied with what actually is, needing to become, to reffirm its existence as a real thing. *Psychotherapeutic material-ism is the paradox of ego striving for its own transcendence,* like consciously trying to fall asleep or, more absurdly, striving to jump free of one's own legs.

THE NEED TO BE THERAPEUTIC

Similarly, the concept of therapeutic materialism applies also to the therapist. True therapy occurs, I think, when the therapist is empty; when all his presence and awareness is with the patient so that there is that intimate connection, so rare and so nourishing, of real understanding.

Only when the therapist is, for the moment, empty of his needs, expecially the need to be a good therapist or a superior human being, can he or she be fully in touch with the patient and with the data of psychotherapy—the feelings, thoughts, and images aroused in the therapist by the client.

When such total contact happens, I only know that I was with the client in retrospect and through inference. That is, I must fabricate and distort my experience to fit the dualistic necessity of subject-predicate verbalization. There is no awareness at such times of an "I" separate from the other. The person/moment is all there is for me, a rare moment of full contact. I am doing nothing. Some words come, flow through me it seems. The client is touched, weeps perhaps, a flash of insight, a significant release and integration. Or the client need not respond in any particular way. Yet, I know that "it" has happened. I clutch gleefully at this incident. *I* have achieved what I have been constantly striving for. I have "felt" that oneness with my client that I am convinced is the essence of good therapy.

In that instant, when I am no longer in the moment, no longer fully with the client, when I am judging what has happened, the therapeutic relationship has ended. Ended by my need to see myself as a "good therapist." Ended by my need to add this incident to my collection of proofs that I am such a worthwhile, integrated person that others grow through their contact with me.

It is this self-contradictory process of ego taking credit for that which results only from being fully in the moment—and therefore momentarily egoless—that I call "psychotherapeutic materialism." It is a subtle kind of neurosis.

IN PURSUIT OF GROWTH

Here is a seemingly insurmountable obstacle to the goal that I've set for myself. How can I ever be enlightened or wholly integrated or empty if all my efforts are merely another more subtle way of affirming the existence and identity of my ego—precisely that aspect of myself I seek to transcend?

Humanists have long been telling us that the natural tendency of human beings is toward growth. Yet psychotherapeutic materialism is one ego identification which stands directly in the way of growth. All such judging and striving maintains a duality. As long as I am judging my feeling or my state of consciousness, I am outside of it and I cannot fully be it. Hence, such judging and striving is antithetical to the achievement of its object: oneness.

An image occurs to me: the ocean shore. An outcropping of rock extending into the sea, strong and narrow. Which, when I restrict my field of vision sufficiently, appears to split the water into two distinct and separate bodies. The action of the waves lapping up on either side makes it seem as though these two are ever straining toward one another, striving with each surge to overcome this rock with prevents their joining together in oneness. When, by simply stepping back and seeing more, by taking an all encompassing perspective, expanding consciousness, I see that the separation of the waves by the rock is only an illusion; that both waves are and always were part of the one ocean, separated only by my choice of perception nad my notion of striving to become one.

It is clear to me that this metaphor applies. The rock for me now is what I've diagnosed as my "psychotherapeutic materialism," an insurmountable obstacle in my path toward psychological integration. Yet, when I really "see," I see that I am already whole, that there is nothing to overcome.

In those moments of emptiness, of letting be, of complete contact with another, I know that I am all that I can be. The value of those moments of "not-doing" does not reside in how far they take me toward my ideal of perfect therapist(or perfect person), but rather such moments are no more or less than fully being. They are valueless.

NOTES

1. Trungpa (1973), p. 13.
2. Ibid, p. 14.

8

Befriending
Emotion

John Welwood

Emotions are our most common experience of being moved by forces seemingly beyond our control. As such, they are among the most confusing and frightening phenomena of everyday life. People often treat them as a nuisance or a threat, yet failing to experience them straightforwardly undermines sanity and well-being.

How can we begin to relate to emotions in a more direct and fearless way? Can we ever befriend our emotions and accept them as part of us? Why is emotion so hard to come to terms with in our culture? What is the difference between uselessly going around in emotional circles and working with emotions in a more healthy way? Is it possible to go more deeply into emotions, go toward them, face them as they are, so that we could allow their energies to expand our sense of what we are? If we could let ourselves feel just what we feel, instead of reacting against it, condemning it, or trying to manipulate and suppress it, perhaps we would develop greater confidence about facing whatever life confronts us with.

EMOTION IN WESTERN PSYCHOLOGY

The subject of emotion is one of the most confused chapters of modern psychology. Anyone wishing to learn about emotion from the literature of Western psychology finds a bewildering array of conflicting theories about what it is, how it arises, and what it signifies. James Hillman, at the end of an exhaustive study of these theories, could only conclude that "no matter how thoroughly amplified, the problem of emotion remains perennial and its solution ineffable."[1]

In Western culture we have a history of treating emotions with suspicion and contempt, as alien, "other," separate from us. The "passions" have usually been viewed as our "lower nature," from Plato onward. Viewing the source of the passions as Freud did, as an "it" (translated in English as "id"),[2] "a primitive chaos, a cauldron of seething excitement,"[3] makes it more difficult to befriend emotions and accept them as part of ourselves. This view of emotions as primitive and alien seems to be a classic Western way of separating ourselves from them. This is in sharp contrast to the meditative approach, which considers that it is precisely our alienation from emotions that makes them become so domineering and uncontrollable.

A dualistic attitude toward emotions, which sees them as something "other," can lead to trying to get rid of them by impulsively acting them out, or by suppressing them. However, neither of these strategies allow us to experience our emotions as they are, face to face. Acting out and suppressing emotions often only keep us separate from them.

Before exploring how to work with emotion in a different way, it is important to understand what emotion is and how it usually arises.

THE SPECTRUM OF FELT ENERGY

Our feeling life has a whole spectrum of expressions, from global and diffuse to sharp and intense. This spectrum of felt energy could be pictured, as in Figure 1, in a cone shape, with a broad and deep base, which gets more narrow and intense as its peak:

FIGURE 1. The Spectrum of Felt Energy.

The Ground of Feeling and Emotion: Basic Aliveness

All our feelings and emotions grow out of a basic life stream coursing through us. The biologist Rene Dubos describes this basic aliveness as a wholesome feeling persisting beneath all the ups and downs of circumstance:

> About the experience of life, most people are under the illusion that they can be happy only if something especially good happens. Oddly enough, there is only one phrase I know to express that life is good *per se,* that just being alive is good . . . the French expression, *joie de vivre. Joie de vivre* simply means that just being alive is an extraordinary experience. The quality of that experience anyone can see by watching a young child or a young animal playing in the spring. It is totally immaterial what goes on, except for the fact that you are alive. It does not mean that you are very happy with the way you live. You can even be suffering; but just being alive is a quality *per se.*[4]

Our basic aliveness is also the source of our sensitivity and tenderness. Because we are fundamentally open and receptive to life, we are vulnerable. Our soft skin, the intricate workings of our senses, brain, and nervous system are all geared toward *letting the world in.* Feeling and emotion are what arise in response to letting the world in.

Our aliveness is not only the source of feelings; it is also contained within them, just as water is the cradle of life as well as a universal element in all living tissues. Like earth, our sense of aliveness encompasses and nurtures us, with specific feelings growing out of its ground. Like air, which, when breathed in, quickens the whole body with a fresh source of energy, our aliveness provides an open space at the core of feelings, which keeps them from ever becoming totally fixed or solid. And like fire, our sense of aliveness has an all-encompassing warmth. Connecting with this aliveness, in which lies our basic sanity and well-being is to discover our most intimate sensitivity, from which all our feelings and emotions arise.

Felt Senses

Between this pure aliveness and the specific feelings and emotions we are most familiar with, we have more global kinds of "felt senses" about the life situations we are in. For example, I may feel anger toward someone, but anger is never all that I feel toward him. My anger is only the tip of the iceberg of a much larger sense of how I relate to him, what bothers me in our relationship, and many other senses for how he affects me and how I have related to similar people and situations in the past. This larger "iceberg" is much wider and deeper than my anger, and can actually be experienced as a global felt sense in the body. We can tap into such a felt sense by asking ourselves, "How does this person feel to me as a whole?" or "How does this whole situation feel to me?"

Because a felt sense includes many different aspects of how we relate to a situation, it may seem vague or fuzzy at first, appearing for instance, as a tightness in the chest or a heaviness in the stomach. Yet we can begin to unfold its meanings by asking questions of it and letting it speak to us. For example, with the client I described in Chapter 4, the felt sense of heaviness in his stomach turned out to contain frustration, disappointment, holding back, and desire to communicate and care more deeply. Unfolding a felt sense can help open up the basic aliveness underneath and reconnect a person with positive life directions that may have been dammed by the entanglement of the situation.[5]

Feeling and Emotion

In contrast to a felt sense, which is often unclear at first, feelings, such as sadness, gladness, or anger are relatively familiar and recognizable. Emotions are more intense forms of feelings. The feeling of sadness may build into grief, the feeling of irritation can become a fierce rage. The distinguishing characteristic of emotion is that it dominates our attention and cannot be ignored, while a feeling can remain in the background of awareness.

THE BIRTH OF EMOTIONAL ENTANGLEMENT

I have suggested that feelings and emotions themselves do not have to be a problem if we can relate to them directly. How then do they turn into such a problem, becoming tight, claustrophobic, or explosive? Suppose I wake up feeling sad. Instead of letting this sadness touch me and put me in contact with what is happening in my life, I may concentrate on how it punctures my self-image of being a together, successful person. In that it seems to undermine the self-image I would like to maintain, I stand back from it and judge it as bad. But when I judge sadness negatively and cut myself off from it, it becomes frozen, losing its tender quality that connects me to life. I get caught up in sad "story lines"—sad thoughts and fantasies which I project in the past and the future (e.g., "What is the matter with me? I'll never get it together, etc."). The more I mull over these story lines, the more I become locked into them. The more sad story lines arise, the sadder I become—a vicious circle that eventually starts building into more intense emotions of depression and despair. As a heavier depression grows out of simple sadness over a specific incident, I may begin to see the entire world, my whole life history and future prospects in this light. My depressed thoughts radiate out in all directions and lock me further into my depression. In this way, my sadness has become thick, solid, and heavy.

Actaully, the word "sad" comes from the same root as the words "sated" or "satisfied" which indicates that it may actually be a kind of fullness, in this case fullness of heart. We often feel sad when our heart—that part of us where things touch us—is full. This fullness, which may want to spill over in tears, is still very tender and alive, as opposed to the frozen state of depression that results from putting away our sadness rather than opening to it. The cycle of feelings giving rise to thoughts solidifies and freezes feeling and causes us to go around in emotional circles, getting nowhere. As we spin around in this emotional confusion, perception becomes cloudly, and we often say or do things we later regret. Cutting through the tendency to get caught up in emotional story lines takes a certain discipline, which psychotherapy and meditation can provide in different ways.

THE THERAPEUTIC APPROACH TO EMOTION

Therapeutic work provides one way to free ourselves from emotional spinning by going underneath the emotion to unfold a larger felt sense—which expresses our whole connection to the situation about which we are feeling so strongly. For example, with the client described in Chapter 4, finding a deeper caring underneath his anger released him from his anger's grip. That rather simple example illustrates what may happen in greater depth over a longer time in therapy. Venting emotions may be necessary along the way as well, but what often seems to release an emotional tangle is not catharsis per se, but letting our feelings speak to us and reveal what they are asking us to look at, what they are telling us about how we are relating to our life situations. It often helps in therapeutic work to separate oneself from an emotion, to personify it and give it a voice, so that it can speak freely to us, without the censorship that might arise if I regard the emotion as "me." Letting emotions open up and speak to us allows "felt shifts"—gaps in the mental logic of emotional story lines—which break up the logjams in our life stream so that it can start moving forward more freely again.

However, one limitation of the therapeutic approach to emotion is its tendency to overlook the larger sense of aliveness that often opens up in moments of shift and release. Exploring feelings may become an endless project, an end in itself, often obscuring the larger aliveness, tenderness, and openness that we can discover through them. Insofar as a primary purpose of psychotherapy is to untangle emotional problems and strengthen identity, it often does not provide means for gaining full access to this larger aliveness, which overflows our personal boundaries.

THE MEDITATIVE APPROACH TO EMOTION

The practice of meditation can provide this access, partly through helping us to face and work with our emotions more directly. While meditating, the meditator does not try to discover the meaning of his feelings, but simply acknowledges their presence and returns to the breath. When surges of emotional turbulence arise, he practices "keeping his seat" and riding them out. In so doing, he may start to glimpse how, underneath the whitecaps of emotional frenzy and the broader swells of feeling, all is quite calm in the depths of the ocean, where our personal life problems empty into larger, universal life currents.

Mindfulness practice helps us become more aware of the gaps and discontinuities that are always opening up spontaneously in the logic of our story lines. For instance, even in the midst of the most intense anger, we might begin to notice flashes of "Why am I so angry? Do I need to make such a big deal out of this? Is this really as important as I am making it?" Meditation allows us to notice how big mind is always available and flashing into awareness, even when we are most caught up in our stories. Although we often feel most alive when involved in emotional dramas, meditation helps us realize our basic ongoing aliveness that is always present in both dramatic and undramatic moments.

TRANSMUTATION

By neither suppressing emotions nor exploring the meaning in them, meditation teaches us a way to feel their naked aliveness and contain their energy, apart from any story lines they suggest. This approach to emotion as a vehicle for self-illumination, for seeing through oneself and one's mental fixations is called *transmutation* in Vajrayana Buddhism as well as in other traditions. The notion of transmutation, going back to the ancient alchemical traditions, implies converting something seemingly worthless into something extremely valuable, like lead into gold. The following exploration of transmutation is simply meant to be suggestive, without presuming to capture or conceptualize its subtleties, which are much more experientially vivid than could be described here.

The first step toward transmutation is to cut through the struggle of self-judgment by accepting emotion as an expression of our own life energy. Instead of seeing emotions as a threat, it is possible to befriend them by allowing them to be just as they are. By not getting caught up in judging them, we can directly feel their actual texture and quality. Transmutation in the Buddhist tradition becomes possible only through meditation practice, in which one learns to face and accept everything that arises in the mind, without losing one's sense of presence. Chögyam Trungpa outlines several aspects of this process:

> There are several stages in relating with the emotions: seeing, hearing, smelling, touching, and transmuting. In the case of seeing the emotions, we have a general awareness that the emotions have their own space, their own development. We accept them as part of the pattern of mind, without question. And then hearing involves experiencing the pulsation of such energy, the energy upsurge as it comes toward you. Smelling is appreciating that the energy is somewhat workable. Touching is feeling the nitty-gritty of the whole thing, that you can touch and relate with it, that your emotions are not particularly destructive or crazy, but just an upsurge of energy, whatever form they take. Transmutation is [to] experience emotional upheaval as it is but still work with it, become one with it.[6]

For someone accustomed to struggling against emotions, this might seem an impossible task—"If I let myself really experience my emotions, maybe I will go berserk!" In most situations this fear indicates how alienated we are from ourselves. By alienating our own energy, making it "other" and then judging it negatively, we may come to believe that emotions are demonic, that we have "monsters" inside us. By treating emotions as an autonomous power, we grant them dominion over us.[7] In their raw state, emotions are fluid expressions of our aliveness, and they are constantly changing, in-process. But our reactions against them and the story lines we weave out of them ("My anger is right because . . .," "My sadness is bad because . . .") turn their fluid aliveness into something solid and heavy. The irony is that in trying to control them, we become controlled by them all the more. So we find ourselves stuck in their grip—which leads to more attempts to control them or to explosive eruptions that leave us further alienated from them.

The first step in taming the lion of emotions, in transmuting their fierce energy into illumination is to befriend it by letting it be, without judging it as good or bad. Running away from a fierce animal or trying to suppress its energy only provokes attack. The path of transmutation is to directly identify with the energy of emotions and become one with it. Although emotions may seem to have us in their grip, as soon as we turn to face them directly, we find nothing as solid or fixed as our judgments or stories about them.

The Buddhist definition of ego as "holding on to ourselves" and controlling our experience helps us understand why it is so hard to let ourselves feel our emotions and let them be. We usually try to keep them from flowing through us because they threaten the control we try to maintain. Since ego by definition is the activity of holding on, "I" cannot let go, "I" wants to ward off anything that threatens this hold. What is possible, however, is to let the emotions wash through me, and in so doing, wash the controlling part of me away with them. If I can really open to the actual texture and quality of a feeling, instead of trying to control it or churn out story lines from it, "I"—the activity of trying to hold myself together—can dissolve into "it"—the larger feeling process itself. If I fully become my sadness, it may intensify for a while, and I may feel the full painfulness of it. Yet really letting myself feel the pain and letting myself dissolve into it wakes me to the feeling of being alive. Emotions, we could say, are the blood shed by ego—they start to flow whenever we are touched, whenever the shell around the heart if punctured. Trying to control them is trying to keep the shell from cracking. Letting ego bleed, on the other hand, opens the heart.

So, if I turn to face my own demons, they dissolve, revealing themselves to be my own living energy. Then I can begin to feel my tenderness, my vulnerability to life, which reminds me that what I really am is a living being who is exposed to the world, interdependent and connected with all other beings. Moving beyond my judgments and story lines to feel this naked quality of my life is a breakthrough that relieves pain and develops compassion for others.

With this kind of experiential understanding, a therapist can help clients face their emotions more directly as well. For example, one man I worked with felt terribly burdened by his extreme hunger for love. The first task was to cut through his critical judgments about his need. ("I should be more self-reliant; this need is terrible.") When he could let himself feel his neediness fully and directly, he was able to discover his aliveness in it, as the following condensed transcript illustrates:

> Therapist: What happens when you let that need be there?
> Client: It says: "I'm unhappy. I'm all alone. I'm scared. It's hard to make it on my own. I need someone to love and care for me."
> Therapist: What if you let yourself have that need for caring 100 percent?
> Client: (long pause) It really shifts things around inside me to do that. . . . When I really go into it, it gives me a feeling of power . . . like I'm deserving. . . . It really feels different. . . . I feel more balanced . . . grounded. . . . There's much more space. . . . There's no desperateness or fear. . . . Letting myself have this need is very nurturing, even though no one else is there . . . I feel full.

Thus, in turning to face our emotions directly, we may get a glimpse of the fullness of life. Emotion, as something we judge and separate ourselves from, may appear overpowering. But as something that touches us, it expresses the dynamic energy of life itself. Transmuting emotion requires a gesture of opening to its energy without backing off or getting caught in emotionally charged thoughts and images arising from it. Tarthang Tulku, a Tibetan Buddhist teacher, describes this process quite exactly:

> What we can do is concentrate on the anger, not allowing any other thoughts to enter. That means we sit with our angry thoughts, focusing our concentration on the anger—not on its objects—so that we make no discriminations, have no reactions. Likewise, when anxiety or any other disturbing feeling arises, concentrate on the feeling, not on thoughts about it. Concentrate on the center of the feeling: penetrate into that space. There is a density of energy in that center that is clear and distinct. This energy has great power, and can transmit great clarity. To transform our negativities, we need only to learn to touch them skillfully and gently.[8]

This may be a delicate maneuver at first. We may have a brief glimpse of a larger life energy, but then soon drift back into story lines. However, the sustained attention that is necessary can be facilitated by meditation practice, through which one can learn to stop being "hijacked" by one's thoughts.

Reacting against emotions—fearing our fear, being angry about our anger, getting depressed about our sadness—is much worse than these primary feelings themselves, for it freezes them and turns us against ourselves. Befriending emotions opens us to ourselves and allows us to discover the intelligence and responsiveness contained in them. Anger can become a means of direct communication, rather than a weapon to hurt ourselves or others. Fear can wake us up to what is actually going on in certain situations, rather than just serving as a signal to run away or hide. We can appreciate loneliness as a longing to share and sadness as a fullness of heart; then they have a certain dignity rather than simply indicating some lack or failing on our part. In judging these feelings, we cut ourselves off from our own aliveness; in feeling them fully, their energy becomes available to us, enlarging our sense of what life is about.

Various metaphors have been used to describe this transformation of emotional energy. Benoit describes it as a "process comparable with that which transforms coal into diamonds: the aim of this process is not the destruction of the ego, but its transformation. The conscious acceptance results in the coal which has become denser, and so blacker and more opaque, being instantaneously transformed into a diamond that is perfectly transparent."[9]

This image of transparency and lucency, where emotion becomes a window onto the vitality of life itself, like a diamond metamorphosed from coal, is particularly prominent in Vajrayana or Tantric Buddhism. *Vajra* signifies the diamondlike, indestructible clarity of the awake state of mind. *Vajra* is itself seen as a quality of life, whose fullest realization is "mirrorlike wisdom." Because it signifies absolute clarity, the Vajrayana (literally, the "diamond path") sees the world in terms of luminosity, lit up with brilliance. Struggling to confirm our self-images creates a screen of confusion that dulls this natural brilliance. Transmuting emotion is one way of turning the dark, murky world of the confused mind into the radiance of clear vision.

This metaphor may make transmutation seem like a sudden change, but it is actually part of a gradual path of increasing friendliness with ourselves. Other metaphors emphasize the gradual, organic nature of this process:

> Unskilled farmers throw away their rubbish and buy manure from other farmers, but those who are skilled go on collecting their own rubbish, in

spite of the bad smell and the unclean work, and when it is ready to be used they spread it on their land, and out of this they grow their crops. And though it is very difficult and unhygienic, as it were, to work on, that is the only way to start. So out of these unclean things comes the birth of the seed which is Realization.[10]

Suzuki Roshi speaks in a similar vein of how the weeds of the mind may be used to enrich one's awakening awareness:

We pull the weeds and bury them near the plant to give it nourishment. So you should not be bothered by your mind. Your should rather be grateful for the weeds, because eventually they will enrich your practice. If you have some experience how the weeds in your mind change into mental nourishment, your practice will make remarkable progress.[11]

What is essential in this approach is to identify fully with basic aliveness, the larger open space around and inside emotions.[12] By realizing this spaciousness, emotional turmoil begins to appear as a smaller drama in the middle of a much larger awareness. When we can dissolve into this larger awareness, this free energy, emotion becomes an opportunity to explore our depths, instead of getting tossed around by the waves on the surface of our being.

Overcoming fear of our own energy can help us develop fearlessness toward the whole of life, known in Buddhism as the "lion's roar":

The lion's roar is the fearless proclamation that any state of mind, including the emotions, is a workable situation. Then the most powerful energies become absolutely workable rather than taking you over, because there is nothing to take over if you are not putting up any resistance. Indian Ashokan art depicts the lion's roar with four lions looking in four directions, which symbolizes the idea of having no back. Every direction is a front, symbolizing all-pervading awareness. The fearlessness covers all directions.[13]

To summarize, this transformative approach to emotions involves: (1) keeping our seat in the middle of emotional turbulence; (2) cutting through judgments about emotions in order to feel them more fully; and (3) identifying with their energy in its power and painfulness. In so doing, we discover the intense tenderness of our aliveness.

In the Vajrayana tradition, genuine transmutation is not considered to be possible without the proper understanding and guidance. Since one could become overrun or inflated by the intensity of one's emotional energy, it is considered essential to have a firm foundation in meditation practice, which helps one to see through one's domination by thought and fantasy, and to develop the strength to no longer be carried away by them. It is also important to work with a living teacher who has an intimate personal understanding of the energies of life, and who can guide the student through the many twists and turns involved in the development of this deeper awareness. Then, through discipline and practice, the confusion of the emotions may become transformed into the wisdom of seeing things as they are.

NOTES

1. Hillman (1961), p. 289.
2. See Welwood and Wilber (1979).
3. Freud (1933).
4. Dubos, in Needleman (1979), p. 59.
5. See Welwood (1982).
6. Trungpa (1976), p. 69.
7. "That which has become an object to me is something which has captured me." Hisamatsu (1960), p. 78.
8. Tarthang Tulku (1978), pp. 54, 52.
9. Benoit (1959), p. 143.
10. Trungpa (1969), p. 23.
11. S. Suzuki (1970), p. 36.
12. See Welwood (1977).
13. Trungpa (1976), pp. 69–72.

=9=

Anger and the Gentle Life

Adrian van Kaam

Our aim in this article is to understand how we may better live and experience human gentleness, culminating in a gentle presence to ourselves and others.

The word gentleness points to an attitude. Expressions like a "gentle gesture," "a gentle word," "a gentle approach," are all said of human behavior that expresses certain inner feelings or attitudes. One can also speak about a "gentleman." Think about the English word. It seems to indicate that gentleness can become a characteristic of a person as a whole and not merely of some of his expressions. Gentleness can become a lasting attitude, affecting or transforming one's personality. Gentleness directs itself to something or someone in a distinctive way; it implies a special relation of a person to himself, to others, to things.

What is it that evokes this gentleness? Gentleness is usually enkindled by something that is precious but vulnerable. Everything that appears fragile and vulnerable and at the same time precious in some way seems to evoke gentleness: a sick person, a child, a pregnant woman, the victim of an accident. All that is small and somehow precious: a baby, a newborn puppy, an old woman emaciated by age and sickness. Yet also something large and powerful can evoke gentless. A person could feel gentle about the boss of a large company who is all bluster and no bite. Gentleness is not evoked by the impressive function and power of the boss but by the vulnerability of inner endearing traits that hide behind a facade of strength. Greatness evokes gentleness in so far as it refers to the vulnerability of hidden precious qualities that one knows to be a deeper characteristic of the person. For behind each one's strength is hiding a person in need of love, understanding, and appreciation.

All that is pure, unblemished, and immaculate can also evoke feelings of gentleness because its exquisiteness seems so fragile and open to contamination: the bright wonder of an idealistic young man, the innocent questions of a child, the unsuspecting spontaneity of an adolescent girl make us gentle in our approach to them. Finally, all that is beautiful can make us gentle for we feel that it can be marred so easily: the perfection of a painting, the radiance of a human face, the attractiveness of a fresh flower. In these and many more ways, beauty touches us and evokes gentleness.

Can I be gentle with myself? From what we have uncovered thus far about gentleness, I can be gentle with myself if I can experience myself simultaneously as precious and vulnerable. I know from daily experience that I am not always faithful to myself. Many times I feel disappointed in myself, experiencing how I prevent my better self from flourishing. In fact, I am often my greatest disappointment. Most people are not inclined to feel gentle towards this disappointing self because they do not look with love at the precious person they are called to be. They either feel indifferent or they refuse to see their shortcomings and limitations. When they begin to see how fragile and vulnerable their precious selfhood is, they feel either frustrated, desperate, or angry with themselves. Such self-condemnation does not give rise to a gentle approach to themselves. At such moments, I want to whip myself into shape. I feel that I have to discipline myself mercilessly, forgetting that I may harm my finer sensitivities and silence my better self.

What is the other self that approaches me so unkindly? It is the voice of my pride and anxious concern to look good in my own eyes and in the eyes of others. I do not accept the limited but precious person I can be. I ask myself only what others may think about me, how I can get ahead of society, even at the expense of the unique potential excellence I have.

THE GENTLE LIFESTYLE

I spent part of last summer writing a paper. My decisiveness to get the thing over and done with made me feel tense and strained. Before going any further, I began to tell myself: "This time try to do your work with ease of mind." So I tried. I began to muse in a leisurely way about my topic. I read thoughtfully material related to it. Only then did I feel ready to write out a few paragraphs or pages. When the work became too much, I would stroll in a nearby park, look at the flowers, follow the antics of playful ducks in the pond. I tried not to let myself become upset, strained or willful. Neither did I try to obtain the results of my study instantly. I was sure my topic would speak to me in its own good time if I would keep myself quietly open for hints, sudden associations, flashes of insight. My faithful readings and reflections would sooner or later show me the main aspects of the question I was dealing with.

So I trusted. I also kept my inner freedom to occasionally close my books, halt my typing, and leave my notes to enjoy the radiance of the sun in the garden or the pleasant breeze along the lanes and meadows of the park. My new way worked. Slowly I could feel the ideas rise, the right words come. A gentle perseverance in my attention to the topic and its expression proved sufficient for the paper to be written.

At first I had approached my task with the anxious drive to get the work over with. Now I had given myself over to the calming effect of a gentle life style. I could almost feel the tautness leaving my head, the tenseness draining from my muscles. No longer was the will to force things out present in me. I did not command my topic to make itself clear at once. I was content to be nothing more than I could be at the moment, content to make as much headway as I was humanly able to. There was no compulsion to be more efficient, more clever or faster than I reasonably could be in a relaxed manner. Gone was the eagerness to hurry up the process of production. The spirit of gentility had invaded my work.

On other occasions my feelings were quite the opposite. At such times I wanted desperately to gain time. The work had to be done as fast as possible, I felt, and the topic itself was not going to play a part in its production. I did not give the topic much chance to show itself to me. I ran through books and articles without really allowing them to affect me. The topic spoke but I could not hear its message because I did not approach it gently, as a reflective person should. Many pages were pregnant with meaning but not for me. Instead I gathered surface information as fast as I could. No time was given to let it sink in, to make it part of myself, to recreate it in my own manner.

For the process of thought and its precise expression, time is of the essence. Gentility allows time to run its course. My concern was to gain time. I typed my information out like a reporter on the city desk. While I was hurrying on, I was concerned neither with the kind of people who would read my paper nor with the people around me and their needs.

By contrast, gentility opens me to what people, events, and things may disclose to me or reasonably want of me. I allow these persons and things to change and affect me when such change is called for. Gentleness is an attitude of letting be, combined with a patient abiding with myself or with the person, task, or problem I am involved in.

I can be busily engaged in a demanding task like writing a paper, organizing a business deal, fighting for a cause and yet be gentle inwardly. One condition is to keep in tune with the real me and with my real life situation and not to become a prisoner of my projects or of the outcome of my task. It is unrealistic to strive after something I cannot reach without overextending myself. Such efforts wear me out. I feel frustrated when I cannot reach goals too sublime for me. Even when I achieve such goals, frustration may still result. I may have so depleted myself by vehement strife that I cannot enjoy my success. It may seem meager in comparison to all I had to go through to make this achievement come true. For too long a time, I may have used my life as merely a tool for achievement in the eyes of others.

In contrast, the gentle attitude leaves room for what is more than mere usefulness. When I am willful instead of gentle, I program my life. Things are not allowed to appear to me as they are. The willful man squeezes every experience in a tight little box tied up with unbreakable strings. His mind becomes a storehouse of these little airtight compartments. He does not allow any new situation to touch the content of his store. What he has done is to forfeit his ability to abide with things as if for the first time. He moves through life as a programmed computer lacking any sense of wonder.

The gentle person is more free. He can take himself and the world as they are because he feels free to be himself and to let all things be with the same gentility. There is a friendly accord between him and his life situation. He does not feel that he has to push himself forward or hold himself back. If he cannot feel at ease with what he is doing, he can put it aside for another time when he can more readily give his all. If the situation demands that he go on with the work at hand—in spite of his reluctance—he gently does what cannot be delayed. He does not allow himself to become upset by the less perfect outcome due to the inauspiciousness of the moment. He takes things in stride. Being a gentle man, he never forces people or situations. Neither would he tolerate anyone who forced himself or others, were he able to ward off such imposition. All people, events, and things, no matter how insignificant, draw his respect. The motto of the gentle man might well be, "I must never force things."

In living the gentle life style, I may discover something else. Gentility stills and quiets the greediness and aggressiveness of the ego. A silenced ego allows me to center myself. While it is helpful to have a strong ego, it is harmful to center my life in that ego alone. Greediness and arrogance might then absorb all of my life. I would be so busy keeping my ego sublime, sane, and successful that no time would be left for a gentle nursing of my deeper values.

Any true gentility mellows the ego, not by weakening its strength but by diminishing its arrogance, its false exclusiveness, its pretense of ultimacy. Any diminishment of the ego's arrogance makes me more available to life.

GENTLENESS AND AGGRESSION

Gentleness is a main condition for wholesome living. Can I then allow feelings of agression in my life? What about attack, taking the offensive, feeling angry?

Aggressive feelings can be wholesome and human. They may keep us alive and dynamic in situations that demand a sharp, swift approach. I may wrongly consider all aggressive feelings to be less than human. I may begin to repress my awareness of any anger and aggression that emerges in me. It is true that nearly all people who want to live gently have difficulty coming to terms with their aggressive feelings. I too tend not to take these feelings in stride. Instead of working them through, I turn them off. Not daring to see them for the human feelings they are, I may malign all indignant feelings as unworthy of me. The price I pay for such denial is incalculable.

Not only may I deny aggressiveness that is misdirected; I may even deny my ability to be aggressive because aggressiveness is removed from my awareness as quickly as it comes up. Anxious repression does not do away with aggressiveness. I can hide but never destroy this potential of my nature and its inevitable upsurge in my life. I may mask aggressiveness with gentleness, but it still comes out as muffled violence. Others sense that my gentleness is a fraud to take advantage of them.

This masking of aggression may not be a conscious forgery on my part. My intention may be honest, my desire to be gentle genuine. What is pretended is a lack of anger that is really there. I alone am the victim of such unconscious pretense. Perhaps I fell into this trap because I pushed myself too fast and furiously into the role of the gentle person. I skipped the work of catching my angry feelings, of bringing them honestly to light, of bearing with them patiently.

Gentleness does not deny anger and aggression. On the contrary, it helps me to bear with even that unreasonable aggression I cannot as yet overcome. Gentleness draws from this affliction a humility that in turn deepens the gentle life style. Being gentle with myself helps me to bring to the fore in the right way, at the right time and place, my reasonable indignation without hurting others unnecessarily. It drives aggressive feelings to the surface, never pushes them underground.

A gentle life style is difficult to maintain when unresolved anger lurks within me. Anger, driven underground, poisons my life. Aggressive feeling when repressed cannot spend its force wisely and moderately. All it does is turn inward and thrive as a hidden explosive power—a counter style of the gentle life ready to pervert true gentility. When it bursts out finally, it does so in an uncontrollable, destructive way.

Anger should be allowed to come into the open from the beginning and spend itself in a wise and moderate way, for instance, in a forthright talk with a good friend. This openness gets rid of beginning anger and allows the gentle life style to be taken up again. After anger has been aired and dispersed in an acceptable way, gentleness may deepen.

The gentle life style should be the usual climate of my life. Moments of anger, expressed in the right way to the right person, should only be interruptions of my basic style of gentle living, passing incidents that do not touch the calm inmost region of gentleness that prevails. Aggressiveness should not become a lasting style of life but only an incidental emergence—necessary in certain social situations for defense of rights and truths, and of the unique role I am there called to play; necessary also for psychic relief and for keeping the gentle life style pure, that is, unmarred by hidden aggressive feelings.

The wages of repressed anger include, in the long run, poor psychological and bodily health, damage to my togetherness with others, and diminishment of my effectiveness. I should accept and work through my feelings of anger and aggression. Insight into these feelings can free me for a more gentle life and make available hidden energy, talents, and abilities.

Taking a healthier view of my potentiality for anger and repression seems in general to foster better health of mind and body.

We must now reflect concretely on how to detect, expose, sublimate, and wisely express aggressiveness without hurting others. So far we only commented on the general compatibility of a gentle life style with intermittent moments of anger and indignation.

GENTLENESS AND SUBLIMATION OF ANGER

All people get angry, saints and sinners alike. Feeling annoyed, angry, aggressive is therefore as human as feeling sad, delighted, loving, tired, or lonely. Gentle persons get angry like everyone else. The difference is that anger and aggressiveness do not dominate their lives. They may be incidentally angry, usually at the right time and in the right way. Also they seem to know better how to handle their aggressiveness.

Growth in true selfhood does not whittle away my capacity to feel angry or aggressive. Neither does it lessen my need to respond in some way to that feeling. Growth helps me to accept my aggresiveness as a human feeling that is undeniably there. The unfolding spirit of man, moreover, offers each person a wider view of life. It is from this perspective that I may see in a new light the persons, events, or things that arouse my anger and aggression. From this wider view, my anger either subsides, lessens, or finds the right expression in the angry situation. This wider vision itself is born not in anger but in gentleness.

It is not enough to enjoy this wider vision of life; I must also know my anger and its source so that it can be illumined and tempered by this philosophical or religious vision. A first condition for this sublimation of anger is knowing fully that I feel this way. Next I need to find out why I am feeling so. Only then can I do something about the way I feel in the light of my gentle vision of self and humanity. My angry "feeling against" can be tempered by a deeper "feeling of." Still it is difficult to realize and accept peacefully that I feel angry and aggressive. A false idea of what life should be like has perhaps made me feel ashamed, guilty, or anxious about my aggressiveness—so much so that I don't dare to admit to myself how angry I sometimes get. Even when I own up to the anger that arises in me on certain occasions, it may still be difficult to pinpoint its original source. This takes insight, reflection, and patience.

GENTILITY AND EMOTIONAL RESPONSE

All of us are born with the ability to feel angry or gentle. Usually such instantaneous responses are not freely chosen. We picked these reactions up from others long before we could talk, or for that matter understand what was being said angrily or gently by the people around us. While we could not yet comprehend, we could sense the angry and gentle moods, feelings and deeds of father and mother, brothers and sisters. Without them having to tell us, we learned from them on the spot how to act angrily or gently.

As children, we listened to the way in which they responded to our own feelings, especially those of aggression or gentleness, when we dared to let them come out. Maybe we were lucky enough to be born into a family that allowed us to bring our feelings out into the open without playing any of them down. They took in stride both our tenderness and aggressiveness. Then, too, they let us freely know how they felt. At home they created a climate in which it was easy for us to know how they felt and what we ourselves were feeling. They realistically accepted the fact that all kinds of feelings may spontaneously emerge in human beings outside the immediate control of their will. Each one in such a family could show how he felt without being condemned and threatened for that.

The result of this climate of relaxed self-expression is an overall gentleness, only sporadically pierced by expressions of anger and aggression. Because the latter feelings are expressed at their first emergence, they do not have time to build up inwardly into a sudden outburst or explosion. The telling of a dissatisfaction becomes more and more like a giving of information about what is beginning to build up inside. The other can take that information into account; it is then easier to rescue or restore the style of gentleness. In such an atmosphere, we would learn early in life that it is alright to feel gentle and loving and alright also at times to feel angry and aggressive.

Like most people, however, I may not have been that lucky. Perhaps my family, and the people in my school, church, and neighborhood, were afraid to admit the emergence of angry feelings in themselves or to tolerate angry feelings that arose in others towards them. As a result, my life of feeling may have become crippled. I may have grown so fearful that my feelings might not be acceptable to any other person that I do not dare to allow them to come through even in the presence of people who really support me. I may have a hard time feeling and expressing either gentleness or anger to my true friends.

As a way beyond this I must stop feeling one way and acting the opposite way when the situation does not make this truly necessary from the viewpoint of compassion or wise diplomacy. When I feel angry, I must not smile sweetly or freeze sullenly. I must learn instead to be humble and courageous enough to let my feelings come out—straight, honestly and simply, yet wisely and not destructively, if the situation allows me this freedom of expression. Surprisingly, when I learn to communicate my feelings at their first emergence to those whom I can trust, it will become easier for me to express them in a modest and relaxed manner, which may restore the atmosphere of gentleness.

It is precisely when I deny my anger or pretend the opposite that it might grow inwardly out of proportion; it can no longer be enlightened and mellowed by my deeper self. My trusted friends, not having received the slightest clue that I am growing mad, may unwittingly add fuel to the fire. My denial and their misunderstanding may finally lead to aggressive outbursts and unreasonable displays of rage, no longer in proportion to the incident that suddenly, like a spark, touches off my accumulated madness. Such displays may poison the atmosphere for a long time.

When I feel angry or aggressive with a good friend, well-meaning family member, or trusted acquaintance, I should let him know it in some way, so that he is aware of my mood or feeling and can take it wisely into account. This openness will also help him to feel trusting when I am gentle with him at most other times of our togetherness. Neither when I feel angry should I get cold and sullen and withdraw my attention and affection from the friend or comrade who makes my angry.

Briefly, if I am really angry. I have to let it come out straight and wisely when possible and beneficial for all concerned. If the situation makes it impossible or unwise to do so, at least I can talk it out with a friend or some understanding acquaintance. If such persons are not available, or even if they are available, I can still speak it out or write it out for myself, run angrily around the block, pound a punching bag, or take an aggressive swim. I must, in short, never allow anger and aggression to bottle up in me and so paralyze my potential for trustworthy gentleness to myself and others.

Once anger and aggression are out in the open, I can cope with them. I can lift who or what angers me into the light of my wider vision of life and humanity. In that light, my anger may melt, especially when it proves to be a mere self-centered, ego-competitive anger or an anger based on the easily threatened insecurity of a self that has not yet found, through growth, true inner strength.

RELIEF OF ANGER AND GROWTH IN GENTLENESS

A fake gentle life does not admit to angry feelings; it does not accept them and try to live with them while quietly mellowing a little day by day. Fake gentle life starts from an idealized picture of myself. "From now on I have to be the perfect pleasant person approved of by everyone." Unconsciously, I may add to this ideal image: "If I never get angry, others will never get angry with me."

I begin to build my personality on the image of the "nice fellow," liked and revered by all. Since this is the image I live by, any show of anger, even the slightest irritation, seems to tarnish my image. Being revered by all is a way to be safe. Any irritation I may evoke in others is felt as a threat to myself.

The price I pay for this role-playing is immense. I can never be myself. Constant attempts to fool myself and others cost me enormous energy. Not growing in true gentle life, I drift into a superficial show of sweetness. I lost out with those who might have been able to like the original limited me but who do not like me now because they are unable to find out who I really am.

There is little difference, then, between either bottling up my angry emotions or letting them out of the bag by kicking the furniture, smashing a teapot, or lashing out at any unfortunate creature who crosses my path. This outburst may relieve my pent-up anger, but it does not promote my growth in gentleness. On the contrary, I begin to develop a violent style of life. My emphasis is on the instant relief of anger here and now. I overlook the fact that the repeated acting out of aggression in numerous here and now moments will have a long-term effect on my life. Rewarded by the pleasant feeling of relief I get whenever I let people have it, I may feel the urge to be even more aggressive the next time the pressure of anger builds up inside. Every time I act out my aggression without restraint, my inner resistance against violent outbursts is lowered.

Immoderate venting of anger may also mean that I have to work it up and express it before experiencing relief. Remnants of this worked-up anger and its expression remain in memory and fantasy. Such remnants make me more sensitive to minor stimuli to anger. After many experiences, I become easily provoked and I may explode more readily. Before I realize it, I have become an angry, explosive person, often indulging in resentful fantasies and perceptions that keep me on edge. I'm always on the lookout for the wrong word, the wrong move. At the slightest provocation, my anger flares up. Such vigilance makes gentle relaxed presence to self and others impossible.

The mature person neither bottles up his anger nor releases it through unrestrained aggressive words and actions. In the beginning, I may not be able to dissipate in time accumulating anger. Therefore, anger may be dammed up, resulting in chronic muscular tensions. In such a case, it may sometimes be advisable to let go, to let the anger out by kicking an old chair, running around the block, or allowing myself to burst out in the presence of a good friend. I should realize, however, that this is only an emergency measure—an exceptional emotional release I should not become addicted to. Otherwise, its repetition may turn me away from the gentle life style.

As we said before, we should not bottle up angry feelings by playing the role of the "nice person" who never feels angry. Now, by warning against an aggressive acting out of such feelings, do we not contradict ourselves? Not really, if we remember the distinction between verbal aggression and talking about my feelings.

If I attack someone with words and actions, I provide myself, him, and bystanders with strong stimuli for more aggression: I create an angry and aggressive atmosphere. It is a different case when I merely describe how I feel, saying, for example, "I feel really angry now." Telling the other I am angry is informative. It may clear the air between us. My honest telling may make him aware that he inadvertently hurt my feelings more than he intended. He is less likely to hurt me again. I may feel even better when my information prompts him to explain that he had not really meant to hurt me.

GENTLENESS, ANGER AND LARGER VISION

The best way of dealing with angry feelings is to raise them up to the light of a transpersonal vision. This movement implies making the objects of my anger and aggression relative, that is, putting them into a wider perspective.

Such a transpersonal horizon will only be powerful enough to calm the stormy sea of angry feelings when I have really made it my own over a long period of time. I must create an alive world of meaning that may in time diminish the overwhelming power of anger and aggressiveness. The transpersonal horizon emerges in me in the long run out of repeated moments of dwelling on transpersonal truths and values and becomes a living awareness.

At the same time, I must try slowly to develop another habit; it too must become second nature for me. This is the habit of relating the emotions that arise in me—in my interaction with people—to my emerging transpersonal horizon, an horizon that opens me up to humanity, history, and the cosmos. In this meeting, emotions sooner or later lose their power to engulf me. I am less likely to become livid with rage. In this way, the mature man to some degree overcomes the self-destructive power of an overwhelming anger. He no longer has to avoid real interest in others. Neither does he have to deny his feelings. He gives his emotions the right place in the light of his transpersonal vision.[1]

NOTES

1. For discussion of the dynamics of anger and aggression, see van Kaam (1974).

10

Things Are Not as They Seemed

Roger Walsh

For some seven years now, I have lived in a state of chronic shock and disbelief. One after another, my most cherished, stable, sensible, common, ordinary, taken-for-granted, and culturally shared beliefs have been shattered. Time and again I have taken the pieces of my shattered belief system and shaped a new, more comprehensive system to encompass the unexpected experiences and information which had done so much damage to the previous one. And time and again the new expanded system has proven too limited to encompass the next set of experiences. I have been forced to recognize that I just don't know.

I don't know whether I'm right or wrong or how correct my currently cherished set of beliefs, assumptions, and world views are. I don't know how my mind works, how deeply it extends, how to control it, how to escape from the all-encompassing realities it appears to create. I don't know what consciousness is, what its limits are, don't even know if the concept of limits applies to consciousness or to us. I don't know how unaware I am or how aware I can become, what the limits to knowledge are, what our capacities and potentials may be, or whether I can accurately assess the the wisdom and the well-being of anyone significantly wiser than myself.

I do feel that I know that I've been wrong, that I've underestimated the mind, consciousness, us, the extent to which we are asleep, sleepwalking, trapped in our individual and shared cultural illusions. I've also underestimated the vastness of human suffering, especially the extent of unnecessary, well-intended suffering. I am clear that I've totally misunderstood the nature of the great religions, the practices such as meditation and yoga, and that I've underestimated the potential sensitivity of perception and introspection and the extent of wisdom that lies within us all.

How did this come about? It began with an entirely fortuitous entry into psychotherapy. Part of my postdoctoral training in psychiatry involved doing psychotherapy, but having examined the research literature and found very little that was unequivocally favorable, I had precious little faith in it. I was in the paradoxical situation of doing something that I really didn't believe worked. I found myself on the therapeutic couch expecting an interesting few weeks but not too much in the way of surprise or major benefit. I could hardly have been more wrong. Not only did I begin to undergo a series of totally unexpected and formerly unknown experiences, but they were of such profundity and impact as to change the course of my life from that time on.

My therapist, Jim Bugental, trained his clients in the development of heightened sensitivity to, and appreciation of, their own inner experience and subjective world. He was remarkably skillful in this, and within a few weeks, I began to find in myself a capacity for subjective sensitivity deeper than anything I had realized was possible. Gradually there occurred "the slowly dawning awareness of the presence of a formerly subliminal, continuously changing stream of inner experience. The range and richness of this internal universe amazed and continues to amaze me. After a couple of months, I began to perceive more clearly a constant flux of visual images that exquisitely symbolized what I was feeling and experiencing in each moment. Here was a previously unsuspected wealth of information about myself and the meaning of my experiences. As my sensitivity increased, I found that the images accompanied subtle physical sensations in my body, and that these sensations were the somatic representations of emotion. With this Rosetta stone, I was helped to a greater sensitivity of my moment-to-moment emotions. Whereas initially I had believed that the inner world must of necessity harbor unwholesome collections of monsters, which I had avoided confronting all my life, I now came to think of this inner world as a very attractive, pleasant source of positive information."[1]

With this heightened awareness as a tool of investigation, I was now able to explore my experience, mind, beliefs, and relationships more deeply than ever before, and what I found was often quite unexpected and contrary to my own and the culture's traditional assumptions. To name but a few, I experienced that, at least within the limits of my ability to detect, I was creating my own experience intentionally. Formerly I had thought of myself as a helpless victim of uncomfortable emotions, symptoms, and defenses, but now I could observe the process by which these were actively chosen and created. Thus I was forced to acknowledge a level of responsibility far more extensive than anything I had previously considered possible.

My belief system was already taking quite a beating. And the more I examined my beliefs, the more I was awed at their power to operate as self-fulfilling prophecies. Even things as apparently physiologically determined as sleep needs proved to be functions of my psychological state and beliefs. Whereas formerly I had believed that eight hours of sleep were an absolute necessity if I was to be anywhere near fully functional the next day, I now began to see the ways in which I created fatigue in order to avoid experiences and literally drive myself unconscious (asleep). From the very day on which I first saw my creation of fatigue in order to escape conscious experience, I found that I needed less sleep per night.

In short, I was beginning to realize that my former beliefs about myself, the nature of mind, consciousness, beliefs, and the extent of our potentials, and parts of the cultural belief system were considerably in error, and that I had gravely underestimated our capacities and the power of mind to create our world-view and sense of self. This is not to say that the process was free of anxiety, confusion, and uncertainty. But it was now very clear to me that I and many others had been very wrong about who and what we are and can become, and I was firmly committed to exploring and attempting to understand these formerly unsuspected potentials.

To some, I may well have looked like the stereotypic seeker lost in a narcissistic search, which Peter Marin and Christopher Lasch,[2] among others, have so soundly castigated. And yet, somehow the process didn't seem narcissistic, or at least no more so than the more traditional educational pursuits I had spent so many years at. True, there was a large element of self-serving motivation, but there was also a compelling sense of the importance of this exploration, an importance not limited to myself alone.

One general principle that soon emerged was that my defenses, biases, and lack of experience limited my capacity to appreciate information or people of greater wisdom than I myself possessed. Moreover, it seemed that not only was I passively incapable of hearing it, but was also at times actively defended against it.

On one such occasion, I went to a public lecture given by Ram Dass in the San Francisco City Hall with approximately three thousand other people. During the course of the evening, he started to outline a multilevel model of consciousness and described the component states in ascending order from the ordinary to the more transcendent. My reactions and those of the audience provided unexpected insights into the nature of our usual state of consciousness and its relationship to apparently more developed states. As he ran through the first two levels, they seemed very reasonable and readily understandable, the third was a little less usual, and the description to the fourth immediately evoked an experience in which I heard his words with perfect clarity, was struck by their import, and immediately afterwards could not remember a word he said. My next memory was of being awakened by the snores of the person next to me, and looking round the hall I saw that approximately one quarter of the audience had very suddenly fallen asleep.

It was not until some two weeks later in a discussion with a psychoanalytic friend that I began to appreciate the implications of this experience. Clearly, I had undergone massive repression or denial resulting in a literal and extremely rapid loss of consciousness, as presumably had a significant number of those people who had fallen asleep at the time I did. In order to repress something, we have to at least partially recognize it and assess it as dangerous. Yet if the descriptions of the higher states of consciousness were recognized and repressed, it could only mean that they were already known and that this knowledge was denied awareness through active defenses. This and related experiences led me to a total reevaluation of the relationship between ordinary and "higher" states. Formerly I had assumed that deeper wisdom was attained through the acquisition of new knowledge and understanding. However, now I was forced to consider the possibility that we already possess the requisite knowledge, that our usual state represents an actively and defensively contracted state, and that higher states are attainable, not by the acquisition of something new, but by the release of current defenses and the resultant expression of already existing capacities.

Needless to say, many of these experiences ran counter to my previous professional training. I therefore began to explore the existential and humanistic psychology literature because my traditional psychiatric and psychological texts contained almost no information on the experiences I was having or implied that they might be pathological. Soon, however, even the humanistic and existential literature began to show gaps in its coverage of the range of experiences which were occurring.

In short, I was becoming aware that either I was becoming increasingly disturbed, which certainly didn't feel true and was not true as judged by the writings in various consciousness disciplines, or that some of our traditional psychiatric models and assumptions tended to misinterpret and pathologize certain nonpathological states and experiences which occurred with heightened sensitivity to experience. Indeed, I began to suspect that a significant number of our traditional cultural values and assumptions about our psychological nature were distressingly incorrect, illusory, and productive of unnecessary suffering. These suspicions were further deepened when I began to practice meditation.

MEDITATION

When I was first exposed to various meditative practices, I found them neither particularly attractive nor helpful. Sitting still and attempting to control the mind proved both physically and mentally uncomfortable. Sporadic ten or twenty minute sittings elicited no discernable benefits, and it was not until almost two years later when I began a daily practice of sitting for one-half to one hour per day that I could detect any real benefits, and even these seemed pretty minimal. If it had not been for the encouragement of friends who had gone further, I would certainly never have continued.

What finally seduced me was a statement by Steven Levine, a meditation teacher and author of *A Gradual Awakening,* that *Vipassana* or insight meditation was a perfect tool for observing the workings of mind. My curiosity was instantly captured, and full of naive innocence, I immediately enrolled in a ten-day retreat. Little did I know what I was letting myself in for. These retreats comprise about eighteen hours per day of continuous sitting and walking meditation performed in total silence and without eye contact, reading, or writing. The practice consists of attempting to maintain continuous awareness of all the experiences, both internal and external, which enter awareness and allowing attention to focus on whatever stimulus is predominant at any time. The intensity of the resultant experiences was quite surprising.

"When one sits down with eyes closed to silence the mind, one is at first submerged by a torrent of thoughts—they crop up everywhere like frightened, aggressive rats."[3] The more sensitive my meditation became, the more I was forced to recognize that what I had formerly believed to be my rational mind preoccupied with cognition, planning and problem solving actually comprised a frantic torrent of forceful, demanding, loud, and often unrelated thoughts and fantasies which filled an unbelievable proportion of consciousness even during purposive behavior. The proportion of consciousness which this fantasy world occupied, my powerlessness to remove it for more than a few seconds, and my former state of mindlessness or ignorance of its existence staggered me. This "mindlessness" seemed much more intense and difficult to deal with than in psychotherapy where the depth and sensitivity of inner awareness seemed less, and where the therapist provided a perceptual focus and was available to pull me back if I started to get lost in fantasy.

The subtlety, complexity, and entrapping power of the fantasies which the mind creates seems impossible to comprehend, to differentiate from reality while in them, and even more so to describe to one who has not experienced them. Layer upon layer of imagery and quasilogic opened up at any point to which my attention was directed. Indeed, it gradually became apparent that it was impossible to question and reason my way out of this all-encompassing fantasy since the very process of questioning, thinking, and seeking only created further fantasy.

The power and pervasiveness of these inner dialogues and fantasies left me amazed that we could be so unaware of them during our normal waking life and reminded me of the Eastern concept of maya or all-consuming illusion.

Attachments and Needs

It soon became apparent that the type of material which forcibly erupted into awareness and disrupted concentration was most often fantasies and thoughts, to which I was attached (addicted) and around which there was considerable affective charge. Paradoxically, it seems that a need or attachment to be rid of a certain experience or state may lead to its perpetuation. The clearest example of this has been with anxiety. At one stage, I suddenly began to experience mild anxiety attacks of unknown origin. At such times, I would try all my various psychological gymnastics to eradicate it since it was not clearly not OK with me to feel anxious. However, these episodes continued for some five months in spite of, or as it actually turned out because of, my resistance to them. During this time my practice deepened and I was able to examine more and more of the process during meditation. What I found was that I had considerable fear of fear, and my mind therefore surveyed in a radarlike fashion all internal and external stimuli for their fear-evoking potential. Thus, there was a continuous mental radarlike scanning process preset in an exquisitely sensitive fashion for the detection of anything resembling fear. Consequently, there were a considerable number of false positives, i.e., nonfearful stimuli and reactions which were interpreted as being fearful or potentially fear provoking. Since the reactions to the false positives themselves comprised fear and fear components, there was of course an immedite chain reaction set up with one fear response acting as the stimulus for the next. It thus became very clear that my fear of and resistance to fear was exactly what was perpetuating it.

It was not, however, until the middle of the next meditation retreat that the reasons for this became clear. After the first few days of pain and agitation, I began to feel more and more peaceful, and there came a sitting in which I could feel my meditation deepen perceptibly and the restless mental scanning slow more and more. Then as the process continued to deepen and slow, I was literally jolted by a flash of agitation and anxiety accompanying a thought—"But what do I do now if there's no more anxiety to look for?" It was apparent that if I continued to quiet down, there would be neither anxiety to scan for nor a scanning process itself, and my need to get rid of anxiety demanded that I have a continuous scanning mechanism, and the presence of the mechanism in turn created the presence of anxiety. My "but what do I do now?" fear had very effectively removed the possibility of the dissipation of both. Paradoxically then, it appears that within the mind, if you need to be rid of certain experiences, then not only are you likely to experience a number of false positives, but you may also need to have them around continuously so you can keep getting rid of them. Thus, within the province of the mind, what you resist is what you get.

Perception

With continued practice, the speed, power, loudness, and continuity of thoughts and fantasies began to slowly diminish, leaving subtle sensations of greater peace and quiet. After a period of about four or five months, there occurred episodes in which I would open my eyes at the end of meditation and look at the outside world without the presence of concomitant internal dialogue. This state would be rapidly terminated by a rising sense of anxiety and anomie accompanied by the thought, "I don't know what anything means." Thus, I could be looking at something completely familiar, such as a tree, a building, or the sky, and yet without an accompanying internal dialogue to label and categorize it, it felt totally strange and devoid of meaning. It seems that what made something familiar and hence secure was not simply its recognition, but the actual cognitive process of matching, categorizing, and labeling it. Once this was done, then more attention and reactivity was focused on the label and its associations than on the stimulus itself. Thus, the initial fantasy and thought-free periods may feel both strange and distinctly unpleasant so that we are at first punished by their unfamiliarity. We have created an unseen prison for ourselves whose bars are comprised of thoughts and fantasies of which we remain largely unaware unless we undertake intensive perceptual training. Moreover, if they are removed, we may be frightened by the unfamiliarity of the experience and rapidly reinstate them. As is noted in the Carlos Castaneda books,

"We uphold the world with our internal dialogue."[4]

Interestingly, the extent of response to the stimulus itself as opposed to the label seems to be a function of the degree of mindfulness or meditative awareness. If I am mindful, then I tend to be focused on the primary sensations themselves, to label less, and to react to these labels less. For example, there was a period of about six weeks during which I felt mildly depressed. I was not incapacitated, but was uncomfortable, dysphoric, and confused about what was happening to me throughout most of the waking day. However, during daily meditation, this experience and its affective quality changed markedly. The experience then felt somewhat like being on sensory overload, with many vague, ill-defined somatic sensations and a large number of rapidly appearing and disappearing unclear visual images. However, to my surprise, nowhere could I find stimuli which were actually painful. Rather, there was just a large input of vague stimuli of uncertain significance and meaning. I would therefore emerge from each sitting with the recognition that I was actually not experiencing any pain and feeling considerably better. This is analogous to Tarthang Tulku's statement that "The more you go into the disturbance—when you really get there—the emotional characteristics no longer exist."[5]

However, within a very short time, I would lapse once more into my habitual nonmindful state, and when I became mindful once again, I would find that I had been automatically labeling the stimulus complex as depression and then reacting to this label with thoughts and feelings such as "I'm depressed, I feel awful, what have I done to deserve this?" A couple of moments of relaxed mindfulness would be sufficient to switch the focus back to the primary sensations and the recognition once again that I was actually not experiencing discomfort. This process repeated itself endlessly during each day. This demonstrates one of the differences between meditation and most psychotherapies. Whereas the latter attempt to change the content of this experience, in this case from depression to positive affect, meditation is also interested in modifying the perceptual-cognitive processes by which the mind produces such experiences.

Perceptual Sensitivity

One of the most fundamental changes was an increase in perceptual sensitivity. Sensitivity and clarity frequently seem enhanced following a meditation sitting or retreat. Thus, for example, at these times it seems that I can discriminate visual forms and outlines more clearly. It also feels as though empathy is significantly increased and that I am more aware of other people's subtle behaviors and vocal intonations, as well as my own affective responses to them. The experience feels like having a faint but discernible veil removed from my eyes, and that the veil is comprised of hundreds of subtle thoughts and feelings. Each of these thoughts and feelings seems to act as a competing stimulus or "noise" which thus reduces sensitivity to any one object. Thus, after meditation, any specific stimulus appears stronger and clearer, presumably because the signal: noise ratio is increased. These observations provide a phenomenological basis and possible perceptual mechanism to explain the findings that meditators in general tend to exhibit heightened perceptual sensitivity and empathy.[6]

Trust and Surrender

These experiences have led to a greater understanding of, and willingness to surrender to, the meditative process. In the West, surrender has connotations of succumbing or being overwhelmed, but here it is employed more in line with its use in the meditative traditions. Thus, with increasing experience I have begun to surrender to the process in the sense of trusting, following, and allowing it to unfold without attempting to change, coerce, or manipulate it.

Furthermore, it now seems clear that allowing experiences to be as they are, and experiencing them without forcibly trying to change them, reduces the deleterious agitation, resistance, and eruption of defenses and manipulation. Moreover, contrary to my previous beliefs, acceptance and a nonjudgmental attitude towards an experience or situation does not necessarily remove either the motivation or capacity to deal with it in the most effective manner. My prior beliefs were that I *needed* my judgments, aversions, and negative reactions in order to motivate me to modify the situations and stimuli eliciting them.

Overall, I recognized that the great meditation teachers really knew what they were talking about. Time and again I read descriptions, explanations, and predictions about meditation, the normal psychological state, the states that arise with more and more meditation, and have scoffed and argued against them feeling that they were so removed from my prior experiences and beliefs that they could not possibly be true. However, by now I have had a variety of experiences which I formerly believed to be impossible and have gained the experiential background with which to understand more of what is being taught. Thus, I now have to acknowledge that these teachers know vastly more than I do and that it is certainly worth my while to pay careful attention to their suggestions. Thus, experiential knowledge may be an essential prerequisite for intellectual understanding in these areas.

FEARS ALONG THE WAY

Having considered myself a relatively fearless daredevil type (hadn't I done high-diving, trampolining, scuba diving, parachuting, and circus trapeze?), I was amazed to discover the extent of my fears as I continued to explore more deeply. Wholly unsuspected anxieties and fears emerged one after another, layer after layer, and this discovery led me directly into a trap of my own making. For what I concluded was that I must be an exceptionally fearful person, and this conclusion molded my self-image and behavior over many months.

Many of these fears represented the surfacing of simple anxieties about social skills, intimacy, performance, and ability. However, another whole family of them were related to my concerns about who I would become and what would happen to me if I continued to explore and open my mind, and they centered around the belief that in some way I would be incapacitated or disabled if I continued.

Each fear presented a new choice about whether to go back to safety or to continue forward and risk the feared consequence. Sometimes I would remain scared and retreat, often using defenses of one type or another to deny that this was what I was doing, only recognizing the fact in retrospect. Abraham Maslow[7] pointed to the dozens of decisions that face us each day and advised as one strategy for self-actualization adopting the habit of always taking the growth choice. I suspect that if anything, Maslow underestimated the number of choices and that it is actually a continuous, ongoing process in which the pulls to self-actualization compete with the fears of awareness, thus creating a dynamic ebb and flow of growth motivation.

With deeper exploration it began to become apparent that these fears, no matter how diverse their apparent concerns, appeared to all be founded on limiting self beliefs. For example, in my very first therapy session, I became anxious that if the therapy was effective, I would never amount to anything because I would lose much of my motivation. I feared that without my conflicts and neuroses, I would be inert and passive, lacking the necessary drives for productivity and achievement.

However, on those occasions when I made the growth choice and proceeded in spite of fear, it always became apparent that there was in fact no loss. What was necessary was to be *willing* to let go of the attachment and to be *willing* to experience the feared consequence. But after having let go, it almost invariably turned out that all that was "sacrificed" was the attachment, not any skill or capacity.

A pervasive early fear was that if I turned my attention inward, I would find a Freudian nightmare. I fully expected to uncover various monsters and bogeymen composed of unbridled emotions and drives such as anger, jealousy, lust, greed, kept in check only by continuous superego monitoring and repression. Invariably, I believed that the experience of becoming aware of this internal world would be highly unpleasant, requiring great determination in the face of unsavory experiences.

Yet, what I found was quite the opposite. True, there were anger, much fear, and other negative emotions, but these paled beside the depths of warmth, joy, caring, and compassion which lay below them. I began to suspect that what has often been thought of as "*the* unconscious" and invariably negative and "idish" was only an initial layer of a far larger more positive unconscious. The curious paradox was that my beliefs in the existence of the internal bogeymen had effectively prevented me from looking inside to discover what was really there and had thus perpetuated the beliefs.

Then there was the fear of aloneness, the fear that if I continued this exploration I would end up as an eccentric outcast whose beliefs and experiences were so different from other people's as to separate us and preclude the possibility of friendship and intimacy. How many people, I wondered, would there be who could understand what I was going through and who shared my emerging values? Surely the deeper I went, the fewer people I could expect to find who would share such experiences. It looked as though the price of deep exploration might be a life apart from all those who had not trodden the same path.

And yet, once again there turned out to be a curious and delightful paradox. True, the further I continued, the fewer fellow travellers there were, but new networks and friendships developed. A further benefit was that in these networks there were always people who had proceeded further than me, and these individuals turned out to be invaluable resources who could point the way to the next steps and to some of the traps to be avoided along the way. The opportunity of being with these people and learning from them proved to be one of the real gifts of the whole process.

On the other hand, those who were not making the same journey, including some of my fellow psychiatrists, expressed concerns about the directions in which I was headed. In one group meeting with my fellow psychiatry residents, it was suggested that if I continued I would probably be unlikely to function well enough to maintain my professional standing and would most likely drop out of psychiatry and possibly "end up selling candles on the beaches in Southern California." In retrospect, it's fascinating to see how closely my peers appeared to be reflecting my own fears and projecting theirs onto me. As we were a fairly homogenous group of somewhat obsessive nature, it's hardly surprising that my questioning of the beliefs and defenses we shared should evoke such strong reactions. Now it all seems very funny, but at the time it was quite fearful, and had it not been for the support and reality testing of my therapist and people involved in similar explorations, I might well have abandoned the exploration and returned to old styles. Since then, I have indeed moved to Southern California but as yet have not started selling candles.

As these and other fears came and went and came again, I began to gain a new perspective on how and why they occurred. Initially, I had thought of them as experiences forced upon me unwillingly. Yet the more I examined them, the more I began to realize that I was actively creating them out of the perceived need to protect myself. It began to be apparent that I was creating my experience and self-sense moment by moment exactly the way I thought I needed to. Fears and defenses were not thrust upon me helplessly but rather were something I was actively and intentionally creating.

The Spiritual Shock

Slowly I began to realize that, contrary to being the opiate and pablum of the masses, the great spiritual traditions were, at least at their esoteric core, roadmaps to higher states of consciousness. Please note that I am not saying that this is necessarily all they are, but I am saying that at their esoteric core, this is at least what they are. This realization answered a question about my own behavior which had been puzzling me for several months. Much to my surprise, I had found myself spending an increasing amount of time with various spiritual teachers, primarily Buddhist and Hindu. While it was true I was learning some useful things about meditation, I could not for the life of me imagine how it was that I ended up in a spiritual setting when my interests were primarily psychological and psychotherapeutic. This was a new and totally unexpected realization since I had previously dismissed religion of all types as merely misguided fantasy. Perhaps this was not entirely unexpected since my own exposure to religion had been in its traditional institutionalized Western form and there was certainly little of the trenscendent in it.

In any event, there was a deepening appreciation of the extraordinary wisdom contained in some of the Eastern psychologies. Much against my will, and with no lack of resistance, I was forced to acknowledge that these traditions and their founders and advanced practitioners knew much more about the workings and depths of mind than I had ever imagined.

Our Cultural Illusions

How could I have known so little and been so wrong? How could my beliefs have been so deficient and ignorant? And how could I have been so unaware of my experience and self? In retrospect, my own ignorance staggers me, and I suspect that if the journey of discovery continues as I hope it will, five years hence I will look back with amazement at my current level of ignorance.

Yet I suspect that my own ignorance, limiting beliefs, and illusions are a reflection and microcosm of our culturally shared limitations. Prior to undertaking this exploration, my own beliefs, fears, and cosmology were pretty much consistent with cultural norms which I had presumably incorporated. If this is true, then we effectively share a mass cultural hypnosis. This sounds like an extreme statement, yet it is hardly a new one. The consciousness disciplines have been repeating it for at least three thousand years. We believe our inner depths and nature are essentially idish, brutal, guilt-ridden, and untrustworthy and must be continually defended against and repressed. These beliefs and fears prevent us from turning inward to the source of our experience to see for ourselves whether or not they are true. Thus, the illusions remain unexamined and perpetuated by the very fears they created.

THE REWARDS OF THE SEARCH

I've emphasized the numerous fears and difficulties involved in the search for self-understanding, but I need to balance this by noting that it's not been all pain and hardship by any means. The rewards have been more than worth it, for no matter how partial and incomplete my own explorations have been, they have also been a source of joy, wonderment, understanding, and meaning. There has been a gradual and fluctuating reduction of fear, anxiety, conflict, and other psychological pain. This is by no means complete, continuous, or permanent. Rather, it seems to have followed a cyclic though gradually evolving course. In the initial highs, I hoped I'd make it, that I might be permanently installed in some blissful state from which I would never fall, and when I did fall, I wondered if it all had been a mistake, if I'd deceived myself and had made no progress whatsover. However, after hundreds and thousands of ups and downs, highs and lows, I am gradually learning to maintain a certain degree of equanimity and not to identify myself quite so fully with the mood of the moment.

Relationships have also been a source of deepening pleasure despite my fears of ending up as a lonely outcast. The heightened perceptual and introspective sensitivity appear to have resulted in somewhat greater empathy and understanding of others. This in turn seems to facilitate the development of compassion. It feels as though I am at least partly more aware of suffering in others. Recognizing the shared nature of our well-intended but unskillful behavior, I find myself better able to understand the ways in which people create suffering for themselves and less likely to judge them for it. This is reminiscent of the French saying, "To understand everything is to forgive everything."

There is also the joy of the *sangha,* the community of people sharing the same journey. With such people I experience a shared purpose which at least partially transcends the usual personality and cultural barriers. All of us are attempting to learn and grow, and since that process is inhibited by selfishness, all of us are trying, no matter how partially or unsuccessfully, to contribute to others in whatever ways are available to us. Sometimes there is jealousy, competitiveness, and resentment, but that too is all grist for the mill.

Jealousy and competitiveness may also occur in response to those who have gone further and learned more than I have, but usually there is also a sense of deep gratitude and appreciation to them for having cleared the road and being available to point it out to me. I can begin to understand the Buddha's statement that,

> Better than a thousand offerings . . .
> Is one moment's reverence
> For the man who has conquered himself.

One of the most satisfying results of all has been an enhanced ability to contribute to the relief of suffering in others. One thing that has become very clear is that we cannot successfully undertake a deep search for understanding and growth for ourselves alone. Contrary to some popular misconceptions, this type of exploration seems to ultimately lead away from rather than towards narcissistic preoccupation and selfishness. True, we bring our selfish habits and neuroses with us as we begin the journey, and I certainly brought my share. And yes, we can certainly pass through selfish preoccupation and ego inflation, and presumably some of us remain stuck there for long periods. But there is a danger of confusing a stage or trap on the path with its goal and possibilities and of assuming that the entire path is a trap. Then, too, there is no shortage of aberrant groups and teachings, yet it would be a mistake to assume that because superficial practices and practitioners exist, profound ones do not.

To anyone who continues the journey for more than a little way, it rapidly becomes clear that selfishness is problematic, in that it reinforces such disruptive motives and states as greed, anger, hatred, and guilt. In Buddhist terms, selfishness is recognized to be unskillful, causing suffering for both oneself and others. Sooner or later, anyone who would go further is required to work to transform and relinquish all forms of selfishness and self-indulgence. Indeed, working to transform one's neuroses and relinquish unskillful habits is the path. In the Hindu tradition, service is regarded as a path in its own right, named karma yoga, and anyone who would explore the farthest reaches of the path and of him or herself must also practice karma yoga. This provides an interesting example of the collapse of the self/other, me-or-you dichotomy, because this type of service benefits both giver and receiver.

As the journey progresses, it feels increasingly vast, awesome, and important. Indeed, it seems to lead in the direction of confronting the most basic and fundamental questions of human existence, the answers to which I had once thought were to be found externally, but which I now appreciate must be searched for within. As my insights deepen, they seem to display their own magnetic power pulling me with an increasing intensity toward them, creating a gentle imperative to be and contribute all that I can.

All this emphasis on the positive is not to say that I have not misused what I have learned. On the contrary, I must confess that it's hard for me to think of many things that I haven't misused. It seems to be characteristic of this game that the ego searches for ways to use any new knowledge, experience, or understanding to aggrandize itself. Even the most lofty goals and experiences may be misapplied in this way, a phenomenon which the consciousness disciplines call spiritual materialism.[8]

Yet the journey continues. Where it will take me from here, I've no idea; the more I open to it, the less predictable it becomes because the growth choice is usually into the unknown. But this much I have learned: no matter how remarkable I believe our mind, our self, and the exploration of them to be, my beliefs usually turn out to be the filters limiting still deeper appreciation of them.

Whether we know it or not, we are all on a journey beyond belief.

NOTES

1. Walsh (1976), p. 111.
2. Lasch (1978).

3. Satprem (1968).
4. Castaneda (1974).
5. Tarthang Tulku (1974).
6. Shapiro and Walsh (1982).
7. Maslow (1971).
8. See Trungpa (1973).

III

WORKING
WITH OTHERS

Introduction

This third and main section of the book explores different aspects of what is involved in awakening the heart through the therapeutic process. We find many overlapping themes developed in the chapters here: the effect of immediacy and nowness in facing another person; the need to stay with uncertainty and move through it, rather than seeking easy solutions; the development of appreciation and compassion on the part of the therapist; acknowledging the real tenderness and vulnerability that goes along with an open heart; and the vital importance of recognizing a core of sanity and health underlying whatever pathology may be manifesting.

The Tibetan meditation master Chögyam Trungpa opens this section by characterizing the helping relationship as one that brings out the therapist's and client's mutual humanness. What helps make psychotherapy a healing encounter is an appreciation of what Trungpa calls the "basic goodness" inherent in all people. What he means by this term is not a conditional goodness which is dependent on being any particular way. It is not a stance or belief of any kind. Every stance, posture, and belief we adopt and identify with creates some inner division, activating an opposite tendency inside us, often referred to in psychotherapy as "the shadow." Basic goodness is not a stance that creates a shadow. Rather, it is more like the radiance of the sun itself, unconditional because it is beyond both our attempts to be good and the shadow these attempts create. Moreover, it still shines even when it is obscured by the clouds of self-destructive or aggressive behavior. The therapeutic task, from this perspective, would be for the therapist to help the client discover this basic goodness by creating an environment of warmth and well-being.

Coming from the existential-phenomenological tradition, Thomas Hora stresses the importance of approaching the therapeutic situation with a questioning mind. Moreover, the right questions are important: not "Why are you this way?" but rather, "What is really going on for you?" What allows real change to happen is experiencing what is actually going on, not standing back from the situation and trying to figure it out. When we really *see* clearly what it is we are doing, our awareness links up with reality, and we become more unified with ourselves. As Hora points out, what heals the client is not the therapist, but the truth. The therapist should get out of the way of the truth coming through. Otherwise, his efforts to help or "therapeutize," as Hora calls it, get in the way of the healing process.

David Brandon expands further on the theme of being there with the client in the nowness of the present, and points out how difficult this is to do. As his examples illustrate, listening to another person is often a process of getting out of the way so that preconceptions based on past experience do not interfere with what the other person is trying to communicate.

In the next chapter, I explore the basic vulnerability that is part of being human and having an open heart. This chapter investigates how we can not only learn to live with this vulnerability, but also come to appreciate it as our link with other people and life as a whole. If a therapist can fully accept his own human vulnerability, he can better serve his clients and help them to find a source of power and strength in the midst of their most difficult crises.

Diane Shainberg addresses the issue of the therapist's openness to the client. Through examples of her supervision of student therapists, she clearly illustrates the difference it can make when therapists begin to let themselves and their clients be, without trying to fit the healing process into a preconceived mold.

Richard Heckler brings a martial arts approach to therapy, describing the effects of meeting the client where he is and entering directly into the core of the neurotic conflict. He also explores how meditation can teach people how to move from safe, familiar adaptations and go through crisis and transition with their eyes open, so that new directions can emerge.

In line with the Western emphasis on pathology, rather than health, traditional psychiatry and psychology focus on a client's history of psychopathology, and overlook the fact that everyone also has a history of sanity in their lives. Ed Podvoll describes how to uncover landmarks of sanity in a person's life by looking at six key areas: repulsion with self-defeating patterns, longing to transcend self-preoccupation, urge for discipline, longing toward compassionate action, experiences of clarity, and a sense of courage. If health professionals pay more attention to those areas, they will be able to mobilize the client's resources more fully and draw on what are already inherent strengths.

In the final chapter, Cason and Thompson describe their work with a home care service for the elderly and disabled, founded and staffed by seasoned Buddhist meditators. Warmth, humor, compassion, and friendliness—the qualities that grow out of awakening the heart—prove especially important in working with people facing old age and death. This article illustrates the principles described in this book in a very direct and extremely human application.

═11══════════════

Becoming A Full
Human Being

Chögyam Trungpa

The basic work of health professionals in general, and of psychotherapists in particular, is to become full human beings and to inspire full
human-beingness in other people who feel starved about their lives.
When we say a full human being here, we mean a person who not only
eats, sleeps, walks, and talks, but someone who also experiences a basic
state of wakefulness. It might seem to be very demanding to define
health in terms of wakefulness, but wakefulness is actually very close to
us. We can experience it. In fact, we are touching it all the time.

We are in touch with basic health all the time. Although the usual
dictionary definition of "health" is, roughly speaking, "free from sickness,"
we should look at health as something more than that. According to the
Buddhist tradition, people inherently possess Buddha-nature; that is,
they are basically and intrinsically good. From this point of view, health
is intrinsic. That is, health comes first: sickness is secondary. Health *is*.
So being healthy is being fundamentally wholesome, with body and
mind synchronized in a state of being which is indestructible and good.
This attitude is not recommended exclusively for the patients but also for
the helpers or doctors. It can be adopted mutually because this intrinsic,
basic goodness is always present in any interaction of one human being
with another.

There are many approaches to psychology and some of them are
problematic. From the Buddhist point of view, there is a problem with

any attempt to pinpoint, categorize, and pigeonhole mind and its contents very neatly. This method could be called psychological materialism. The problem with this approach is that it does not leave enough room for spontaneity or openness. It overlooks basic healthiness.

The approach to working with others that I would like to advocate is one in which spontaneity and humanness are extended to others, so that we can open to others and not compartmentalize our understanding of them. This means working first of all with our natural capacity for warmth. To begin with, we can develop warmth toward ourselves, which then expands to others. This provides the ground for relating with disturbed people, with one another, and with ourselves, all within the same framework. This approach does not rely so much on a theoretical or conceptual perspective, but it relies on how we personally experience our own existence. Our lives can be felt fully and thoroughly so that we appreciate that we are genuine and truly wakeful human beings.

When you work in this way with others, it is very powerful. When someone begins to feel that he is not being pigeonholed and that there is some genuine connection taking place between the two of you, then he begins to let go. He begins to explore you and you begin to explore him. Some kind of unspoken friendship begins to develop.

Although I am speaking as a Buddhist teacher, I do not believe that therapy should be divided into categories. We don't have to say, "Now I'm doing therapy in the Buddhist style," or "Now I'm doing it in the Western style." There is not much difference, really. If you work in the Buddhist style, it is just common sense. If you work in the Western style, that is common sense, too. Working with others is a question of being genuine and projecting that genuineness to others. The work you do doesn't have to have a title or a name particularly. It is just being ultimately decent. Take the example of the Buddha himself—he wasn't a Buddhist! If you have confidence in yourself and you develop some way of overcoming ego, then true compassion can be radiated to others. So the main point in working with people is to appreciate and manifest simplicity rather than trying to create new theories or categories of behavior. The more you appreciate simplicity, the more profound your understanding becomes. Simplicity begins to make much more sense than speculation.

The Buddhist tradition teaches the truth of impermanence, or the transitory nature of things. The past is gone and the future has not yet happened, so we work with what is here—the present situation. This actually helps us not to categorize or theorize. A fresh, living situation is taking place all the time, on the spot. This noncategorical approach comes from being fully here, rather than trying to reconnect with past events. We don't have to look back to the past in order to see what people are made out of. Human beings speak for themselves, on the spot.

Sometimes, however, people are obsessed with their past, and you might need to talk with them about that somewhat, in order to communicate with them. But it should always be done with a present orientation. It is not purely a matter of retelling stories in order to reconnect to the past, but rather it is a question of seeing that the present situation has several levels: the basic ground, which could be in the past; the actual manifestation, which is happening now; and where the present is about to go. So the present has three facets. Once you begin to approach a person's experience in that way, it comes alive. At the same time, it is not necessary to try to reach a conclusion about the future. The conclusion is already manifest in the present. There might be a case history, but that history is already dying. Actual communication takes place on the spot. By the time you sit down and say hello to the patient, that person's whole history is there.

You see, we are not trying to figure people out based on their past. Instead, we are trying to find out their case history in terms of who they are *now*, which is really the point. I always do that in interviews with my students. I ask them how old they are, whether they have been outside of America, whether they have been to Europe or Asia, what they have done, what their parents are like, and all the rest of it. But that is based on *this* person rather than on *that* person. It is quite straightforward. The people we are working with might be dwelling in the past, but we as their helpers have to know where they are *now*, what state of mind they are in at the moment. This is very important. Otherwise we may lose track of who a person is now and think of him as someone else, as if he were another personality altogether.

Patients should experience a sense of wholesomeness vibrating from you. If they do, they will be attracted to you. Usually, insanity is based on aggression, rejecting oneself or one's world. People feel that they have been cut off from communication with the world, that the world has rejected them. Either they have isolated themselves, or they feel that the world is isolating them. So if there is some compassion radiating from your very presence when you walk in to a room and sit down with people, if there is gentleness and willingness to include them, that is the preliminary stage of healing. Healing comes from a simple sense of reasonability, gentleness, and full human-beingness. That goes a long way.

So the first step is to project ourselves as genuine human beings. Then beyond that, we can help others by creating a proper atmosphere around them. I am speaking literally here, extremely literally. Whether someone is at home or in an institution, the atmosphere around them should be a reflection of human dignity, and it should be physically orderly. The bed should be made, and good meals should be prepared. In that way, the person can cheer up and be able to relax in his environment.

Some people may regard the little details of the physical environment as mundane and unimportant. But very often, the disturbances people experience come from the atmosphere around them. Sometimes their parents have created chaos—a pile of dishes in the kitchen, dirty laundry in the corner, and half-cooked food. Those little things may seem incidental, but they actually affect the atmosphere a great deal. In working with people we can present a contrast to that chaos. We can manifest an appreciation of beauty, rather than just pushing the crazy person into a corner. The appreciation of the environment is an important part of Tibetan and Zen Buddhist practice. Both traditions consider the atmosphere around oneself to be a reflection of one's individuality, and so it should be kept immaculate.

The conventional therapeutic approach is to try to straighten out people's minds first, then give them a bath, and finally help them get dressed. But I think that we have to work with the whole situation at once. The environment is very important, and yet it is often overlooked. If the patient is presented with a good meal and is acknowledged and received as a special guest, which is what he or she deserves, then we can work from there.

We are talking about creating an ideal, almost artificial life for seriously ill people, at least in the beginning, until they can pull themselves together. We may actually bathe them and clean their rooms, make their beds and cook nice meals for them. We can make their lives elegant. The basis of their neurosis is that they have experienced their lives and their world as being so ugly, so full of resentment, so dirty. The more resentful and ugly they become, the more that attitude is reinforced by society. So they never experience an atmosphere of compassionate hospitality. They are regarded as nuisances. That attitude doesn't help. People are not really nuisances at all. They are just being themselves given their circumstances.

Therapy has to be based on mutual appreciation. If people feel it is just your "trip," they may not like the environment you create for them. You may present them with a nice tray of food, but still they may be outraged if they know that your attitude is not genuine, if they feel your generosity is hypocritical. If your approach is completely unified, if you treat your patients like princes or princesses in the fullest sense, then they may want to respond. They may actually cheer up and begin to extend themselves. They may begin to appreciate their bodies, their strength, and their existence as a whole. It is not so much a matter of finding techniques that will cure people so that you can get rid of them. Rather, it is a matter of learning how to actually include them as part of a good human society. It is important for the therapist to create an atmosphere that makes people feel welcome. That attitude should infuse the whole environment. That is the point.

The ability to work with another person's neurosis, or even their craziness, ultimately depends on how fearless you are when you deal with them, or how inhibited you feel. It depends on how much you are embarrassed by somebody or how much you can actually extend yourself. In the case of a mother's relationship to her infant, there is no problem because the mother knows that the child will grow up and one day become a reasonable person. So she doesn't mind changing diapers and doing all sorts of things for her child. Whereas if you are dealing with people who are already grown up, there is some kind of basic embarrassment which has to be overcome. That embarrassment has to be transformed into compassion.

Crazy people in particular are very intuitive. They are somewhat brilliant and they pick up messages very easily, even just the flicker of your thoughts, and that goes a long way with them. Usually they chew it, or they swallow it, or they throw it out. They will make a lot out of it. So it is a question of your basic being and how open you are in those situations. You can at least make an attempt to be open at that moment, which is a tremendous commitment to training and educating yourself. Then there is the possibility of developing fearlessness.

It is necessary to work patiently with others, all the time. That is what I do with my students: I never give up on them. No matter what problems they come up with, I still say the same thing: just keep going. If you have patience with people, they slowly change. You do have some effect on them if you are radiating your sanity. They will begin to take notice, although of course they don't want to let anybody know. They just say, "Nothing has changed. I have the same problems going on all the time." But don't give up. Something happens—if you take your time. It works!

Just do what you have to do to keep them going. They will probably keep coming back to you. You are their best friend anyway, if you don't react too neurotically. For them, you are like a memory of eating in a good restaurant. You remain the same, and they keep coming back to you. Eventually you become very good friends. So don't jump the gun. It takes time. It is an extremely long process, but if you look back at it, it is very powerful. You have to cut your own impatience and learn to love people. That is how to cultivate basic healthiness in others.

It is very important to commit yourselves to your patients fully and not just try to get rid of them after they have been cured. You shouldn't regard what you are doing as ordinary medical work. As psychotherapists you should pay more attention to your patients and share their lives. That kind of friendship is a long-term commitment. It is almost like the student-teacher relationship on the Buddhist path. You should be proud of that.

=12=

Asking The Right Questions

Thomas Hora

There is a story about an American professor who went to Japan to study Zen. He was introduced to a Zen Master, and this Zen Master invited him to tea. They were sitting at a table and the Zen Master was pouring tea. He kept pouring even after the cup was full and the tea was spilling over. The professor was saying, "You are spilling the tea!" And the Zen Master said, "This is your first lesson in Zen. To study Zen, the mind must be empty of preconceptions or else there is no room for anything to come in."

There are many things that seem very logical, natural, rational, and realistic, and yet they are not necessarily true. For instance, we are led to believe that it is important to remember everything from our past so that we might improve the present and prevent it from influencing the future. A lot of energy is expended in helping people to remember in great detail their past, what happened, why it happened, and who is to blame for it.

There is a story about a man who was in analysis for about a year or two. His main problem was nail-biting. One day he met a friend who asked him: "How do you like your analysis?" He said, "It's great, I tell you, everybody should have it. It is wonderful!" "Well, have you stopped biting your nails yet?" asked the friend. The man said, "No, but now I know why I do it." A French psychiatrist once said: *"On ne guérit pas en souvenant, mais on se souvient en guérissant."* In other words,

"We don't get well because we remember, but we remember as we get well."

Now in existential psychotherapy, we do not probe the past, we allow it to reveal itself in the course of gaining a better understanding of what is. There are certain questions which become superfluous in existential psychotherapy. The question "Why?" becomes completely superfluous. We don't ask the question "Who is to blame?" or "What should I do?" Mainly we ask two questions:

1. What is the meaning of what seems to be?
2. What is what really *is?*

The therapeutic process is an encounter situation where many aspects of the patient's mode of being-in-the-world reveal themselves. What is needed is open-minded receptivity which is devoid of preconceived ideas about what should be and what should not be. If we make a practice of observing our thought processes, we find that most frequently our thoughts have a tendency to revolve around what should be or should not be. If our consciousness is released from these preconceptions, we are much more able to perceive what really is.

Psychotherapy could be described as an endeavor to discern the good beneath the pathology. What is pathology made of? It is made of misperceptions. For instance, last week we had a case presentation here of an individual who misperceived the difference between dominion and domination. To exercise dominion is healthy, but to twist it around into dominance is a sickness. Now we can help a patient understand how he misperceives something and clarify to him what is existentially valid. Thereby he discovers that he really has healthy intentions which have become distorted through misinterpretations and misperceptions. So we could say that pathology consists of misconceptions of what is good, what is true, what is existentially valid. Earlier we said that existential psychotherapy is not interpretative but hermeneutic, elucidating, clarifying, helping people to see more clearly the existential issues. The interpersonal perspective intends to help people to get along with other people. Anybody can learn that, but it is not synonymous with being healthy. The existential approach aims to help people come into harmony with the fundamental order of existence.

What is the fundamental order of being? To understand it better, we must become aware that there are several obstacles to coming into harmony with it. And one of them is operationalism. What is operationalism? It is a concern with how to do things even before we have found out what is what is. There is a certain bent of mind which is always concerned with how to do things. This interferes with focusing attention on that which really is. It is necessary to place the "how to" concerns into secondary place so that we may be more fully aware of what is.

When we sit with a patient, the patient presents to us certain problems, and if we know the right questions to ask, the meaning will then reveal itself to us. The emphasis must be on *revealing* itself to us. Sometimes inexperienced therapists who have not yet been liberated from the operational and calculative way of thinking and seeing life have a tendency to try to figure it out. Meaning cannot be figured out; the meaning of phenomena reveals itself to us. If we take a ping-pong ball, submerge it in water and let go of it, it will invariably pop up to the surface. It is similar with meaning. If we let go of trying to figure out the meaning, it will spontaneously reveal itself to us.

Let us take swimming as an analogy. What would be the right question to ask about swimming? Some people have a hard time learning to swim because they are inclined to ask, how do you do it? If we are going to ask the wrong question, we are going to have a hard time learning anything. People who have difficulty in learning to swim probably have in the back of their minds the wrong questions. How do you do it? What would be the right question? What is swimming? Swimming is floating. The essence of swimming is floating. Once we understand that, doesn't it make it easier to learn to swim?

Now the question arises, is floating passive? Is it correct to say that we surrender ourselves to the water when we float? If we were to surrender ourselves to the water, we would drown. What is required in order to float? What kind of activity is required in floating? Attention. Floating is an activity occurring in consciousness. Floating is not passive, floating is not surrendering to the water, floating is not relaxing. It is the quality of consciousness which is alert, attentive, and responsive to that *invisible power* present in the water which is called buoyancy. If we judge by appearances, floating may seem passive.

But we must not judge by appearances, we need to understand what is really involved. It is a quality of attention. How would we describe the quality of attention which is required for successful floating? The primary requirement is to love floating. We have to love it and we have to be responsive. In other words, the essential quality of consciousness which is required for floating is *loving responsiveness to the invisible power upon which we are endeavoring to lean.* This power of Love-Intelligence provides us continually with what is needed to understand the meaning of phenomena, it gives us the intelligence to clarify them, and it inspires us with right solutions to whatever seems to be the problem. Psychotherapy is not *done* by anybody; it is allowed to occur. It is not passive; neither is it active. It is reverent, loving responsiveness to that which *is* from moment to moment.

It is interesting to consider the fact that some people swim with great effort, while others swim effortlessly for hours on end without getting tired; they don't even get winded. And the same goes for life and for psychotherapy. The difference lies in the quality of awareness. If we believe that we have to do our own swimming, it will then be a very strenuous, exhausting exercise, and we will be poor swimmers. But if we understand that there is a sustaining power present, then it becomes easier and easier. Similarly, if we believe that we have to get somebody well in psychotherapy, that we have to cure him, that we have to personally change him, we will have a very strenuous job, and we will get exhausted and frustrated.

This reminds me of a story about two psychiatrists who worked in a professional building. At the end of the day, they would ride down together in the elevator. One was an elderly gentleman, very dapper and neat looking, the other was a young man and he was exhausted and tired looking. One day the younger man said, "I don't know how you do it. All day long you were working, seeing one patient after another, and yet you are not showing any tiredness at all. I am exhausted after listening to all those patients. Tell me how do you do it?" The older man replied, "Who listens?" Of course this is not what we are trying to do. There is a way of working actively, effectively, and effortlessly by letting Love-Intelligence do the work.

What is the requirement on the part of the therapist for good communication to come into being? What is it about some therapists that they have no problems in communication? There are some individuals who can go into a mental hospital and sit down with a patient who hasn't spoken for years to anybody, and pretty soon the patient will start talking, whereas others may have tried for years to speak to this patient and he would get worse every time he was approached. What is this mysterious quality? Is it magic? No, it is motivation. The therapist must have the right motivation. In order for communication to take place in a meaningful and therapeutically beneficial way, there are certain requirements. One of the first requirements is that the therapist must be free from his desire to therapeutize. This is not easy. The desire to therapeutize may mean to the patient that he is being intruded upon and manipulated. The quality of presence in every one of us is different and it is determined by our value system and by our motivation.

One of the most frequent motivations of a psychotherapist is to therapeutize. This is inevitable, especially among those therapists who have an operational approach to life. If the therapist's mode of being-in-the-world is an operational one, his patients will manifest a great deal of resistance. Nobody likes to be therapeutized. So what then is it that can facilitate communication? There has to be a quality of *letting be.* Many people misunderstand the principle of letting be as leaving alone. There is a very subtle but radical difference between letting be and leaving alone. Letting be is a reverent form of love, leaving alone is neglect. Letting be is rather difficult to learn.

Let me just quickly comment on the word "acceptance." Who are we to accept or not accept anyone? The moment we think this way, we have immediately set up a certain kind of structure wherein we are superior to the patient. The category of acceptance is better left out, we are not acceptors nor rejectors, we are there to understand whatever reveals itself from moment to moment, and we are available to comment on it in case someone is interested. If not, we will sit there in quiet receptivity to that which *is* from moment to moment. It is total unobtrusiveness in the spirit of love. We are available to the patient. We sit with him in that spirit of availability and help to clarify whatever he may desire to know or to understand.

Previously we were talking about influencing. Influencing is a great curse in life—in friendship, family life, business, and profession—and it is absolutely poisonous in therapy. Certainly we have no right to try to influence our patients in any direction whatsoever; however, we can be influential by the quality of our presence and by our availability to clarify what we have understood and what is asked of us. When we sit with a patient in that spirit, there is usually no difficulty in communication. Pretty soon the patient begins to ask questions, and more and more questions arise. Whenever something is asked, we are there to comment on it to our best understanding. If we happen to understand *what* is, the question *"how?"* does not arise. Therapy is a hermeneutic process of clarifying whatever needs clarification. And it is the clarity of understanding of certain issues that has the power to heal the patient. The healing power is not in the therapist, it is in the correctness of his clarifications. It is the truth that heals, not the man who bears witness to the truth. "The finger pointing to the moon is not the moon," say the Zen Masters. So this way we don't do anything, the patient doesn't do anything; therapy isn't being *done,* it is spontaneously unfolding as a progressive process of clarification, dawning.

Yen-Hui was a disciple of a famous Taoist sage by the name of Chuang-tzu. This Yen-Hui was also a prominent figure at the Imperial Court and was to become an adviser to the emperor. This emperor happened to have a great predilection for chopping off the heads of his advisors if they made a mistake. Yen-Hui was afraid of this job and came to his teacher for advice. He said to his teacher, "I don't think I am sufficiently enlightened to be safe in this exalted position." Chuang-tzu said to him, "In that case, you must retire and practice mind-fasting." Yen-Hui asked, "What is mind-fasting?" Chuang-tzu gave him the following instruction: "When you want to hear with your ears, don't listen with your ears; when you want to see with your eyes, don't look with your eyes; when you want to understand with your mind, don't think with your mind. Listen, see, and understand with the tao.* Yen-Hui retired and spent three years practicing this discipline. After three years he returned to his teacher and said, "Master, I think I am ready." Chuang-tzu said, "Well, prove it." And so Yen-Hui said, "Before I practiced mind-fasting I was sure I am Yen-Hui; but now, after I have practiced mind-fasting, I have come to realize that there never was a Yen-Hui." His teacher said, "You are ready."

Now what did he mean by this? If he never was Yen-Hui, then what was he? And if Yen-Hui never was, what are we? Yen-Hui discovered that he was not a person with an ego of his own, a mind of his own, opinions of his own, that he was a manifestation of Love-Intelligence. He became a beneficial presence in the world who does not lean on personal opinions but on inspired wisdom. Such a man lives in safety.

The aim of existential psychotherapy is to help people attain authenticity of being. In order to know what is true, we have to face up to what is not true. The strange thing about human existence is that, unexamined, existence tends to be inauthentic. What is the derivation of the word person? It is *per-sona* (mask). In Greek tragedies, the actors held appropri-

---

*Tao is the Chinese word for "way." In this case it means the larger life stream in us, or big mind. [Ed.]

ate masks in front of their faces. They were literally putting up a front. In reality, there is no such thing as a person. Yet we are all conducting ourselves in life as if we were certain kinds of persons. We speak about personality make-up, and we study it and try to improve it. What is make-up? Isn't it pretending to be what we are not? A make-up can either enhance the appearance of an individual, distort it, or detract from it. We do not say that this shouldn't be or that it should be, but let us understand what is, what really is.

The issue of anxiety has puzzled psychotherapists for years, and there are many theories and speculations about it. Various techniques were evolved as to how to help people cope with it. But as long as we are, unconsciously or ignorantly, living inauthentic lives, pretending to be something other than what we really are, there will be always anxiety. Anxiety is fear of being found out that we are not what we appear to be.

Neurotic anxiety can be contained, can be controlled, can be suppressed, can be hidden, can be drugged, but it cannot be healed until man becomes authentic. It is easy to know what a person is, but what is what really *is?* What are we, really, underneath the mask? Is it so horrible that we have to hide it? Are we so awful that we have to put on personality make-up to make ourselves acceptable to our fellow man? What is the meaning of this game of hide-and-seek we are playing throughout life? What are we hiding?

Existential anxiety was spoken of by Heidegger as the "dread of nothingness." Heidegger's main theme is worth considering, especially in the context of what we have touched upon here. He said: "Nothingness by contrast to all that seems to be is the veil of being." What did he mean by that? We mentioned the dread of nothingness. Children often express an ambition to be somebody. "When I grow up, I want to be somebody." What is the meaning of that? Now this would indicate that we want to feel that we are something. In psychology, we speak of role-playing and functioning, but when are we what we really are? And what is it? We can go through life never having met with ourselves, never having found out the truth of our own being. Is it important? Is there any advantage to it?

Existential literature frequently refers to alienation; what is alienation? Mostly it is separation from the truth of what we really are. We have become so involved with our pretensions; we expend so much energy on improving our masks; we are so much concerned with functioning, role-playing, influencing, and being influenced, that as time goes on we become more and more alienated from the awareness of our true self-identity.

What is the method whereby we would endeavor to attain the goal of authenticity? Actually, it is very simple. All we have to do is to learn to ask the right questions. The entire field of psychotherapy is victim of an unfortunate choice of questions. What are the questions that are asked most often in this field of endeavor?

The first question is: Why did it happen? This is a *cause-and-effect* question. It is assumed that something has happened, it must have had a cause or a reason. This sounds very logical, but unfortunately it is not valid in a broader context.

The second question: Who is to blame for what happened? This is a *personalistic* question. Nobody is really to blame. There is neither cause nor culprit.

The third question: What should we do about it? This is an *operational* question. It presumes that we can fix whatever went wrong.

The fourth question: How should we fix it? is a *process* question. It presumes that the repair that seems necessary entails a certain process.

These questions are misleading. Whenever we successfully answer these questions, we have embarked on a "wild goose chase."

To speedily attain the goal of realizing the truth, there are two valid questions which we may ask.

The first is: What is the meaning of what seems to be?

The second is: What is what really *is?*

=13=

Nowness In the Helping Relationship

David Brandon

In meditation practice, the most elusive point is nowness. You focus all energy on the ingoing and outgoing breath. The door swings open and shut. You strive for that still point of the present and see it eternally escaping the grasp. Nowness is a flowing river. You may get your fingers wet, but the quality of riverness flows through your clutching hands.

The emotions drift in the current. They are logs and branches which seem to arrive carefully labeled anger, greed, and fear. Each of these has attached to it a further label saying bad and horrible. What is the nature of the energy before I label and make my decisions about value? I struggle to discover but the river flows ever faster.

Nowness is with us, of us, yet always elusively evading our grasp. Bringing ourselves into the here and now sounds deceptively simple but is essentially very difficult. We divide life into a series of events and happenings which are seen as big and small. We mainly live our lives by concentrating on those events and people seen as large and important. Living becomes a series of time holes punctuated by occasional big happenings. Falling in love can mean that I live suspended between the especial meetings with my loved one.

Other times and moments—traces of the past and shadows of the future—crowd into our awareness of the present moment. Sometimes they are clear; often rather foggy. Nowness practice does not mean excluding the past and future but an awareness of the subservience of both to the present moment.

> The essense of meditation is nowness. Whatever one tries to practice, is not aimed at achieving a higher state or at following some theory or ideal, but simply, without any object or ambition, trying to see what is here and now. One has to become aware of the present moment. . . .[1]

I continually fall short of those standards which I set myself in contrasting the present situation with the might-have-been. The here and now is an important discipline in helping clarify this continuous friction and punishment. It is the difference between asking myself "How ought I to feel?" and "How do I feel?"

Now is the only time when we can actually do anything. I can be guilty about the past, apprehensive about the future, but only in the present can I act. The ability to be in the present moment is a major component of mental wellness. We commonly admire certain people as having "presence" and usually mean, in part, that they seem to be rooted, to communicate a sense of dignity in the now.

To what extent can we bring our perceptions and energies into what is happening all around us when that is happening? How much of our energy seeps away into anxiety and apprehension? The ability to exclude irrelevant worries and anxieties about past experience and future happenings is of great worth. Many present perceptions are so intensely colored by past experience that I can hardly see a particular person at all. Frequently, I observe others through the superimposed shadows and reflections of significant people and events in my life.

I had recently taken to avoiding a certain student in the coffee room. I feel that she is bitter and angry in her dealings with me. Each time we meet, I bring this belief and memory. I am hurt and respond angrily and dogmatically although I feel near to tears.

I hardly see her. She becomes a walking symbol for the thousands of times that people seemed unkind and unjust.

Frequently, it is difficult for me even to hear certain people. They talk on particularly painful wavelengths, so I turn down the emotional sound. They penetrate the superficiality of certain images I am trying to broadcast. Often I have so much radio static and personal commercials, such an unquiet mind, that their words and feelings are hardly audible. My attention becomes distracted by personal problems or by what children are doing outside the window or in simply being bored by a client's words.

Good listening has an enormous quality of nowness. The listener has made no prior decisions or laid down any precious structure of his own in relation to the speaker. Chögyam Trungpa identifies three kinds of ineffective listening:

> In one case, one's mind is wandering so much that there's no room at all for anything that's being said. One is just there physically. This type is said to be like a pot turned upside down. In another case, one's mind is relating somewhat to what's being said, but basically it is still wandering. The analogy is a pot with a hole in the bottom. Whatever you pour in leaks out underneath. In the third case, the listener's mind contains aggression, jealousy, destruction of all kinds. One has mixed feelings about what is being said and cannot really understand it. The pot is not turned upside down, it doesn't have a hole in the bottom, but it has not been cleaned properly. It has poison in it.[2]

Many of the helping questions contain assumptions as to what the answer will be. Questioning and listening which does not structure the answers, except minimally, is a great art.

I was writing a book with a friend who was physically handicapped. Anne had been a Beauty Queen until paralysed in a car accident. I asked her very carefully what it was like to be handicapped. "Funny" was her reply.

"But you can't mean funny. . . ."

"Yes I do—when I was a little girl, I used to dream about being a fairy princess who was waited on hand and foot. And it came true."

"But there must be pain and disadvantages."

"Of course. You see if I had not been in the car accident, life would have been very different but not necessarily better. This way I was forced to explore myself, to meditate. I have become a strong person."

I was not listening to Anne. She was trying to tell me something quite opposed to my conceptions of physically handicapped people. She was telling me something outside my range of expected answers. She was asking me to unlearn—always very painful.

Helpful listening is simply listening. It is a form of meditation wherein the speaker becomes the object of the concentration rather than the breathing or a mantra. The focus of the helper's concentration is the sound of the speaker's voice and the possible meanings of his words.

I felt really in harmony with a man whose wife and family had just left him. His physical health had been deteriorating for several years, reducing his mobility and enjoyment of life considerably. Black depression shrouded him. He had tried to take his life several times. He talked to me at some length about suicide. One question which was repeatedly and pressingly asked was "Can you see any reason for me to go on living?"

I evaded the answer. I dodged through every psychotherapeutic bush. "How can I know the answer to that? You have to find your own reason." My nowness was that I could see every reason for his wish to die, but social workers were "not supposed to tell people that. It might prove destructive."

This man wanted a genuine answer from me. I thought deeply about his whole life—the depression, poverty, his failing health, and the loss of family. Finally I replied "I can see no reason to go on living in your case. I can see clear reasons for wishing to die."

I felt afraid. It seemed an enormous risk to say that to him. What kind of responsibility would I have if he finally killed himself? How would I feel? How is he to respond to my answer? My mind raced off into the future etching complex mental patterns. Months afterwards, when the depression had largely disappeared, he told me that my answer had been helpful. At the time when it seemed everyone was simply giving an unthinking response of pity and sympathy, he had urgently needed an honest answer to that important question.

One of the most difficult skills in group work is that of simply staying with the group members. Your task as leader is to follow the energy of the group and avoid putting your own interpretative patterns and expectations on them. Sitting quietly watching someone work on their personal problems, my mind is buzzing with analogies to past experiences. "Doesn't she seem just like. . . . I wonder whether she had a poor relationship with her brother and that that influences the way she. . . ."

Nowness means the ability to throw away those intellectualizations when the client goes off in an unexpected direction. How often have I compelled some poor client to come back from some pathway of exploration simply because I was holding firmly to my view of what he *ought* to be doing? I use my power to make what I believe to be true, probably to the detriment of the client.

Talking in therapy can be a way of trying to be in any other time and place except the present one. Pascal puts it precisely: "We never remain in the present. The truth is that the present commonly wounds us." It wounds us primarily because of our yearnings for different times and places. We crave better professional status, more money, less heavy caseloads. Our clients crave more money, better houses in an improved environment. Our lives become a series of loosely linked "if only" experiences. "If only I had time to do that. . . . If only I had the money to buy that. . . ."

When visiting a residential establishment, fieldwork setting, or voluntary society, I commonly ask what people are doing. How do they spend their day, their working week? Seldom do I receive an answer which relates directly to the question. Usually the question evokes a whole patchwork of dreams and visions covering deep frustrations and disappointments.

People find it difficult to say what they are doing at present. They describe what might be happening in a few months' or years' time. Residential homes particularly weave a web of fantasies around their casual visitors. Present activity seems unbearable because it falls so short of the visions which the social worker needs.

In Western society, we are constantly encouraged to take our minds away from the present. We are afraid of boredom. We learn to occupy ourselves desperately; to do several things simultaneously. We feel best when busy. Our minds split off in different directions. We watch ourselves with rapt concentration. Our conversation is carefully edited before it goes out onto the air. It is screened for social acceptability. "How will what I say influence the way others see me?" Such activity is more concerned with becoming somebody rather than being someone. We learn to package ourselves, to protect certain kinds of images rather than simply to be.

Our actions and the events in our lives are seen in the context of some overall personal plan which goes "right" or "wrong." We do things to achieve status, love, or power. We learn to manipulate others and to minimize the social costs of various actions by not taking responsibility for them. Most of our activity becomes an integral part of this life plan. Life becomes like the numbered dots which children connect up with a pencil and turn out to be the shapes of donkeys or camels.

The shapes we draw are ego shapes. They link our actions to a conception of self-image. Our perception of both ego and role provide us with some insurance and security in a world where there seems much risk. We insure against surprises by writing scripts and stories into our lives. We offer explanations of ourselves. We draw patterns of consistency around others and then get angry when they step out of the shape. R.H. Blyth puts this process firmly in its place:

> We are only apparently a unity, a stream of innumerable selves following one another like a series of cinematographic pictures, so quickly that they seem one continuous whole.[3]

This illusion of shape, solidity, and continuity is what we call ego. Nowness lies in the absence of the bubble of separation between watcher and watched; a lack of awareness of self. Nowness is the essential direct experience; the unity between helper and helped.

The Buddha told a parable in a sutra:

> A man travelling across a field encountered a tiger after him. Coming to a precipice, he caught hold of the root of a wild vine and swung himself down over the edge. The tiger sniffed at him from above. Trembling, the man looked down to where, far below, another tiger was waiting to eat him. Only the vine sustained him.
>
> Two mice, one white and one black, little by little started to gnaw away the vine. The man saw a lucious strawberry near him. Grasping the vine with one hand, he plucked the strawberry with the other. How sweet it tasted![4]

What magnificent nowness!

A few years ago, I attended a Westernized Zen sesshin—three days of intense meditation. We went to bed at midnight each day, in a remote Sussex manor house, and awoke to the sound of the gong at 5:45 AM. The very long day was spent working in the garden, walking in meditation or sitting opposite another student, both of you wrestling with a koan. Each person received a koan from the Master. Mine was "What are you?"

I tried to hold the question in my head but it kept leaking out. It whirled rapidly round and round and was consistently disturbed by other thoughts, like noisy shooting stars, intruding and tumbling in. Literally hours and hours were spent looking into another student's eyes and trying to answer the question "What am I?" My legs and spine ached throughout the first day and my bottom became quite numb. My body was so painful and stiff that it was difficult to focus on the question at all.

Whatever we did—whether eating, walking, or working, we had to hold on firmly to the question. At the beginning of answering, my mind threw up a whole range of attractive rubbishy phrases. I was dizzy with images and symbols of seashores, mountain glaciers, crystals, slowly opening flowers. Then I went through a period of monsters—black cloaks, lurking shadows, and pitch blackness. All were in some way part of me but none comprised the whole.

Thoughts about my family and job came flooding in. I tried to keep my aching spine erect. The answers became even more flowery and poetic. They were bright, shallow images, perfumed and too clever by half. "I am a question echoing in an empty mind." My mind darkened and the squirrels played out on the large country lawn. I envied them. They had more sense than to try answering such ridiculous questions.

I saw that I was a candle. A small rather unimportant flickering candle. But the next question was "Who lit the candle?" How could I be both the candle and the one who lights it? My mind squeezed intensely on this curious paradox. Physically my legs and arms were taut; my chin was stiff and set and teeth held painfully together. Quite suddenly the image of a candle which I had been trying to hold on to had vanished.

I looked at myself intently. I was a knot. My whole body and mind had become tight and taut like a knot. But who tied the knot? Who was responsible for the tension and frustration? Of course I knew who lit the candle and who tied the knot. Nobody had tried harder than I to solve the problem and loosen the ropes. It was simply unfair. It was a trick question and there was actually no solution at all. It was like catching sunbeams. I remembered being small and throwing my jacket over sunbeams on the grass.

Now I seemed lost. Everything lost its clarity. Now I just clenched my fists, first in anger and then in despair. I answered "I am a person who cannot answer the question." The question rolled around my head like a noisy ball. It became difficult to concentrate. I began to convince myself that I did not have the necessary precision to obtain an answer. My mind was a fuzz. Perhaps in the next reincarnation. . . .

Outside the wintry afternoon gave way to darkness and a biting wind. I walked up and down in a very large, high-ceilinged stable. My stride quickened and I kicked out at pieces of stick and stones. The question came over and over again like a pendulum "What am I? What am I?"

The words became a shout and then a whole scream of anger from a tense face and mouth. "What am I? I am a bloody idiot who does not know what he is. Who cannot answer a simple question." My cries got louder and louder. Rain and wind carried them back to me. This shuffling, shouting, scruffy figure in the stables punched at the air. Every muscle was tight. I was going to burst.

At the very moment of bursting frustration; at the very height of all the wind, rain, and fury, I was aware, quite softly, that I was actually keeping the answer at bay. Like an old and discreet friend, he had been patiently waiting to come in all this time. He came in and my whole body relaxed and jumped, felt good and warm. NOW I was now—the answer was NOW. I am/was/shall be everything which unfolds and moves, thinks, questions, and talks at that moment in time. It was far more than a purely intellectual realization—it bathed me with my goodness, everyone's goodness. Goodness happening now. I shouted happily "Now, now, now." I and the question had become friends.

NOTES

1. Trungpa (1969), p. 52.
2. Guenther & Trungpa (1975), p. 83.
3. Blyth (1960), p. 101.
4. Reps (1971), p. 32.

=14=

Vulnerability and Power in the Therapeutic Process*

John Welwood

There is a central experience we all have, which is essential to being human, and which some of us have more frequently, or at different times of our lives, whether we're classified as "sane," "neurotic," "psychotic," "enlightened" or "unenlightened." This experience is at the core of both the existential and the Buddhist perspectives. For existentialism, it is the source of existential anxiety. For Buddhism, it is the basis of the path toward what is known as "enlightenment," "awakening," "liberation."

The experience I am speaking of is one that nobody actually likes to talk about very much. It is also easy to ignore because we've developed a number of habits and routines to avoid facing it. There is no ready-made term for this experience that I know of. So I am inventing one and calling it a "moment of world collapse."

I'm sure we're all familiar with these moments when the meanings on which we've been building our lives unexpectedly collapse. Suddenly they lack weight and substance, no longer influencing us or holding us up as they once did. Before, we may have been motivated for success—

* Adapted from a presentation at the conference, "Open Ground: Existential and Buddhist Approaches to Psychotherapy," cosponsored by the California Institute of Integral Studies and Naropa Institute and held June, 1982, in Oakland, California.

making money, providing for our family, or seeking to be loved. Now, suddenly, in this moment, we wonder why we're doing all of this, what it's all about. We may look around in vain for some absolute, unwavering reason for it all, some unshakable ground, yet all we see is the inexorable passing of time and our hopeless attempts to grasp on to something solid.

At the same time, when an old structure falls away and we don't have a new one to replace it, we usually feel a certain inner rawness. That kind of tenderness and nakedness is one of the most essential qualities of our humanness, one which we are usually masking. When an outer shell or facade or mask falls away, we get to touch what we might call our *basic vulnerability*. The experience of basic vulnerability which accompanies moments of world collapse is one that I have come to know quite intimately through meditation practice. As an existentially trained psychotherapist who has practiced a Buddhist style of meditation for many years, I would like to explore not only the place of these moments of world collapse and basic vulnerability in these two traditions, but also how they can awaken deeper qualities of humanness in the therapeutic relationship.

In the existential approach, the feeling that accompanies these moments is called "existential anxiety" or, in Kierkegaard's words, "dread (*angst*)." It is seen as an ontological anxiety; that is, it arises from our very nature as human beings. And it comes in those moments when we perceive the intrinsic groundlessness of all our personal projects. Anxiety about death is one special case of this.

In existential thought, this kind of ontological anxiety is distinguished from neurotic anxiety, which is self-manufactured out of our attempts to distract ourselves from this deeper anxiety. Worrying about what people think of us or worrying about whether we are "getting somewhere" serves as a smokescreen that keeps us from having to face this larger existential dread. It sometimes seems that we are almost in love with our neurosis, because it occupies us and gives us something concrete to hold onto, unlike those moments of world collapse, where there seems to be nothing.

In the existential tradition, Sartre's notion of nausea, Camus's investigation of suicide, Kierkegaard's alienation from all the rational, philosophical, and religious structures of his world, Nietzsche's attempt to establish a set of values based on life rather than fear—all grew out of a keen perception that the old meanings that served human life and society so well were no longer holding up. After the Industrial Revolution, the old structures of the society that guided people's lives no longer worked. As Nietzsche said, "God is dead." Existentialism, failing to find any absolute, unshakable ground for justifying what we are doing with our lives, was an attempt to *create* meaning out of a person's own individual existence. This meant that the *only* source of meaning was your own individual action—which was a new perspective in the history of our culture. And this is wonderful in a certain way because it creates a heroic outlook on life in which each person must find and create his own meaning in a meaningless world. One archetype of that effort is the myth of Sisyphus, as Camus talked about it, where, although the rock keeps rolling down the hill, Sisyphus rolls it up again and somehow finds heroic meaning in that. This is a sense of "let's keep plugging," despite all the obstacles. In this approach, however, existential anxiety is a given; there's no way to finally overcome the sense of dread. After all, there is never any guarantee that the personal meanings you create for yourself are going to hold up for very long, especially in the face of impermanence and death. What's meaningful today is not necessarily meaningful tomorrow, and what's meaningful throughout your whole life may not be meaningful at the moment of your death. You may cast a look backward at the moment of your death and say, "What did I do?" So, from an existential point of view, since self-created meaning does not form any absolute ground, anxiety is inescapable.

Like existentialism, Buddhism is also a response to moments of world collapse. The Buddha himself, as an Indian prince, was born into a world of complete meaning—his life was programmed for him by his society and his father. He was scheduled to inherit his father's kingdom, yet he found his life permanently altered by four moments of world collapse: when he saw an old person, a sick person, a dying person, and a wandering holy man. The shock of these encounters, undermining all the meaning that had supported his life until then, started him on his own personal search. He tried the various ascetic practices of his day, and finally decided to just sit in meditation and see if he could get to the bottom of the whole thing. What he discovered after six years, among other things, was the central fact I'd like to emphasize here—the illusory nature of the self. He saw that the self had no real solidity or continuity. Ordinarily, the self that we know is constructed by identifying with objects of awareness that come and go—such as the occupations we perform, the things that we own, our personal history, with all its dramas and achievements, the intimate relationships we hold most dear. All these things we hold onto, as something to identify with, go to make up an identity. The word "identity" comes from a Latin word that means "the same." So having an identity literally means that we are trying to be the same from day to day. Our identity holds us together, and we use it, among other things, to avoid that experience of our world collapsing, which is so frightening.

Why do we need to identify so thoroughly with the things that come into our awareness? Here is where the Buddhist approach seems to go a little deeper than existentialism. The meditative experience upon which Buddhism is based teaches us that the nature of consciousness itself is radically nonsolid, open, receptive to the world. Now that sounds quite similar to what many of the existentialists have said as well. Sartre, for example, speaks of the human being's nostalgia for the solidness of a rock and the definition of a tree (What he called the *en-soi*, the in-itselfness of things).[1] The tree is just a tree. What is a human being? My father is my father; a tree is a tree. Who am I? We want to possess that same kind of solidity that we perceive in the Other. Yet, from a Buddhist point of view, the very fact that we can take things into us and let them touch us, or see Other as solid at all, means that we are not solid, but rather, empty like a mirror, open like space. Unfortunately, we tend to treat our spaciousness and nonsolidity compared to Other as a lack, something that should be filled up and made solid. So, first we assume that what comes into us has an independent, solid existence in itself, and then we ask ourselves, "Well what am I in comparison? Who am I?" In envying the seeming solidity of Other, we fail to appreciate that the nature of our consciousness is to provide a space in which things can stand out and be revealed. Here is where meditation practice can be extremely helpful—in teaching us how to relate to our nonsolidity in a different way.

Before showing how moments of world collapse and basic vulnerability relate to therapy, I would like to describe how I personally made the transition from existentialism—essentially that heroic attempt to create my own meaning—to Buddhism. During the early 1960s, I went to Paris—when I was in my early 20s and extremely influenced by the existentialists. That was the place to soak up that existential feeling of the time. The existentialists were my personal heroes because the world that I had grown up in didn't make much sense to me, and these were people who were at least trying to create a sense of meaning for themselves and for the world too. So I'd sit in the cafes that Sartre frequented, and I'd walk along the streets that Rilke wrote about. Even the stones, the streets, and the walls in Paris had a certain existential quality. I would walk along the bridges over the Seine that I imagined Camus had thought about throwing himself off. It was wonderfully romantic and painful. But somehow it didn't feel satisfying just to accept the absurdity of the world and heroically struggle on from there. Fortunately at that time, just when I was starting to feel that I had rolled the rock up the hill a few too many times, I came across the writing of Alan Watts and D. T. Suzuki.

The one book that changed my world view on the spot was Watts' *Psychotherapy East and West*. In one reading, I suddenly saw a way out of the existential impasse. The real problem wasn't that human life was absurd or that there wasn't any absolute basis for unshakable meanings. Somehow the problem lay instead in the nature of the self that we try to create. This understanding somehow made things workable in a new kind of way for me. Anxiety, meaninglessness, and that mood of despair did not have to be denied; they could even be a stepping stone to something else. Existentialism tries its best to somehow fill up the void that opens up when the world collapses with new meaning. But I saw that Buddhism does not try to fill it up or overcome it in any way, but rather provides a way to go into that emptiness further. In fact, when I read the playful stories about Zen masters, it seemed that they were even enjoying that emptiness. That was really a radical shift in my perspective at the time. The moment of world collapse could be seen, in the Buddhist context, as one moment in a larger picture or journey, rather than as any final or ultimate one.

What you discover in mindfulness meditation is that a stream of thoughts, feelings, and perceptions keep coming into awareness and pass away, moment to moment. The mind tries to grasp them, hold on to them, and identify with them, but this never really works. You can't hold on to anything. You keep trying to come to some conclusion about things, but every position the mind takes is succeeded by a different one a few moments later. This provides a very direct experience of impermanence and lack of solidity of self. Yet this need not lead to existential terror. If you stay with the process of meditation, you often find that you start to relax a little bit into the spaces between the successive moments of trying to grasp on to something, that you can't just keep grasping. You have to let go for a little bit before you can grasp again, and let go and grasp again. When a thought comes, you grasp and try to do something with it, either identify with it or disidentify with it, fight it or own it or disown it—but then there's this moment of letting go in between each grasping where something happens that is not grasping. In these cracks between each successive grasp, there is a sense of something different. And as you practice, relaxing into these open spaces, you discover some kind of emptiness there, a larger background in which the grasping is taking place, which we could call the "open ground" of our experience. This discovery points toward a different kind of liberation than the existential freedom to make meaningful choices. It is the beginning of a path beyond existential despair.

I think many of us know that life is continuously changing, that the nature of life is to move forward, and that we can't move forward unless we let go of where we have already been. In other words, freedom requires leaving old structures behind. We know this rationally, yet how hard it is to let go, and how painful it is when old structures collapse on their own.

Meditation provides a way of learning how to let go. As we sit, the self that we've been trying to construct and make into a nice, neat package continues to unravel. Then we can clearly see how we are constructing it, how we are trying to maintain it, and how we only cause more pain and discomfort by continuing to pump it up.

The illusory nature of the continuous self is not an idea unique to Buddhism. We find it in the Western tradition as well, though it comes out of an essentially philosophical analysis. Hume, for example, said, "For my part, when I enter most intimately into what I call myself I always stumble on some particular perception or other."[2] Here he is saying nearly the same thing: what we are mainly aware of are the objects of consciousness. "I never catch *myself*," he says. William James also came to the same conclusion. He found that the continuous self was a belief constructed out of the endless sequence of thoughts which overlap and, in the process, pass along an illusion of ownership, "like the log carried first by William and Henry, then by William, Henry and John, then by John and Peter, and so on. All real units of experience *overlap*."[3] "Each thought dies away and is replaced by another, saying, 'Thou art mine and part of the same self with me.' "[4] It's this trick that each thought has of immediately taking up the preceding expiring thought and adopting it which creates the illusion of a continuous self. This sounds very Buddhist. Sartre also talked about the illusion of selfhood when he said, "The essential role of ego is to mask from consciousness its very spontaneity. Everything happens as if consciousness were hypnotized by this ego which it has established, which it has constructed, becoming absorbed in it as if to make the ego its guardian and law."[5]

But without a path that helps us discover a larger sense of what we are, we might well wonder, "So what if the self is a construction—we are still left with existential anxiety." Since the meanings on which we build our identity are continually changing and passing away, this means we will continually be going through a series of identity crises. Especially in an era of future shock, when meanings the culture holds valuable change more and more rapidly, the identity crises will escalate at a comparable rate. So, having discovered the insubstantiality of the self, we still seem to need some path, somewhere to go from there.

This seems even more essential for our clients in therapy. Helping them understand that the self is a fiction does not in itself relieve their suffering. In therapy, there is often a crucial moment when many clients start to see through the old self. As a meditator, I'm keenly aware of these moments when a client realizes, "I don't know who I am." It can be a wonderful moment actually, but many therapists and clients would rather not face this. It often comes at a point in the therapy when the old structures have unravelled and started to collapse and before some new direction has emerged. It's an in-between place.

There is not much in Western psychology to prepare people for how to deal with such moments. Most of our therapies are guided by a *personality* theory. And most of us usually think we *should* know who we are. After all, others seem to walk around knowing who *they* are. But if we look inside ourselves and find nothing that we can hold onto, this scares us. What we may not realize is that no one *really* knows who they are, that this is the nature of our being, and that if we have a true self at all, it somehow lies in the heart of the unknowingness that we face when we start to look inside ourselves. And if we can "hang out" on the edge of this unknown, we may discover how to let ourselves be, without having to be some*thing*.

As the old maladaptive structures start to break down, the client often looks at the void opening and asks, "What now?" What do we as therapists do at that point? Do we try to substitute new structures? Do we let the client dangle there in space on the edge of the abyss?

For me, meditation provides some context for working with those moments. I had a strong sense of this personally during a three-month retreat with my meditation teacher. About six weeks into it, I found my world radically collapsing at a level of intensity that matched the old existential days, perhaps even magnified a few degrees. I found I didn't really believe in the self that I was constructing and holding onto for dear life, even though I thought it was a better self than I'd ever had before. And yet, if I let go of that, what then? I knew I would fall, and I didn't know where I would land.

Yet there was something about working with that fear in a practice environment that helped a great deal. I found that I *could* let myself collapse. The atmosphere of the practice environment encouraged that in a friendly kind of way—other people were also practicing, and the whole purpose of being there was to let your world collapse, to keep going, and to find something of importance in doing that. I don't want to say it was "meaningful" because I didn't necessarily find some new meaning there, to be used as a basis for constructing a new and better self-structure. And yet neither did I fall back into that sense of meaninglessness that existentialism had provided relief from.

Letting go of the need to be something, to be some*thing,* giving up that struggle for meaning, if only briefly, is like clearing something out, reducing mental clutter. This allows us to discover what is called in the Buddhist tradition "basic intelligence" or "buddha nature"—that clarity and openness we talked about as the ground of our consciousness. It's not just the neutral openness that appears in existentialism, or a scary emptiness, but it has a brightness and sharpness that cuts through fog, cuts through obscuration. It's like a light that doesn't allow anything to block it. And the more you sit and practice meditation over time, the more it starts to come through and cut through all of the fog that you are creating, all the things you are trying to hold onto which block that light. It seems to have its own energy which shines right through all of the rationalizations and other tricks that we play on ourselves.

A therapist often tries to focus on the content of clients' problems to steer around clients' underlying sense of utter vulnerability, of not knowing who they are, of not having anything ultimately to identify with. Yet I see this vulnerability as the essence of human nature and of consciousness. As humans, we are the animals that stand up erect with a soft front, fully exposing our front to the world. By doing that, we also take the world fully into us, all through the front of our body. To have sensitive skin means that it can be easily punctured. This literal softness and tenderness is reflected in our psychological makeup as a basic sensitivity, where we often feel quite raw, beneath all our problems and concerns. In touching this vulnerability, a client may connect with a basic aliveness that can shift the way in which he holds his problems. This is a different approach than giving the problems primary importance, although problems can be a vehicle for helping us contact this sensitivity. In my work, I don't actually try to make someone feel that vulnerability—it seems to come up at some point on its own.

It's interesting to note that the word "vulnerability" usually has a pejorative meaning in our culture. I think that's because we identify vulnerability with a loss of power. If we say that someone is vulnerable, it usually means he is weak, overly sensitive, and easily hurt. I distinguish what I call basic human vulnerability from another kind of vulnerability—the fragility of the ego, the shell that we construct around this soft receptive center where we take the world into us. Because we feel so sensitive and raw, we usually try to protect our tenderness with a facade or a mask that gives us some distance from the world. But this shell is fragile and always susceptible to being punctured, if not demolished (in moments of world collapse). Other people can usually see through our facades; death or other circumstances inevitably break open this shell. Having to maintain and patch ourselves up creates a certain brittleness—and this is the vulnerability that we usually think of in our culture as something weak. In fact it *is* weak because that kind of fragility puts us at the mercy of things that continually threaten to puncture our shell. We have to try to control situations so we do not feel threatened. On the other hand, getting in touch with our more basic human tenderness and vulnerability can be a source of real power.

I would like to illustrate what I am talking about here through a case example. A client in his mid-thirties, call him Ray, came to see me with the presenting problems of exhibitionism and alcoholism, as well as fear of homosexuality and severe problems relating to women, despite a basically heterosexual orientation. His mother had abandoned him at about age six, and he'd been adopted by an uncle. The uncle was a "macho" type of person who was not able to be intimate and tender with him. Nonetheless, he came to identify very strongly with the uncle, a man who could not express his softness.

I've chosen this client to discuss because all his symptoms kept pointing back to this issue of vulnerability in one way or another. For example, his exhibitionism was one of those strangely appropriate symptoms that are symbolically perfect. It was a way of exposing his vulnerability, while also maintaining some kind of control and power.

His fear of being homosexual was connected with the fear of his softness. His alcoholism—getting drunk and "busting loose"—was a way in which the child in him could get out from under his heavy control, so that he could be spontaneous and feel his aliveness fully. And finally his coldness toward women was clearly related to a fear of being at their mercy and being in a vulnerable position again.

Oddly enough, Ray's experience of being a man was a sense of being "on edge" all the time. Those were his words—"always on edge." One image he had of this was of driving a car on the freeway and being held back by people who were driving too slowly. This symbolized the way he was actually driving himself. He came to discover that it allowed him to feel in control, to feel like a man.

What I did with Ray was to "hang out" with him in those raw places which came up as we worked together. I never introduced the word "vulnerability"—that came from him. But it was clear that that part of him wanted to be recognized and included in his life. What seemed to be important for him was to discover that vulnerable didn't mean victimized. One day he said, "It's okay to be hurt. That doesn't mean that I'm unloveable." He started to see how he created anger and struggle with women in order to feel strong rather than soft.

Ray had another fitting image of being on edge, which he generally felt as a tightness in his upper torso. He saw himself hanging on the side of a cliff. We came back to that often, that experience of holding on to the edge of the cliff, and what he could do there. One time he explored climbing to higher ground. Other times he explored letting go and falling. Another image he had was of being out on a limb. Being in love was like being on a limb for him. This is not an uncommon feeling, actually. But if the love wasn't fully returned, or if his lover left him, he would fall into the abyss again, with all those dreaded feelings of terror, emptiness, groundlessness. In one session when he felt he was out on a limb, I asked him to shift his attention from his panic to the feeling of "nothing there if she leaves me." He found that something warm happened inside him as he let his attention go into that void that was opening beneath him, which surprised him. He actually saw it as red and yellow. This experience started to break the set in his mind that vulnerable equals victimized.

In some ways, Ray was in a classic "macho" bind—he had to hold on to himself tightly, which kept him always on edge. And yet an occasional helpless look in his eyes, his childlike need to get drunk and bust loose, as well as his willingness to keep coming and working on his problems, told me that the tenderness in him was longing to find some outlet or expression.

What I most remember from the time we spent together is that sense of being there together, hanging out on the edge of that cliff—exploring what it was like to hold on and what it was like to let go and fall. I suspect that somehow being there together like that made it okay for him to feel vulnerable. He realized it didn't have to mean annihilation, disgrace, humiliation, dishonor, or abandonment. Within the past year Ray has married and stopped drinking, and he's still working with his vulnerability on a deeper level, especially now that he's married. But he is definitely starting to get in touch with some gentle strength inside himself, which is very nice to see.

Perhaps someone might object, "Well, maybe it's all right for someone who has an intact ego to discover his vulnerability, but what about people whose world is collapsing all the time, and who cannot get themselves together?" I would work with clients who have an inadequate protective shell differently from those who have an intact set of defenses. If their roof is *always* caving in, then my focus might be on building firmer supports. In that case, I would put greater emphasis on a person's grounded interaction with the world, so that he could develop ordinary self-confidence and self-respect. If the belief in self is ultimately a fiction in *absolute* terms, still there may be *relative* usefulness in this belief, especially for those who have never developed any sense of groundedness or confidence. Even someone who has poor defenses or who splashes his emotions all over his environment has still probably not made a friendly relationship with this tender, soft place inside. Establishing this kind of friendliness and trust is an important step even with highly disturbed clients, so that their vulnerability is not a source of panic.

The more therapists fear this place of vulnerability in themselves, the more likely they are to think, "If we let people go near this existential void, this state of basic raw vulnerability, what will happen? They might go over the edge!" In fact, Ray had that experience earlier in his life when he was high on drugs. He felt his whole world falling apart and checked into a mental hospital for several weeks afterwards. That reinforced his feeling of, "I can't go near that scary place in myself again. It's out of bounds." But I think that the so-called "freak-out" that happens is not because of that void. Rather, it is an extreme reaction to that void. It is getting frozen into a panic about it. So it is *how* we relate to the emptiness which is important. And this is where meditation can be of value, especially for therapists, in giving them some kind of experience and confidence in working with their own vulnerability, so that they do not panic about the possibility of their clients going over the edge.

To conclude, I want to say something about power and strength, in the sense of inner strength, groundedness, and the ability to act effectively in the world. I don't think we can have real power without a sense of real vulnerability. The other kind of power, the one that Ray was holding onto, has no strength. It is an attempt to have power *over* and so becomes top-heavy and easily toppled. Trying to maintain control in this way makes us very vulnerable in the weak sense, the ego sense. Because our attempts to control things are easily threatened, we have to guard ourselves more tightly. Tying up our energy in this kind of defense system drains us of our strength. The power and strength that come from relaxing into our nature and feeling out the most raw and tender places inside ourselves is quite different. It's like the Taoist image of water as the most vulnerable and soft of the elements. Anything can penetrate it; it does anything you want it to do. And yet, for wearing away what is hard and tough, nothing surpasses it. The bridge from basic vulnerability to this real human power is gentleness. Gentleness can cut through the panic which surrounds our vulnerability. In fact, gentleness is often a very natural response to vulnerability. When you see a newborn child, or a young animal, or a friend who is in pain, the natural response is gentleness. Not so, usually, with ourselves—strangely enough. We have to somehow *learn* to be gentle with ourselves.

Meditation, which involves the practice of letting our world collapse, and of staying with ourselves through that, teaches us how to be gentle with ourselves. And if we start to develop that gentleness with ourselves, we can also be gentle with others in that same kind of way, which helps them relate to their own vulnerability. Buddhism describes this basic vulnerability as the seed of enlightenment already in us. It is said that when this "tender heart" is fully developed, it becomes very powerful and can cut through all of the barriers that we human beings seem to create. In its fully enlightened form tender heart becomes transformed into "awakened heart," *bodhicitta*.

Thus, the mutual vulnerability between client and therapist—as in any important relationship in our lives—seems to be a crucial factor in how two people can affect each other. If we look at the god and goddess of love in Greek mythology, we see that Aphrodite was associated with instruments of war and Eros was armed with arrows. This suggests that to connect, to be able to love means being able to let yourself be wounded. We could say that vulnerable means "able to connect." This implies that, as therapists, we can't really connect with a client unless we can somehow be vulnerable *with* that person.

DISCUSSION

Aud.: What do you mean by "meaning?" Does meditation provide a way of finding new meaning?

J.W.: Most psychotherapy attempts to find meaning where there apparently was none before. I see meaning as structure, as form that we create or discover through our interaction with the world. I haven't talked about that here, but that is largely what I do with clients—we discover and unfold new meaning together.

The interplay of meaning and meaninglessness is a dialectical process. We develop meaning-structures as a child to help us make sense out of the world and navigate through it. But there is often a period around adolescence or early adulthood when we start to question those meanings. And this may lead to the sense of meaninglessness that the existentialists talk about. Existential therapy helps people unfold the implicit meaning in their lived experience, which is much deeper and wider than the preconceived meanings that they try to impose on their experience. I do not want to denigrate the search for meaning, because it is powerful and important to find the organic meaning in our lived experience. Beyond the search for meaning, another step we could take is to discover some kind of meaning-free-ness (rather than meaninglessness in the existential sense), where we are free of the struggle to find meaning. The open ground is meaning-free. We create meaning and structure out of it. But these structures can get too dense and thick unless we can let them dissolve back into the meaning-free open ground. Zen *koan* practice is designed to break down our attempts to find meaning. If you struggle to find the meaning of a *koan,* it doesn't work. Giving up that attempt to find the meaning of the *koan* opens up another kind of awareness.

Aud.: Is it your role as a therapist to speed up the disintegration of old structures? Do you bring meditation into your therapy practice?

J.W.: No, I don't try to speed anything up but try to go with whatever the client's process seems to want to do. If the therapist is with the client's process fully, and the client is working from his own moment-to-moment process, that in itself furthers forward movement. If I were trying to make something happen faster, that would not be the kind of gentleness that is called for.

Therapy is about form—people finding new meaning and building more adaptive structures for living. The realization of no-self only leads toward greater sanity and well-being if we already have a grounded bodily sense of being-in-the-world. If we have this grounded sense of our existence, we will be able to bounce back from a period of world collapse and probably be the stronger for it. Schizophrenic and borderline people, lacking this relative ground, only get swept away by perceptions of groundlessness. Therefore, it is appropriate to help those who lack this ground develop form and structure to guide them in ordinary living.

What I have emphasized here is not form, but the emptiness that surrounds the forms we create, like the vast reaches of space surrounding our planet. Meditation is the discipline par excellence for learning how to appreciate and function in that space. I feel that meditation practice has its own integrity and context that needs to be respected. It has its own form—sitting with a straight posture—which grounds us and helps us "keep our seat" when opening to the greater emptiness that surrounds our lives. I don't try to mix it with therapy, which is more of a vehicle for developing meaning and healthy structure.

Aud.: If you deny that we have a continuous self, who is it that is witnessing and experiencing all of this?

J.W.: To answer this fully would require a much more lengthy philosophical discussion than we could get into here. To put it briefly, our awareness is both active and receptive. "I" is a convenient way to refer to the active part of this process. "I" as an active awareness has no form that can be grasped. At the same time, there is a set of habits, patterns, and structures that I can observe in my life, *post factum*. This is the "me" that the "I" observes. These structures tend to continue and repeat (this is what is meant by *karma* in the Buddhist tradition). "I" can observe these patterns and infer from them the existence of a solid, continuous self. But "I" can never directly experience that self. Moreover, no one has ever been able to find out who owns this active awareness. This was what the Buddha discovered through six years of meditation—there is no Wizard of Oz behind the whole show. Assuming that there is an "I" that owns this awareness creates unnecessary complications.

NOTES

1. Sartre (1953).
2. Hume (1888), p. 252.
3. James (1967), p. 296.
4. James (1890), p. 339.
5. Sartre (1957), pp. 100–101.
6. Welwood (1982).

=15=

Teaching Therapists How to Be With Their Clients

Diane Shainberg

In supervising psychologists and social workers during their clinical training in psychoanalytic psychotherapy, as well as more experienced therapists, I have noted certain recurring difficulties which I would like to discuss along with some ways that therapists can move closer to resolution of these treatment issues.

Early in supervision, the supervisee characteristically feels more tense with "the patient" than with other people in his life. He is scared simply to be with and experience the other person in the room without thinking about interpretations, meanings, theory, conclusions, images of how things should go, or what to do. When uncertainty occurs because there is no known direction or model for the interaction, the therapist often feels anxious. He is anxious merely observing the patient.

Supervisees often say, "I don't understand what is going on," or "I don't know what the patient is saying," or "I don't know what to do." The assumption behind these remarks is that it is possible to know accurately what is going on or that there is a knowable "it," and that therapy is a process of understanding what is in the head of the patient rather than one of interactional participation. There is an illusion that once one knows what "it" means, then some form of *doing* the technique can be practiced on the patient who will then be *helped*. Trainees initially experience patients as radically different from themselves: the patients know nothing and are to be worked on by the supervisee who knows or should know everything, because therapy consists of a prescribed technique.

The work of the supervisor is to show that the work is ongoing, that there is no "way," that one never knows for sure the experience of the other, and that it is in the mutual participation of discovering the essential quality of the patient that the healing takes place. Human relationships are so complex that one can never completely understand what is taking place, and therefore total resolution is impossible. It is this new event of mutuality, of ways of seeing and being together that create a new sense of inner strength in both participants. Along with the common fear that one is not doing thereapy the right way, there is an ignorance about the possibility of learning from the patient and finding out for oneself.

A second supervisory observation is that therapists work during and after sessions to match theory to patient, past experience to present. To apply theory and interpretation implies the wish to change or fix. They do not understand that true knowing is being able to observe and describe what is going on in the present in accurate, concrete, and complete detail. This is different from wanting to change or get rid of or compare or assume a fixed meaning about what is happening.

We do not change or fix but over time get to know the patient as he actually is and lives. In this way, we facilitate his getting to know himself more clearly, at which time he feels increasingly ready to change.

It is the task of the supervisor to enable the supervisee to become more aware of what actually takes place in the session—behaviors, experiences, and transformations of himself and the patient. It has been my experience as a supervisor that many therapists drown their empathy or appreciation of the patient's struggle by worrying that they are not doing enough for the patient, or that they are doing the wrong things.

Following are several clinical examples of how supervision has enabled the therapists to loosen their deterministic view of the patient as someone different who must be treated with interpretations in order to be healed.

After ten interviews, one trainee stated that there was "no relationship" with the patient. He saw this man requesting medication because he felt hopeless about his job and his future. The therapist felt he could not reach the patient and was angry that the patient was unresponsive to his efforts. The therapist felt the patient's hopelessness was "irrational" since he was young and intelligent and only "saw the dark side of everything." This is an excerpt from the tenth session:

Therapist: (after a few moments' silence) What's going on?
Patient: (staring at floor) Nothing.
Therapist: How are you feeling?
Patient: Okay. (shrugs)
Therapist: What are you saying with that shrug?
Patient: What?
Therapist: Your shrug?
Patient: Uh. . . .
Therapist: Are you aware you shrugged?
Patient: No. . . .
Therapist: You shrugged your shoulders. What could you be trying to say?
Patient: (smiling) I didn't know I shrugged.
Therapist: Well, to me it indicates you're leaving it to me to get things going here. Is this how you feel, you'd like to leave it up to me to start things?
Patient: What?
Therapist: Your shrug says you're leaving the session up to me to get going. Is that how it feels?
Patient: I don't feel anything.
Therapist: Did your last therapist start sessions usually? Is that your experience?
Patient: I don't remember. (squinting, a common facial gesture)
Therapist: Did you feel pretty free to talk to her?
Patient: She was nice.
Therapist: You felt you could speak to her comfortably.
Patient: It's hard to remember.
Therapist: It must have been tough for you with her going.
Patient: (no response)
Therapist: What did you feel when your therapist left?
Patient: Nothing.
Therapist: How come?
Patient: I don't know.
Therapist: What is it you don't know?
Patient: What?
Therapist: You started holding your head in your hands when we started talking about Dr. X. Is there maybe a connection between your gesture and Dr. X's stopping her work at the Clinic?
Patient: (silence) I'm very tired.

This therapist clearly had a fixed notion of how therapy was to go, what the patient was saying. However, he had no idea as to who his actual patient was and little interest to find out. My work with this therapist first was to focus on the fact that he had a relationship with his patient, an intense relationship illustrated in his feeling angry and frustrated with the man while in the session. This is the antithesis of "no relationship." I focused on how he felt while with this man and although he could say frustrated or angry, he could not go much further. I suggested he observe himself in the next session and focus on his feelings being with this person and to forget helping him for one week as he could not help until he knew more what was going on in his patient that he did not yet know. It was clear to me that this therapist had theoretical ideas that he saw as existing in this man's head, but could not find a way to facilitate the patient's opening up to him.

The therapist came in the next week and reported a "scary" thing that had happened to him in the session observing himself; he could not stop himself from talking, he could not bear silence. I suggested he had trouble being with this man as it might bring out certain feelings in himself, but suggested he again focus the next session on observing his feelings being with this man.

In the next supervisory hour, he reported a desire to change patients into people who could work more productively. He had *images* of what kind of patient he wanted. I said I was interested in his work with the person he actually had. I asked what he had felt in the session. He said that he had observed himself feeling "no feelings, a numbing." He said he was surprised at how deadened to his patient he could be; he blamed himself and the patient. I asked what else he could say of the deadening experience, and he said he had in the session "lost interest, wanted to close his eyes, and was aching with numbness." I stated that now he had *some feel* for what the patient was living through, how painful this state was, and how his thoughts, theories, knowledge, and explanations had functioned so far to pull him out of this pain, away from what was happening inside his patient. I then suggested in the next session he *give his total awareness to listening and attending to what he saw* and then we would go into it.

Following the twelfth session, the trainee came in and for the first time ever was silent with me. I was also silent a while. I asked him what he had actually seen, and he began softly saying that he found it impossible to put into words what had happened in the session. I asked what he had seen and he said with much feeling, "His hands." Then he was silent. We did not have to go further into this with words. A form of contact had taken place where the division between therapist and patient had momentarily lapsed, where there were two people who could now perhaps begin to be with one another in uncertainty beyond theory, labels, images, and conclusions. This therapist could now begin to see what was between himself and his patient, not what he thought therapy should be. He could begin to be aware of his own thoughts and feelings that created the environment of the work. He could now begin to get to know who the patient actually was, letting him be more, giving him the space to heal. The therapist told me he felt an impact from this experience, and he connected it with feeling interested in learning who his patient was. He wanted for the first time to find out who his patient was in fact. With this attitude, I felt, he could be in such a way that the patient would begin to share his thoughts and feelings with him.

The next supervisee I want to describe was a graduate student in clinical training, having worked two years with patients before beginning supervision with me. She was assigned a female patient from the day program of the clinic. The patient had one brief hospitalization and one of the supervisee's first questions was whether this girl would be "a treatment candidate for analytic work."

She described the therapy as "not working" and said, "I can't seem to make contact." She described asking many questions after which the patient would reply, look down, and remain quiet. "Why is she coming to see me?" she asked me with a touch of impatience. The supervisee felt "unbearable tension" to the point where she asked the patient after the first two sessions, "Would you like to talk about anything else?" and when the patient said "No," she ended the sessions twenty and thirty minutes early.

In telling me this, the supervisee spoke of feeling "terrible" and "ashamed." She was blushing, said that she could not think of any more questions to ask, could not stand to sit in the "frozen silence." I asked her what her thoughts were during those two sessions and she said, "They were racing, trying to find questions to ask." I asked what she was aware of in the session in the form of thoughts. As she told me what she was thinking, it was clear that she could not match her real patient with her image of "patient." She was drawing conclusions, alternating between being angry with herself, calling herself "incompetent," and labeling the patient "untreatable." She thought about asking to have the patient reassigned, then thought that maybe she would have other untalkative patients like this in her practice so she better "stick it out." She thought that in fact there was no point in her staying in the room since she did not have "the technique" yet to work with this patient, and this, she eagerly stated, she "had to get" from me.

I asked the therapist after she described her thoughts how she would feel having a conversation with this patient. She became visibly angry, held herself in check, said that she did not see therapy as "conversation," that she would not be able to "do this." "What?" I asked. "Have a conversation with her." I asked her what would be the difference between having a conversation and a therapy session. She was getting more angry and said, "Come on. If this girl were someone I knew, I could easily talk to her. . . .I can talk to just about anybody. *But she is a patient.*" I asked for the difference between patient and person. We got into a discussion of how out of her anxiety largely created by her image of what a therapist does, she hung onto learned dualistic notions of how therapist and patient talk to each other, rather than being open to finding out how in fact one could actually talk with this particular and unique patient she was seeing. The issue was to be in an inner state of mind to find a way—to want to find out how to be with this patient so that the patient would begin to talk, not to have preconceived notions.

She then said that she did not experience the patient in the same way as she would "a fellow human being." She could not feel other than that the patient was "so far a test of my being a therapist." I said she had turned the patient into an object "to be worked on" at this point. She said she felt the gist of it was that "if *it* is a person you can feel free, but if *it* is a patient you have to do something to change things. Otherwise what are you doing there?" I did not comment on her use of the word "it" but heard it as how remote she experienced the patient at this point from herself, as though the patient were not her fellow being sharing the human condition of suffering, daily conflict, having a mother and a father, being in fear, facing the inevitability of death. She did not remotely feel that she and her patient shared the same life struggles.

I asked her to tell me of her actual experiences as soon as the patient entered the room, to get an image of this event. She closed her eyes and described a tightness in her chest, a slight dullness in her head, she remembered opening her eyes wide in order to stay awake, a flash of fear when she thought that she would have to be with this patient for fifty minutes, an increasingly dulled feeling as time went on, her mind going blank, a wish to get out of the room, then thoughts flooding such as "maybe I can't do this work. I don't know what to do." She said she wanted to "have a good hour," that when she had such an hour, she felt "full of energy, almost elated."

I asked her if she felt she was looking for pleasure with this patient. "Sure," she said, immediately. "Then when you don't get it, what?" She said that she never thought of it that way, but that if she did not get some pleasure, she felt things were not right with her work, which she she did not want to feel. I asked if she felt perhaps she was dependent on pleasure in her work that perhaps pateints could not give her. She said that one's work is supposed to be pleasurable, or to bring satisfaction. I asked, "Are you interested in the actuality of the work? Do you want to see what it is in fact? You want your patient to give you pleasure or to help you feel okay, but this can't always be." The supervisee was upset and talked of the patient's "manipulating her," saying that she felt this patient could talk if she wanted. She said that if a person is not motivated to come, why spend your time with them. "Let someone else do that kind of work," she said angrily. "I don't want to waste my time."

I suggested that we temporarily discard notions of how therapy was supposed to go, and observe with attention how this therapy was going in fact now with the two people in it. I suggested this therapy be seen as a new beginning, never described before, and to participate in whatever came up as a new event for both parties. Since her book knowledge and theory had not been so helpful thus far, I suggested we leave it temporarily and focus attention on attending to what was taking place in the session. I told the supervisee, "Focus all your attention on seeing as clearly as you can the way this person behaves and what you think and feel being with her. Do not try to find meanings, make connections, or understand. Observe what takes place and your responses."

In the next supervisory hour, the supervisee was less tense. She began saying she was interested to realize that to observe was hard for her, although it had always sounded easy. She was aware that a lot of time she was wanting to fit the reading she had done on the schizoid person into what she was seeing in front of her, and this made it difficult for her to see the person as is. She said during the particular session she felt relief. "I realized I could see whatever I could see, that it was my own eyes seeing." She laughed, and I said, "You could be in the session with your own eyes."

This led her into an association of how I did not criticize her when she told me that she could only stay with the patient for thirty minutes in two sessions. She remembered my saying, "You can only be who you are at this time," and felt that thought relieving. I said, "I let you be as you have let yourself be in the last session." She said, "I never thought of letting the patient be."

In the next session, she talked about how she had seen how frightened she was to look, but she said that one thing she had been able to see was the way her patient looked up at her occasionally as if to say, "Will you go away?" I asked for her response to what she saw, and she said that she guessed the patient was aware she ended the sessions early, that maybe the patient wanted to feel that she could stand being with her and was afraid she could not. I said she had gotten a great deal out of the look.

Again I asked the supervisee to spend the next session attending to what was taking place and then we would discuss it. Having a focus in the session undercut her need to do, to figure out, but it also enabled her to begin to feel something during the session for the patient for the first time.

She came in the next supervisory hour and reported that what she had *seen* was that her patient "gave her fear." She talked of "feeling the fear." "It is contagious. It is not only coming from me." This was the first time in eight sessions that there had been any mention of the word "feeling" while with the patient. I appreciated this, seeing the fear as a change in her capacity to be present as a participating person during the session, and I told her this. My face must have mirrored my appreciation of this change in her as she smiled warmly.

We then talked of the "power" this patient had over her as she experienced it. We found that the patient could in her eyes validate or invalidate her belief in herself as a helpful person, a good person, a separate person. She said that it seemed right now that the central fact inside herself with this patient was "I am afraid." I asked her to watch what happened with her fear as she did not avoid it. She slowly said, "I don't think I've ever been able to look at how scared I am. I'm scared to just be in the room with another person and not know what's going to happen. Why should this be? Even in my own analysis I can't face how scared I am of people. My patient is also scared." This was her first noting of her patient being similar to her: a fellow being.

The schism between patient and therapist, between therapist and person was beginning to lessen. This schism had created internal pressure such that no empathy was experienced by the therapist and wanting to find out was reduced to psychodynamic formulations or conditioned images of how therapy works. In the next session, the supervisee reported, "I see her wanting to talk, then cutting it off. Her eyes get afraid and she backs off." The therapist, through listening and attentive observation, was beginning for the first time to see movement in the session. She was seeing the shift in the patient from being open to talking, to being anxious, to closing down in her particular way—withdrawal, moving out of relating. I asked how she had seen that the patient wanted to talk. She spoke of an expression in the patient's eyes, which she saw as "wanting to say something but feeling afriad." I asked, "What expression?" She said the word that came to her was "intelligence." She then said this was the first time she had felt the patient was intelligent. She had also seen how messy, "disgusting," the patient was in her dress. She described the patient's blouse not meeting her pants, the flesh "hung out," and this upset her, as did the way the patient's hair was dyed in such a way that it was "dyed looking." I asked her how she felt with these facts of who her patient was, and she said she was angry. She then went into an intellectual discussion of how important it was to look "good" in this society.

I said that what we had just seen in supervision paralleled what went on in the treatment, where now the therapist was responding as the patient did during the session. The patient had come in, open to being in the moment with her. The therapist was also open to participating. Then the patient had gotten anxious and cut off this being present together, just as the supervisee had done now with me through getting intellectual. We saw how in this process both participants in the therapy were mutually closing off the anxiety of openness.

Then I asked the supervisee how this transformation of an intelligent person in the room with another intelligent person had occurred out of the frozen terrain we had begun with in supervision, where the patient and therapist were unable to be in each other's presence for the full session. It was clear to me that the supervisee did not grasp the depth of this transformation where two strangers frozen in distant terror are beginning to want to talk together. I spoke of this transformation and the depth of it—I stated that the first phase of the work is getting comfortable being with the patient.

In this supervisory hour, a common teaching focus came up, the therapeutic relationship. Although we use this word glibly, few beginning therapists appreciate how meaningful this relationship is in the lives of their patients. Although they talk about it, they do not see the being together as a centrally important fact of the treatment, as are the moments when patients and therapists are together engaged in sharing in the moment, beyond words, time, roles. These are the times where trust is developed, where there is a getting acquainted with a sense of being who you are, letting the other be, when patients learn they can be with another person and be respected for who they are, as is. They are the times that give us hope, hope that we can find new possibilities in life. Their occurrence is pointed out to the supervisee as they come up in sessions described.

The first focus in supervision has been the supervisee listening and observing *what is*. The second focus is to enable supervisees to live in what is, not avoid it, to *let be what is*. We explore what blocks their being able to let the patients be as they are.

This patient is called a "slob." The supervisee wants to call this "bad," as it keeps other people away. So the therapist is inwardly wanting her patient to be a different way than she is and feels an inward pressure for this. She wants to remove the "sloppiness" and leave the person, but the person *is* sloppiness. With liking or disliking, there is pressure on the patient to be different. This pressure creates a strain, and the patient reacts to this pressure rather than feeling free to exist in the relationship with the therapist as is, and then to discover in this freedom her own way to be, not to have it imposed. The supervisee must first *see* the strain she puts on the patient, how she contributes to it with her own likes and dislikes, her own values. This second area of supervisory work is for the supervisee to discover where she actually is with the patient *as is*.

Attention to accepting or not accepting the patient as is led us to discuss the pressures this particular patient had had in life prior to the values the therapist laid on her. The supervisee gave me some history of the patient. At the age of six, she had been sent to a children's institution and separated from her only sibling, an older brother. Her mother was ill at the time, but the patient was not told that her mother was dying of cancer. It was only after her mother's death that her father told her that her mother had been sick all this time. The patient then pleaded to live with her father. The patient became sick in the institution, was placed in the infirmary, and it was at this point that the father came and took her out.

At this point in the history, and five months into supervision, the supervisee stopped. Her face turned red and she said, "Oh . . . God . . ." She said, "I can't believe it . . . I completely blocked it out." There was silence. Then, "When I was eleven my mother and father split . . . my mother said goodbye to me and my sister. My mother went off to Europe. I was scared she wouldn't come back. My sister and I were sent to a school with nuns where we lived for almost a year. It was horrible. My father didn't come to visit so often. My father would come, and I would beg him to take me home, and he would say he couldn't take care of all of us. Then I got sick . . . they took me to the infirmary and I had a fever and then soon after, my mother came back and I went to live with her . . . I can't believe I blocked this out when I heard it from Julie. [long pause] I've always thought I was too sick to be a therapist. This has really plagued me." There was silence and some tears.

I asked the supervisee what she heard herself saying. She answered in a way that is meaningful for all therapists. She said, "At the beginning, I was scared, and I knew it. But I didn't know, or wouldn't let myself know, how much I felt the same as the patient, because that meant that I wouldn't be able to help. So I felt the patient way way out there, like a piece of equipment to be fixed and I had to find the right parts. You can't imagine how far away. I didn't feel the patient at all really. I heard the words, and was worried trying to figure out what to do to help. It's hard to admit to myself that I don't still feel much. You said it's okay to be scared. It's so strange to see all this as human, that my supervisor is human, to say 'you've been scared,' or to feel it—very hard. I'm still having trouble letting in how we're all human. God, it's so big." There was no need to talk about it. We could finally *be it*. We shared this simply being human together as this supervisee would now be able to in her work with patients in years to come.

This supervisee feels she is creating therapy with her patients out of the unique nature of their interaction. She has learned to discriminate when she and the patient are open, when there is anxiety, the forms her anxiety takes in both of them. She sees how she actually lives in the presence of the patient, how she is affected by the patient's pattern of interacting. She can discuss these patterns as they come up in the treatment between them when the timing is right or as they emerge in the patient's life. She can make some discriminations regarding tolerance for anxiety. She learns how to let her patients be without her demands—giving the patient the emotional space to find out too how she is authentically. Images from the past have been loosened so that what is going on in actuality is observed more clearly. The supervisee is more engaged in relating without so many thoughts of what to do, how she is not doing the right thing, clogging up her emotional availability. She has experienced some moments with her patient and supervisor in which people were human without self-consciousness. She has been empathic and that is a touchstone for further work. She gained the strength from the supervisory relationship to drop the images of how therapy should be a bit and to live with the unknown. She becomes interested in who the patient is, how she behaves with her and the others. She became interested in the patient's thoughts, feelings, images, sensations, wants. The therapist learns she does not know at times. She learns if she is interested to find out or not. She learns that the work of therapy is moment-to-moment awareness of what is actually taking place. It is not knowing in advance.

Often patients do not know clearly what they want, think, or feel. They do not feel they can create their own fates from within. They are dependent on others for self-esteem and direction. They can bear minimal anxiety, have little patience. They experience little connection to having caused their own difficulties. They disrupt the relationship when they are not treated in the way they expect or when results that they want are not forthcoming. All this makes for a difficult person to be with and a process where the supervisee feels the patient conveying "Help me. Do something to make my life better. If you don't, you are incompetent or ungiving. I will hate you or leave or lose respect for you." For most supervisees there is intense anxiety at times being with such a person.

Thoughts begin to come quickly at such moments in session. Thoughts of the therapist often are: "What should I do, why don't I know what to do, what is the matter with me, I'm confused. I don't know what's going on here, the patient will find this out. What will happen when he knows I don't have answers? What does this mean? What is the patient trying to say to me? If I could figure it out, something could happen. What can I say that will bring all this confusion together? I'm getting mad. I'm more than mad. I'm furious. What's the matter that I get this way? How can I call myself a therapist? The patient is healthier than me. He reduces me to shaking fury. How can I not show this? I'm going to lose him. I need the money. Will I ever be able to do this work? The patient is right. We haven't gotten anywhere. Why can't I feel anything for this patient? I am hearing the words, but I don't feel."

As the therapist continues thinking during the session, he is wanting to avoid the inner upset, wanting to help, not knowing what to do. The fact is that there is little space with all these thoughts for listening to the patient. The endless noise of thoughts keeps the therapist from being emotionally available for listening to the patient. Therapists can become aware of how much they are involved in the process of thought in the session and what they think. Usually they will discover that their focus on thought does not actually help the patient.

I try to point out to supervisees in this process that thoughts will continue; however, as we see that they do not help us, we will not take them so seriously. They will continue, but we will see that they are impediments to the work. The thoughts roll on, but we do not cling to them once we see that they close us up. Supervisees come to see that it is their own thoughts that are at times their greatest enemies in the treatment process.

There is a key transformation in the supervisee when he is open to observing his patient as is, letting his patient be, dropping previously held judgments of himself and his patient, loosening ideas on how the therapy should go. The supervisee becomes aware of how his lifetime conditioning to accomplish, to get better, to get more, to please, to be liked, to have things comfortable, to avoid violence, to be thought of in a certain way, to avoid anger, terror, hopelessness block genuinely letting be *what is* with the patient and himself in the treatment. As this happens, he is able to feel more comfortable with his patient, to have his presence be the healing environment in which the *being is the doing*.

=16=

Entering Into The Place of Conflict*

Richard Heckler

I want to base my discussion here on a process that happened between myself and a teenager I was working with. I had been asked to consult at a juvenile detention home from an Aikido point of view. I worked with a number of young male adults for about three months. There was this one boy who came bursting out of a big metal door the first day. He was about six feet three inches. He knew we were going to be practicing martial arts, so he threw a kick at me, and I had to get out of the way.

He said, "I'm so angry I could kill someone." As I looked at him, I believed him. He had been in offender homes and juvenile prison before. What I said to him was, "Well, I'll show you how to do that. I'll show you how to kill somebody." This stopped him for a moment. His eyes got big, and I saw that he had a whole story line about what people had told him in the past. Whenever his aggression came out, people would say, "Keep your hands in your pocket," or "Turn the other cheek," or "Go get a soda." He had a history of a broken home, of being isolated and rejected. So when I said, "I'll teach you how to kill somebody," a look of doubt came over his face. I said, "I just want one thing from you. I want you to commit yourself to coming to every one of these sessions we do, three times a week." He agreed to that. In that moment we made contact, and I saw that he probably would come to every session.

*A talk presented at the "Open Ground" conference.

In the first session, I was showing him some pressure point or strike, and it became obvious that he was so eager and excited that he had no sense of center, no sense of ground. He was fumbling around with his hands. So I said, "Wait a minute. You won't be able to kill anybody like that. What we have to do is to develop some other things first." The other things we started to develop over time were certain bodily principles of centeredness, groundedness, extension, of how to organize excitement or energy, and blend with incoming energy. I can describe this briefly, but it took about three months to actually teach him these principles. Every time I would show him a pressure point or a strike, he would fumble around, and we would go back to the principles of center, ground, and so on.

During this process, a change began to happen. The best way I can describe that change is that his attention started to come back to himself, instead of having his bull's eye on whomever it was he wanted to kill. His interest began to shift from his revenge to what was happening in himself as he began to experience himself in new ways. One time toward the end of our work when we were moving around the mat and throwing each other, there was a real sense of playing together. I don't know if he would like that word. But he turned to me and said, "You know, it's easy to kill somebody. But it's more interesting to find out about myself. It's not as easy, but it's more interesting." Something very fundamental was changing inside of him. It was something to do with the way that he was starting to develop a new interest in his mind-body process.

The process that he and I went through over three months illustrates a number of principles that are important in working with people. I learned these principles not only through my Aikido training, but also through my practice of Buddhist meditation—both of which have influenced how I relate to myself, my clients, my family, and my work. Meditation practice has shown me that it is important to see and work with people where they are, and not to cover up the situation with techniques that I might have learned in my training.

Specifically with this boy, when I first saw him, I saw that he was a killer in some sense, and I recognized the killer in myself in him too. Instead of saying to him, "You shouldn't do that," I saw that his aggression was the basic doorway through which I could relate to him. All of the messages he had received in his life had been: "Do anything but feel your aggression. Try to be a good boy." When he came out and kicked at me, I saw that he was essentially saying to me, "This is the way that you need to relate to me." So that is where we started from.

One of the things that sitting meditation has taught me is that as I sit, I'm not sitting to make myself better; I'm not sitting to get somewhere or to have a good time; I'm sitting because I'm committed to look at *what is* with myself, so I can begin to see and experience my mind-body process. For those of us in the helping professions, it is easy to immediately want others to be in our mold, to have them change in a certain way, or maybe even to impress them with what we might know. But my experience is that if I stay with people, the first doorway they open—whether it is pain, aggression, or whatever—basically has its own intelligence. We do not have to try to skirt their neurosis or make it into something else. Their neurosis itself is an actual energetic experience that can be worked with as it is. In the case of this young man, we could see that unfocused, uncontrolled aggression as his neurosis. And yet it had a tremendous amount of energy in it that made him very available. Whether I thought it was good or bad was irrelevant to the fact that this was how he put himself out into the world.

In the Japanese martial arts, there is a movement called *irimi,* which means entering into the place of conflict. If someone is attacking you, instead of trying to block it, run away from it, or be detached from it and pretend it isn't happening, what you do is actually enter into that attack. And at the last minute, you turn so that you are not hit, but you are at the place of origin of the attack, standing next to the person. Usually if someone grabs me, my tendency is to want to punch him. I get defensive. That is not *irimi.* That is not moving into it. *Irimi* is facing the conflict, not so much with an attitude of, "I'm going to stand up to this," but with a sense of openness to it, being willing to see what is happening there. I don't have to like the attack, but I can still move toward it because it is coming at me. It is possible that inside the problem there may be a solution. To take the energy of the attack and to redirect it is a way of neutralizing the aggression. This is what I taught this boy to do.

When I work with people, I often encourage them to enter into their neurosis more fully. Not in the spirit of, "Let's figure it out," or "Where did it come from?" but rather: "What is the actual feeling, the energy, the excitement in the neurosis? What are the sensations in it? What are the temperatures of it? What are the pulsations and rhythms of it, and how can that be worked with?" Of course, someone might feel, "Well, if

I enter into that, I'm going to get more aggressive, or who knows what might happen?" Well, it's true, anything could happen. But I ask people to move into their conflicts in a way that allows them to experience their own excitement and energy. When I use the term "excitement," I am referring to what other cultures and traditions call *ki, chi, elan vital, prana*—our most basic energy of aliveness. It is the ground from which all our living emerges. From my practice of sitting I have learned that when something arises, I don't have to move away from it, figure it out, or block it. It feels healthier just to be with it, face it, and see how the energy of the neurosis takes on a structure.

I work with people somatically. The word *soma,* from the Greek, refers to the living body in its wholeness. Our somatic reality is the experience of life in and through the body, which includes feelings, thoughts, emotions, actions, symbols, images, and sensations. Working with people somatically does not necessarily mean body work where I put my hands on them and manipulate connective tissues, although that might happen. I can also work with people's thoughts, feelings, and actions as expressions of the living body. I don't pay so much attention to what my clients know or what more they could know. Most people I work with seem to know enough already. What I ask people to do is to start touching their living body and allowing a different kind of wisdom that is not cognitive to arise from it. I encourage them to see what kind of information comes out of arching their backs, or feeling a tightening in their diaphragm or a trembling in their legs. I ask people to pay attention to that information, to be in it, and settle into their own kind of energy patterns. Usually when people come to me, they wonder, "Why is this happening?" or "What should I do about it?" The questions I put to them are: *"How* are you doing it? How are you inhibiting yourself? How are you discharging your energy prematurely? How are you throwing your emotions away? How aren't we making contact? How *are* we making contact? How do you escalate your excitement? What does it feel like when we stand here and meet each other and share this kind of intimacy?" I keep trying to bring the attention back to *how* we are. And I find that if I sit every day and ask my clients and students to have some kind of disciplined practice of their own, these "how" questions start to be evoked and become a source of information about how to proceed.

When we sit, we are sitting just to see what is and at the same time we're discovering something more—what Trungpa calls the "basic goodness" deep within all of us (see chapter 11). When I work with people, I translate that into first seeing what is with them, listening to the sound of their bodies, seeing how their experience has shaped their bodies, their breath, their postures, their ability to gesture, to reach out, to take, to say no, to make demands, to strike. This is what I want to see first—what is. From there I look at what wants to become. I know that there will be new structures, forms, and shapes that will come into manifestation. Some people have tremendous rage that they have kept down. Others have tremendous joy that they have never expressed. Sometimes it's deep grief over someone who died years ago that has never been expressed. So, after seeing what is, and the energy of that, I try to gently encourage that energy to take whatever further shapes need to come forth.

Something else that I have learned from sitting practice is how I block these new directions from emerging by berating myself for being a certain way. I get in a fight with myself, and the tension of it locks me into a very solid identity. Yet in the middle of this struggle, all of a sudden I may wake up and find that all that is happening is that I am in the middle of this room, doing nothing but sitting there. And that has taught me when I am working with people to help them notice the ways they create an identity out of fighting with themselves, or resisting themselves, or trying to make themselves something other than they are. If they can just let themselves see who they are, they can allow new forms and structures to come into being, and when these have had their time, to allow them also to die and allow further structures to come forth.

I think what helped that aggressive young man to start moving from being a tough macho guy who was going to cut someone's throat to feeling a certain gentleness and intimacy with himself was some kind of glimpse of what Welwood calls the "open ground" (see chapter 14). What he would experience were moments in which he had no identity. In these moments he suddenly wasn't the tough killer nor was he yet feeling his own sense of aliveness. He was in between these two identities. And when he was in that place, I just encouraged him to stay there, not in the sense of holding on to that place, but from the perspective of seeing what it was like to feel himself there somatically. So he felt what it was like to be unbounded: he wasn't bound into the identity of "tough guy," and he wasn't yet a new person who was a little bit more gentle and compassionate. There were no boundaries in that place, no sense of form.

Normally, boundaries define who we are and who we are not. A child I work with, for instance, will become sick when his mother is sick. His lack of boundary creates confusion about the difference between his experience and that of his mother. His sense of identity is merged with her in an unhealthy way. In this sense, boundaries are defined by what we identify with. When we identify strongly with something, we are bounded by that; it provides the boundaries in which we operate. When we become unbounded, we are undefined. Our previous identity is no longer useful or intact. When our old boundaries collapse, everything, at least momentarily, is open-ended. If I suddenly lose my job, for example, and I have been strongly identified with it, I am no longer sure of who I am. When I become unbounded, it is always terrifying. But meditation has taught me how to hang out in that place and keep my eyes open. When I sit, and this happens again and again, I begin to realize, "Oh yes, of course I'm terrified here, and what else? Of course there is death and my fear of death, and what else?" So the practice of meditation provides a kind of environment in which being bounded and then being unbounded can both exist, and I can keep going on from there. If I become unbounded and start to relax into that, there is actual richness and creativity in that experience. And if I can stay with that, I can encourage others to experience that place as well. When this young man's macho identity was beginning to crumble, I didn't try to say, "Now you can be kind and gentle." That would have kept him from feeling this unbounded place of "Well who am I now?" If we can stay with that experience, it has an intelligence in it out of which the next structure or form will come.

Sometimes I use the metaphor of the cup and the quart. We have a cup of something in our hand and across the table we see a quart container. There is a possibility of expansion. The first thing we realize is that we have to put down the cup to go get the quart. There's a moment when we put down the cup and are reaching for the quart and we don't have either one of them. The old known boundaries are gone. We're traveling through space to get to the quart and we wonder, "Is this going to be worth it? Is this right? Will I ever reach it? Is the quart full? The cup wasn't so bad." There is a strong tendency to come back to the cup, to the known, to the familiar. The quart looked good while you were holding the cup, but when you're not holding either one of them, you think, "Maybe my arm isn't even long enough to reach the quart."

Many of the people who come to see me are going through this kind of life transition, moving from the known into some new, unfamiliar territory. They may be letting go of something, or starting something new, or feeling stuck on some plateau where nothing seems to be happening. There's a way to enter that unbounded space, but few of us have any training in how to let go and just experience the transition. Something in us seems to want to let go, but how do we do it?

As I sit and follow my breath going out, there is a space just before the in-breath comes back in. It might occur to me at that point that the next breath may not come, and I may suck it in, not letting it happen by itself. But if I can let myself keep experiencing that moment when nothing exists, right at the end of the exhalation, I begin to learn how to let go. For a brief instant I am nobody and I live without a tightly bound identity. Learning to let each moment take its own shape in this way has greatly helped me in working with people who come to see me about major questions and transitions in their life.

17

Uncovering a Patient's History of Sanity

Edward Podvoll

There are two kinds of psychological history that we come to know in working with people in psychotherapy. One is the history of pain, discouragement, missed opportunities, unfulfilled hopes, and unrealized possibilities in relationships. Such a history of neurosis has a compelling quality that can freeze the therapeutic relationship into an endless dissection, searching for the origin of inhibited development. The implicit question becomes, "Where did things go wrong?" Such a story is frequently filled with fear, guilt, blame, and aggression; it resembles the history of nations at war, where one war inexorably triggers another in the ageless recycling of insult and territorial revenge. The story line threads together a variety of memories with an explanation of why one event follows another and how one got to be the way one is.

On the other hand, embedded within the history of neurosis is another kind of history—the history of sanity. The history of sanity is episodic and often appears fleeting and subtle. This history of wakefulness, dignity, and patience is often lost by people in despair. To perceive the history of sanity, we need the curiosity and effort to look beyond immediate appearances. When the psychotherapist relates directly to wakefulness and becomes curious about the history of sanity, a different kind of relationship can develop: one of mutual appreciation and trust, not based on dependency, hope, or even memory.

The question arises of how to relate to the history of sanity, "what to look for." There are certain signs and landmark events that characterize wakefulness and sanity in another's life, but they can hardly be recognized unless therapists first experience and identify them in themselves. This is why the personal discipline of mindfulness-awareness meditation can be so important for the development of the psychotherapist. Only by examining the experience of wakefulness in our own lives can we recognize and appreciate it in others. The practice of meditation is the most direct way of studying the nature of our own minds. It is a tuning process, making us more sensitive to psychological and interpersonal experience.

With that kind of training, a natural curiosity begins to develop about the other person's sanity and we begin to feel drawn to it. What we see occurring first in our own, then in another person's experience, is an *intrinsic instinct toward wakefulness*. It is first sensed as a flickering, and from that flickering there can occur an enormous curiosity. We find that instinct to be as strong and as omnipresent as any described by Freud and his students.

While most other drives appear to involve striving towards personal security, self-fulfillment, or pleasure, the instinct toward wakefulness is the urge to penetrate beyond the continuous cycle of ego's self-justification and aggrandizing daydreaming. The most subtle aspect of the history of sanity is how one works with that instinct. The signs of that instinct are manifest in the most severe psychopathology, as well as in mild neurosis. It becomes the choice of the patient whether or not to develop that instinct, and it becomes the option of the therapist to encourage and enrich that development.

We are always startled to see how people in intense despair, locked into a hallucinated world, can suddenly step out of the grip of delusion in a moment of communal crisis, as for example during a fire in a hospital. Less dramatically, we see any number of people who, in spite of their own turmoil, act wakefully in a crisis, maybe even showing the "best" of themselves. Something allows them to immediately drop their preoccupations and act appropriately, possibly even wisely.

A brief clinical example might be useful here. A man who is in a state of impending manic excitement has a hectic quality to his ideas, stories, anecdotes, memories, and plans. The pressure of his words makes him difficult to listen to and follow. At some point, we acknowledge this difficulty. Following this, a spontaneous gap frequently occurs in the patient's streaming thought processes. A moment of confusion is punctuated by the question: "Where was I?" Then there occurs a somewhat tortured return to the point, and the process of escalation begins again.

This natural occurrence comes from the sensation that he has gone too far in the elaboration of a daydream: a sudden awakening followed by a struggle about which way to go. The whole thing often happens very quickly and usually we notice it only after the fact. The above example was taken from psychotherapy with a skilled musician. His musical discipline had been strengthened in the course of psychotherapy to the point where he could play his sight-reading exercises while entertaining a complex train of disturbing and self-condemning yet fascinating thoughts. His musical discipline, which allowed him to cut short the wanderings of his mind, gradually expanded into other areas of his life. The spontaneous returns from "flights of ideas" began to increase and gather during the psychotherapeutic sessions. He recognized that he had always had a latent ability to let go of thought patterns, even as a child. From that point, he began to develop some confidence that he was not at the mercy of his thought processes. The patient was able to use the pressure of a chain reaction of thoughts as a sudden reminder. From that he was better able to *discriminate daydream from reality.* He then began to exert the effort to come back to the point and from there developed the courage to work directly with his twenty-year-old habitual tendency towards a manic state of mind. This is an example of the sharp, intelligent quality of sanity that can manifest moment to moment even in the midst of psychopathology.

Certain signs of the history of sanity can be recognized in both the development and the present experience of all neurosis and psychosis:

REPULSION

First, there is a sign of *repulsion:* fundamental estrangement and a feeling of nausea about one's way of living. It might last for a brief moment or it might endure for years. One is simply sick and tired of unceasing daydreams, hopes, and fears, and the endless cycle of habitual patterns of thinking and acting. The patient says, in one form or another, "I'm tired of this because I see through things." That discrimination requires a moment of clarity, a sign of active intelligence. The ability to discriminate that something could be different in one's life means that something different has been glimpsed. Where and when has that happened? And how can one carry through with that? Perhaps it has been in relationship with one's grandfather, a teacher, or oneself during a particular year of school. It might include subtle or subconscious distinctions between what is healthy and what is not, and it frequently occurs at the height of neurosis itself.

An unnameable feeling of guilt can develop because one cannot live according to the more wholesome vision. It was at such points that the insane John Perceval would look into the mirror and lacerate himself with the word *hypocrite,* later echoed in his hallucinations. In the same way, each landmark event or moment of wakefulness in the history of sanity can be distorted into an aggressive drama. That is the basic perversion: the turning away from intelligence. But with the help of a therapist, the situation need not go that far.

It is the sense of repulsion that usually leads one to a psychotherapist. Quite early in the psychotherapeutic relationship—during the initial allegiance toward sanity—the heightened discrimination between what is healthy and unhealthy may take the form of token actions such as giving up smoking, chronic nail biting, or obsessional masturbation. These are more likely to happen when the patient has recognized that such activities are mindless, that they have the qualities of absorption or trance.

BEYOND SELF

From the moment of repulsion there occurs a *longing to transcend the sense of self.* This longing can become manifest in an instant or over a period of months. For example, a patient in crisis often arrives at the statement, "I don't know who I am any more. I used to know, but now I don't." This might happen from the shock of awakening from a manic spree, from psychotic delusion, or from a dream. During moments of depression, the statement might be made, "I don't know myself any more. I have lost myself."

When we try to find out who this self really is or was, there usually occurs an immediate confusion, followed by a series of confabulations. Then tenuous attempts are made to construct a cohesive story that describes the nature of self. A feeling of uncertainty, of cloudiness and doubt undercuts each attempt to materialize a consistent sense of identity. But we forget that it is a futile task. No wonder that the syndrome of "identity crisis" has become such a popular conception. Even though the attempt to manufacture a self made out of a series of habitual patterns may yield a momentary sense of security, there remains a gnawing doubt about the creation. Discontentment or loneliness arises, not simply because one cannot safely live up to an ideal image but also because there is a clarity and awareness that one is actually more than that. One senses that the limitations of that image are not only false and arbitrary but that they also constrict and inhibit one's health.

One of the primary origins of psychosis is the desire to transcend the sense of self, to arise fresh and purified from an abandoned and transfigured self. This leads to unwitting mental manipulations through which a former identity can be discarded and a new self hallucinated. Suicide, of course, would be the ultimate perversion of a desire to transcend self.

Unlike the conventional psychological models of "ego" that view identity as formed bit by bit from childhood through adolescence into adult life, the history of sanity exposes the quest for identity as a perpetual crisis. In adults it can be recognized as a primordial anxiety. In children it may translate itself into a sense of fragility or a threat to bodily survival. The perpetual crisis is not in failing to achieve a substantial enough identity but in recognizing that it is an unstable state, a delusion, and always falling apart. The history of neurosis points to the anxiety, self-consciousness and embarrassment of self-fabrication, while the history of sanity emphasizes the clarity of perception behind the anxiety.

THE URGE FOR DISCIPLINE

From repulsion and a longing to transcend one's conditioned personality there usually develops a desire for making things more straightforward: a sense of pruning or paring down, an urge towards *simplicity and discipline*. It could be as simple as beginning to make schedules for daily activities or meeting a therapist regularly. It could happen in a moment of cleaning one's desk before working. From the point of view of the history of sanity, the therapist would be particularly curious about the details of the experiences of discipline that have taken place in the patient's life. The reasons why the history of discipline should be so precise are twofold: to find out exactly what another person understands by the nature of discipline and what his or her relationship has been to it; and secondly, because there is a possibility that within that discipline, there has occurred some insight into how mind and body work. The practice of a discipline might have sharpened one's ability to perceive smaller moments of psychological time. It might be exactly that quality of precision that will allow the recovery of health.

An episode of discipline often stands out. One woman experiencing despair and suicidal preoccupation recalled a year of her otherwise futile college experience during which she went swimming every day. Not a dramatic memory, but the daily discipline had become a focus of her life; she had a sense of "taking care" of herself properly. Consequently, she studied in a more orderly way and felt some sense of development taking place. Rejection by a boyfriend ended all this. Her statement, "If only I had that kind of energy again," turned out to be a comment on the accuracy and effort that resulted from her simple discipline. Within such episodes of personal discipline, people often talk of a feeling of dignity, not necessarily because they were happy, but because there was a sense of doing something correctly and relating straightforwardly and pointedly to the rest of their lives.

Each seemingly mundane attempt at discipline carries within it the urge to work with one's state of mind, by directly connecting or synchronizing physical and mental activity. It might be athletics, survival disciplines, art forms, cooking, collecting stamps—any of which can become highly discriminating disciplines that sharpen the senses and create further vividness and appreciation for the sensory world. These experiences can become directly intertwined with the psychotherapeutic relationship. The discipline of the relationship itself can become a prototype of how one works with one's state of mind and life situations in general. When the manic musician, mentioned earlier, became irritated by even the most simple daily structure that might harness his energy, he said, "It's too much for me. I can't do it." When asked what he would reply to his young music student who voiced the same hesitation many times, he said, "I would tell him to start again and take it very, very slowly." His own advice soon became a useful guideline in the psychotherapy.

COMPASSION

The history of *longing toward compassionate action* is continually present in the lives of our patients. It is this compassion that is the key to psychotherapeutic work of any kind. Generally, compassion arises out of the developing basic warmth to oneself, but for most of our patients much self-hatred has accumulated over the years. Nevertheless, patients manifest compassionate urgings, even in moments of extreme despair, and are unable to recognize them. An elderly woman whom I had worked with for several months said, "I have become obsessed with myself, I don't seem to care for anyone else anymore." I replied that that couldn't be true because I felt her recently caring a lot about me.

The experience of compassion and its relationship to recovery is rarely talked about in psychotherapeutic writings. One striking exception is Harold Searles who refers to "a therapeutic devotion that all human beings share." About the course of recovery he has observed, "The more ill a patient is, the more does his successful treatment require that he become, and be implicitly acknowledged as having become, a therapist to his officially designated therapist."[1]

ENVIRONMENT OF CLARITY

Many moments of any psychotherapeutic encounter are marked by a *sense of clarity* and complete presence. Actually, such moments are continually happening throughout our lives. Even our dreams bear the imprint of this intelligence. At the moment of awakening from a dream, we frequently find that the whole dream experience is totally clear, translucent, and even brilliant. At that moment, we are beyond reflection, before interpretation or analysis. It is a naked experience of clarity that becomes clouded over and forgotten.

These barely perceptible moments of clarity are highlighted within the context of disciplines that synchronize or balance body and mind. A young rock climber bitterly complained about the meaninglessness and oppressiveness of his life. His ordinary adolescent life was sullen and confused, but while climbing he felt accomplished and thoroughly awake. No matter what problems occupied him in his internal dialogue, while climbing they were cut through as every foothold and piton placement became a life-or-death possibility.

Within that framework, he described how he would work with the tendency of his mind to wander. At that point, he would allow himself to come back to the sensation of his body hugging rock or the wind whipping around him. If this was particularly difficult, he would remind himself to wake up with the saying, "Come to your senses!" It was not only the exhilaration of accomplishment that he longed for, but also the sense of sharpness and precision that can arise out of fear. When such experiences were clarified so that he could appreciate them within the context of psychotherapy, he became able to recognize their natural and spontaneous occurrences in the less dramatic aspect of his life.

The clarity of the therapeutic environment is crucially involved in the practice of psychotherapy. The qualities of wakefulness, crispness, and simplicity provide an extremely important environment for patients to observe the shifts in their state of mind. It is that kind of atmosphere that helps awaken the patient to the natural history of sanity.

COURAGE

Finally, it is important to talk about *courage* and history. In his autobiographical journals, Charles Darwin asks, "Why don't the psychologists ever talk about courage?"

Because the experience of courage in the history of sanity is so connected with the experience of fear, it is useful to have a patient look into the moment-to-moment psychological structure of fear. Fear is particularly observable during the stages of recovery from a psychosis, when one feels so vulnerable and tender. One young woman vividly described a cycle of fear occurring that turned her "blood into ice-water" and culminated in shaking chills that drew her irresisitibly to crawl back into bed. This was especially exaggerated at the moment of awakening in the morning.

At first, her descriptions were only of intense fear. When her attention was turned toward the nature of that fear, she began to notice a preliminary phase of "overwhelming brightness." Then there appeared the thoughts, "I can't go on, I can't get up." She felt herself pulled back to "dimness, warmth and coziness." Gradually, she saw the oscillations between brightness and fear in a variety of life situations and understood them as a habitual regressive tendency accumulated over many years of psychotic episodes. Her psychotherapy consisted of arousing her courage to work directly with her fear, and at the same time, her environment was arranged so that she could relate with many courageous people.

Even in the case of what seems to be irreversible damage, we find that a quality of courage is not only necessary for recovery but is the nature of health itself. The experience of psychotherapy offers many opportunities for courage, both in the patient and the therapist. The patient's courage takes many forms—for example, the effort to follow a path out of addiciton or the weaning from chronic psychoactive medications. The therapist's courage also takes diverse forms, but the most comprehensive of all is the ability to be in a relationship beyond memory, repetition, or transference.

Something quite interesting occurs when the therapist practices a discipline of courage: courage becomes a quality of the therapeutic relationship, and as that expands into the total therapeutic environment, it begins to attract and motivate the intelligence and healthiness of everyone involved. The practice of psychotherapy involves a therapist in the whole sequence of events, from revulsion to courage, just as it does the patient. The conventional psychotherapies have attempted to describe in great detail the history of neurosis or pathology but often neglect the development of elements of sanity such as wakefulness, inquisitiveness, and curiosity.

From the point of view of the history of sanity, the therapist can begin to recognize, even within the crudest symptoms, aspects of healthiness. This means that psychopathology is not something to be eliminated but to be worked with in its momentary detail, because it is primarily seen as the result of obstruction to intelligent impulses.

When a therapist begins to recognize the enormous richness and fertility of another person's psychopathology, he can begin to relax and work with people exactly as they are, without the slightest desire to change them. Out of that, a vivid sense of appreciation and compassion for others develops. When a therapist practices a contemplative discipline, he may find that his own path toward greater awareness is not so very different from the patient's path of recovering health and sanity.

NOTES

1. Searles (1979).

=18

Working With the Old and Dying

Ann Cason and Victoria Thompson

Dana Home Care offers an alternative to nursing home care for the elderly and disabled, based on principles arising from the practice of meditation. There is a world of difference between caring for someone in their home and caring for someone in an institutional setting. People who have been uprooted from their environment are often confused and disoriented, particularly the elderly. Since institutionalism is generally the result of some crisis demonstrating the inability of the person to function independently, the overall trauma is immense. When done properly, in-home care is a much gentler approach. Clients can remain in a familiar environment and be helped with domestic details they are no longer able to manage. Although the daily routine of dressing, cooking, cleaning, and doctor's appointments are very important in themselves, they also provide a unique opportunity to work with the client's state of mind.

During the last two years a number of concepts have become the ground of our work with old people and dying people. The concepts emerged as we began to discuss what we were doing with our staff.

Usually, when people think about old age and death, they think of these as experiences they have not had yet. Death is something yet to come, mysterious and fascinating, and at the same time frightening. Our approach is that old age and death are actually very familiar. In fact, they are psychological experiences that we have constantly. When you wake up with a hangover and a mouth tasting of cigarettes, feeling like a chimney sooted over, that jaded quality is old age. It is the sense that experience is not fresh, that there is not any hope or reason to go on. That experience is familiar to all of us. We also experience death constantly when we are separated from people or things that we love.

The care of the old and dying in this country is unique. Medical personnel are the only ones that work with such people. There are a few social service agencies and some other people who are well-intentioned, but the majority of the population does not relate to the aging or dying except as problems they cannot handle. This taboo has come about because people are uncomfortabe with the familiar quality of those experiences. Old age and death are not alien—they are right there with us all the time. In our work, going in with some sense of familiarity is the first opening in a genuine relationship. It's tricky, though. While we believe that old age and death are familiar experiences, we have no documented proof to that effect. There is no proof that physical death and what we experience as loss or separation are the same thing. We take a leap of faith, accepting the familiarity of it and at the same time not really knowing, not really being sure. Not knowing is actually a great source of delight and fresh air. If any of us really knew, a computer could do the job. Being able to make a gesture or opening to these situations, treating them as familiar, but not really knowing, is tremendously generous and warm. It comes down to a very ordinary level. When we see an old person huddled in bed, clutching the covers and looking like a corpse, we can feel the presence of death and treat that with friendliness.

This involves us in a recognition of our own mortality. Our own tender beating heart is going to stop at some point, and the blood will stop running through our veins. That sense of mortality we share with the client cuts through the petty concerns and obsessions that we both have. Knowing this enables us to step into peoples' lives with a feeling of having something in common. What they are going through is what we are going through, and so we can work with them.

Another underlying concept that has emerged derives from the Buddhist view of mind. A simple way of describing what mind is would be to say that we and our world are the same thing. There is no difference. With our clients, for example, we can see from their doilies, their pictures on the wall, their knick-knacks, their habits, likes and dislikes, that their world and who they are are the same thing. As we step into their world, we are stepping in with our world. We also create an atmosphere—with the way we are feeling, the kind of attitude we take or how we are dressed. We take these things into their world and there is a quality of merging. There is a moment of confusion, not knowing whose world is whose, as well as much uneasiness on the part of the client and ourselves. Nothing is predictable because of this blurred quality. We do not have to focus on our clients as if they were bugs under a microscope. We do not have to examine them in detail in order to know who they are. If we can take their whole world as a message and allow it to give us some idea of how to work with them, within that relationship both of us can relax. We do not have to be so focused on them, and this creates less of a burden for them to bear.

So we accept the familiarity of the situation, that death and old age are not alien to us but are part of our experience. We accept goodness and mortality as something that we share. This is the basis of our work.

Older people can have a great sense of isolation. There is a diminishing or loss of faculties. Eyes and ears no longer work very well, and this cuts the person off from the rest of the world. Mobility is reduced—arms and legs do not work. It becomes harder to go out into the world as well as one did once. When one is over eighty, there is a good chance that one has lost a mate, and perhaps, too, friends have gone into nursing homes.

This kind of isolation brings up anger and depression. Your faculties are not working and you are lonely. You know how it is when you have a good friendship—it is sparky and good. When you are old and you have not had that for a long time, it is depressing. Your world becomes smaller and more narrow. You are confined to one house, frequently one room in that house, sometimes even one bed in that room. Yet, as your world becomes smaller and smaller, a strange thing happens. You become highly aware of the atmosphere and all the details within that atmosphere.

There is also a general sense of groundlessness that comes with old age, when you are letting go of your life. There is fear of death and uncertainty about whether you can even make it through the day. This groundlessness and fear are so expansive that a reaction of contraction and solidification occurs. People become extremely attached to their detailed routines, with very strong ideas about the way things should be. This is a very interesting situation. Expansion and contraction are happening at the same time.

When we first go into a person's home, the question comes about, who are we and who are they? We have all kinds of ideas. Old ladies ought to be clean, old men should not drink too much. We have to let go of this a bit. We try to suspend our judgment and take notice of the environment that is there. What is the atmosphere? We look at the drapes on the wall and we hear about how they chose the color scheme forty years ago. We look at all the little doilies, the 1939 World's Fair ashtray, all the pictures of the family, all the books and all the prescriptions. We get to know something about that person and what is important to him.

When we go in, we try not to have too much armor. We do not go in as professionals. We do not have uniforms or a lot of notebooks, forms, and professional paraphernalia. Without too much armor, we can let the situation touch us. We have what you might call a touch-and-go approach. We might go into Eliza's house and sit down. She starts telling us about how bad she feels. Her joints hurt and nobody cares about her. You find yourself sinking into her painful state. Then all of a sudden, there is a little reminder, and you let go of that state. You can have a sense of humor about it. You just feel her experience then let go of it a little. You might also feel that Eliza ought to be doing this or that. You can let go of that too.

It is a continual process: going in very gently, paying attention to the environment, being touched, touching, and letting go. This happens all the way through the relationship.

In getting to know an elderly woman such as Eliza and her world, we get some sense of what her personal journey is, what she has been doing all her life, what things have meaning for her. Usually we come into contact with a person when there has been some break in that journey. This may be due to a broken hip or some other physical infirmity, compounded by the severe depression that can go along with old age. We get to know this person and make friends with her. We find out about her journey and what the break in it has been. We find out what the discipline has been and work with that so that her journey can be reestablished. It is very simple. It might be playing bridge with somebody so that her confidence about playing bridge comes back. Then that person might be able to go out and play bridge with her friends once again. We let the situation inform us about what needs to be done.

True fellowship allows some relaxation to take place. This comes through appreciation, interest, and curiosity about someone sharing who they are and who we are. Friendship is really a very ordinary thing. Many people come to us because they want to work with dying people. They have some idea that working with a dying person is sitting by the bedside, holding his hand, and giving him counsel during the last few moments of life. In our experience, this is a romanticized view.

Actually, working with the elderly or the dying is very boring. You are sitting there. They have had their drink of water and you have rubbed their feet. There is not much more you can do, and it is very boring. What you do with that boredom is very important. If you cannot handle it, you scurry around and do all kinds of unnecessary things. The ability to be there with the boredom is the great gift of the meditation practitioner. We are very much used to boredom, so it does not induce as much panic as it does for most health-care professionals.

In the same way, we can be straightforward with people about death. When they give us an opening, we do not back away from it. We do not say, "Well, you never know, you might live forever." This is usually the role of the family,—always in the role of covering it over, which becomes very Kafkaesque. Here is a dying person and everyone is talking about the vacation they will be taking this summer. We can step into that situation and answer, "Yes," when the person asks "Am I dying?" We can be with them and be sad with them. We take our cue much more from the client than from some formula. We let people talk about their own idea of death. One person might talk about being alone, very alone. There are all kinds of concepts. It is very important for us not to project our own ideas about death anytime during the relationship and especially at the last moment before they die. If we do that, there cannot be any genuine communication because we are too busy maintaining our own position. So, on our part, there is a sense of respect and gentleness toward a dying person's view.

Our approach is that we honestly do not know what happens after death. There is really no way we could know. We might have our beliefs, but for other people it is not a matter of beliefs; they are going through a door we have not gone through yet. They have to go through it alone. Basically, what we talk about is feeling a genuinely sad parting—that we will miss that person when she goes. It is simply caring for the person the way she is.

Many of our clients have the attitude that since they are suffering, they must have done something bad. This is a problem when one gets old and is going to die. If God had been good, and you had been good, then it should have worked out that you would be immortal. Somehow it turns out that you are suffering and bedridden and falling apart and about to die. It must mean that either God does not exist, or is bad, or else you are bad. A great sense of punishment comes up, an attitude which is very hard on the client. The fruition of our work is when some of this has relaxed. We work toward an appreciation of impermanence on the part of these old people. This can open the way to some humor or even delight in their situation.

We ourselves have to appreciate impermanence too, and be willing to let go of our desires for our clients. Beatrice is a good example of this. We brought her through psychosis and a broken hip. We watched her open up and work with the world. Now she is starting to decline because she is getting ready to die. We had hoped for a well-received death and a sense of good journey, but we have to let go of that idea too. She is going to die and we have to let go of her. We will not see her anymore.

We must let go of whatever our hopes are for the person. There is always a tendency to want to confirm ourselves and feel that truly we are doing a good job, that people care a lot about us, and that we are fine people. Actually, the more intimate we become with people, the more complaints we get. This is very irritating because we think we we should be appreciated for the good work we are doing. The more we put into it, the more we think we should be appreciated, yet we are more likely to find that people think we are taking advantage of them, charging too much money, or not attending properly to them. This is frustrating, but it seems to be part of the intimacy. The closer you get, the more their crankiness emerges and the less they are on their "best behavior." You just have to keep going, dealing with that, patiently and attentively.

There are all kinds of reasons not to do this kind of work at all, and yet, somehow, we are doing it and it is fascinating. The reward comes from the intimacy of being so involved with someone else's life. It is like being a servant in a way, having a tremendous presence in someone's life that we would not have otherwise. We have to accept the groundlessness of the situation. We are just there, doing it, and in one sense, there is no real reason why.

At the same time, we do have some kind of feeling for the situation. We have a sense of fruition about dying. One lives as completely as possible and one dies as completely as possible. It is a matter of being fully engaged in experience with as much awareness as possible. In working with clients, the way to approach death is the same as the way to approach life. We present some atmosphere of acceptance and invite the client to take part in that with us. If the client does so, then there is some intuition about what to do and some genuine communication. It works for us as well as it works for the client.

CASE PRESENTATION

Beatrice, a 79-year old widow, fell and broke her hip in November 1977. She was living alone in her home at the time, and the accident was quite traumatic. She spent five hours on the floor, dragging herself to the telephone. She was finally able to call her daughter who arranged for her to be taken to the hospital. After surgery and a long period of recuperation and physical therapy, Beatrice and her daughter began to discuss future plans. They were faced with the choice of a nursing home or home care. It was at this point that Dana Home Care was called in.

We first saw Beatrice at the hospital in December 1977. She was seated in a wheelchair, a tiny yet sturdy-looking woman, alert and pleasant. She had obviously spent a great deal of time "cogitating," as she put it, on whether or not to go home. Even at that first brief meeting, Beatrice seemed far away and somewhat introspective. She is quite deaf, and it was difficult to evaluate how much this feeling of distance was the result of her failing faculties.

The second time we went to see Beatrice at the hospital, we took with us the couple whom we had hired to live with her when she came home. Beatrice greeted Brad and Janet very nicely and said she hoped they would enjoy living with her. Throughout this visit, Beatrice would ask us if she should get up, which chair she should sit in, and so on. She seemed overwhelmed and unable to make the simplest decisions. She did not express this confusion directly, but continued to maintain a social front.

The next day, we took Suzanne to see her at the hospital—she was the staff member who would be working with Beatrice. As we came in, Beatrice said, "Don't go near the bathroom. There's bombs in there, and if you go in, they'll explode." She proceeded to tell us a long, rambling story about adding an extension to her house. Very little of what she said made any sense.

Over the next few days, the hospital reported that Beatrice was combative, abusive, and incoherent. Her doctor ran tests and found no physiological explanation for her behavior. He then prescribed Haldol, a major tranquilizer, which reduced Beatrice's combativeness but did not diminish her confusion. After prolonged discussion with her dauther, who had visited all the nursing homes in the area, we decided to bring Beatrice home.

We set up a twenty-four-hour care program. Brad and Janet would live in with her, covering most evenings and all nights. Suzanne and other staff members would cover the mornings, afternoons and some evenings. Because of Beatrice's depression, we decided that short shifts of no more than five hours would be best. Our care plan was to get to know her and provide for her basic needs (personal care, meals, house upkeep, etc.).

When Beatrice came home, her extreme suffering was very apparent. She was fearful and confused. She did not want to get out of bed, wanting all the drapes drawn and refusing to eat because, she claimed, there was metal in her mouth. She "saw double, felt double, and heard double." She was terrified of falling and had to be tied into her bed or chair. In the midst of all this suffering, there seemed to be a great deal of intelligence. Our task was to create an atmosphere that would allow this basic intelligence to flower, through communication and appreciation.

For the first two weeks, while providing her basic care, we also paid attention to how we handled ourselves and tried to discover the things she cared about by "tuning in" to her environment. There was a bird feeder by the window where birds and squirrels fed. The house was full of books and classical music and was very tidy and clean. The neighbors told us that Beatrice always had the nicest yard in the neighborhood and that she loved flowers, plants, and trees. Her orderly closet was hung with clothing which reflected a discriminating taste.

At weekly staff meetings, we shared our experience of Beatrice, cheered ourselves up, and discussed the minutest details of her care and how we could work together.

It seemed that Beatrice had been a hardy person who never did drive but walked everywhere. She came from pioneer stock and thought of herself as a pioneer type. She had arthritis and was told to keep active or she would be in a wheelchair. Walking and activity were important to her. She loved the outdoors, watching birds, working the soil, helping things grow. She had always been an avid reader and had an interest in music and theater. For yardword she would dress in a scruffy manner; when she went out, though, she was always stylish and meticulously well groomed. She was intelligent and sharp, with a salty sense of humor.

As we got to know her better, a plan for her care began to emerge.

We started by gently insisting that she get dressed everyday. We combed her hair, put on lipstick and had her stand in front of the mirror to look at herself. Getting dressed made her angry for a long time. One day while helping her dress she began praying, "Dear God in heaven only you know how this woman's mind works. Please protect me. Thank you. Amen." During this period, the staff did not get taken in by Beatrice's feeling of incapability, anger, or depression. There was a definite sense of feeling her pain but being able to let go, to see through it, even to the humor of the situation.

Suzanne brought in fashion magazines and began looking at them with Beatrice. Janet brought in fresh flowers from the florist, and they had tea parties at four in the afternoon.

The physical therapist came and gave the staff exercises for Beatrice so she could begin walking again. For an active pioneer type, walking was very important. Her whole sense of journey had been broken by not being able to walk. This was also true of reading. The staff began reading to her, providing large-print books and encouraging her to read. This was a busy period for Beatrice and the staff. She had exercises to do, had to walk every day and was encouraged to help with dusting and drying the dishes. She also worked with clay, painted with water colors and frequently listened to music.

Although working hard and making progress, Beatrice started talking about her feelings of emptiness and loneliness. She did not know what to do with herself. She felt this was a "queer" way to live, and referred to her home as an institution.

One day Beatrice discovered a basket of Christmas cards that had come while she was sick, that she had forgotten. She got busy and read them all, remembered all the people who had sent them and started writing letters. For several weeks she wrote letters and remembered. She began thinking of her life before the accident. As memories began coming back, she became very angry.

She alternated between clinging to the staff and getting angry at her situation. This, again, was a difficult time for the staff, listening to her anger, her complaints and "poor me" attitude. Still, there was genuine appreciation for Beatrice, and we could see that she was getting better.

We decided that Beatrice needed encouragement toward more independence and confidence, and so we agreed to cut down her care program very gradually so that she would have some time alone. We started with only thirty minutes alone. She resented this and felt she was being left alone only for our convenience. Gradually she grew pleased with herself and became less fearful. We finally settled on a care program where the live-in couple would fix breakfast and dinner, and provide morning care from 9:00 to 12:30. Beatrice was now alone afternoons and many evenings.

She gradually moved from confinement in the house to walking outside to long walks around the neighborhood. Soon she went out into the world for shopping, hairdresser and doctors' appointments, and occasional meals in a restaurant. On holidays she visited her family in Denver.

There is no true resolution to this case. Beatrice reached her peak several months ago and now is starting to decline. The communication book at her house is full of the details of her life: how her teeth fit and what the doctor said about her toenails or the swelling in her ankles, whether to walk or not, shopping lists, and what to eat if constipated. There is some sense of our having made a relationship to boredom and of having slowed down to appreciate the details of her life.

Now, with faculties failing more, there is for Beatrice a certain amount of frustration and isolation. She tries to mail letters and forgets to put on the address, then gets frustrated if someone reminds her to do it. She might say, "Well, if you hadn't created so much confusion around here I might have remembered." She thinks there is a little girl who lives in the alley who cries and wants to get in. When something is missing she is sure the little girl took it. There is a feeling of sadness, watching our old friend decline and get ready to die. Our goal now is not to help her get better, but to maintain the atmosphere of communication and appreciation which will lead to some realism and sense of humor about our common situation. The other day Beatrice said, "People live and get old and they die. There's no sense getting morbid about it."

Notes on Contributors

DAVID BRANDON is head of the Division of Applied Social Studies at Preston Polytechnic Institute in England. He has spent twenty years as a social worker and has directed research on homeless young people for the English government. His books include *Human Being Human* and *Zen in the Art of Helping*.

ANN CASON and VICTORIA THOMPSON are cofounders and executive directors of Dana Home Care, an innovative service for the elderly and dying with branches in Chicago and Boulder, Colorado.

ERICH FROMM was a leader in the development of humanistic psychoanalysis and one of the first Western psychologists to take an active interest in Eastern thought. His books include *The Art of Loving, Escape from Freedom, Man for Himself,* and *The Sane Society*.

RICHARD HECKLER, cofounder of the Lomi School, is a director of the Tamalpais Aikido Dojo and has taught and lectured widely on body-oriented counseling and psychotherapy. He is currently working on a book on this topic.

THOMAS HORA is an existential psychiatrist in private practice in New York. He is author of *In Quest of Wholeness* and *Existential Metapsychiatry*.

JACK KORNFIELD was an ordained Theravadin Buddhist monk for three years in Thailand and now teaches Insight (*Vipassana*) Meditation at retreats throughout the country. He is Director of the Insight Meditation

Society in Barre, Massachusetts. He also holds a doctorate in psychology and is author of *Living Buddhist Masters*.

MOKUSEN MIYUKI is an associate professor of religious studies at California State University, Northridge, and is also a Jungian lay analyst.

JACOB NEEDLEMAN is a professor of philosophy at San Francisco State University and director of the Center for the Study of New Religions at the Graduate Theological Union, Berkeley. He has been a trainee in clinical psychology and a research associate at the Rockefeller Institute for Medical Research. His books include *The New Religions, A Sense of the Cosmos, Lost Christianity, Consciousness and Tradition,* and *The Heart of Philosphy*.

EDWARD PODVOLL is a psychoanalyst and past director of the Chestnut Lodge Hospital in Maryland. He is presently director of the Contemplative Psychology Progream at Naropa Institute, and he is working on a book applying Buddhist psychology to the treatment of psychosis.

RAM DASS (aka Richard Alpert) has taught psychology at Stanford and Harvard and is a teacher and student of Hindu thought. His books include *Be Here Now, The Only Dance There Is,* and *Grist for the Mill*.

JOSHU SASAKI ROSHI is abbot of Cimarron Zen Center and Mt. Baldy Zen Center in the Los Angeles area. He has taught Rinzai Zen throughout the United States and Canada and is author of *Buddha is the Center of Gravity*.

DIANE SHAINBERG is a faculty member and supervisor at the Postgraduate Center for Mental Health and the National Institute for the Psychotherapies in New York. She has studied Vedanta and Tai Chi and is presently a practicing student of Zen Buddhism. She is author of *Healing in Psychotherapy*.

ROBIN SKYNNER is a psychiatrist who has taught psychotherapy for eleven years at the Institute of Psychiatry and Maudsley Hospital, Britain's principal psychiatric training center. He was the first chairman of the Institute of Family Therapy in London. He is author of *Systems of Family and Marital Psychotherapy*.

KARL SPERBER is a psychologist with the Oneida County Department of Mental Health in New York, where he directs the Child Guidance Clinic. He has cultivated a long-standing interest in Oriental culture and has studied Taoism, Zen, and Aikido.

CHÖGYAM TRUNGPA is the founder and president of Naropa Institute of Boulder, Colorado, and the author of *Born in Tibet, Meditation in Action, Cutting Through Spiritual Materialism, Myth of Freedom,* and *Journey Without Goal*. He is a scholar and meditation master trained in the Kagyu and Nyingma lineages of Tibetan Buddhism and one of the most influential teachers of Buddhism in the West. He has founded a network of meditation centers in the United States, Canada, and Europe. ADRIAN VAN KAAM has been an existential psychotherapist and a professor of psychology, as well as an ordained Catholic priest. He is founder of the Institute of Formative Spirituality at Duquesne University and editor of *Studies in Formative Spirituality* (formerly *Humanitas*). Among the more than twenty-five books he has written are *The Art of Existential Counseling, Religion and Personality, Existential Foundations of Psychology,* and *The Mystery of Transforming Love.*

ROGER WALSH holds both an M.D. and a Ph.D. in neurophysiology. He is presently on the faculty in the Department of Psychiatry at the California College of Medicine on the campus at the University of California, Irvine. His books include *Toward an Ecology of Brain* and *Beyond Ego.*

JOHN WELWOOD is a clinical psychologist in private practice and director of the East/West Psychology Program at the California Institute of Integral Studies in San Francisco. He has also taught at the University of Chicago, the University of California, Antioch, and the California School of Professional Psychology. He is an editor of the *Journal of Transpersonal Psychology* and author of *The Meeting of the Ways: Explorations in East/West Psychology* as well as a forthcoming book on intimate relationships.

Glossary

All non-English words defined are given in Sanskrit, except where otherwise noted.

Abhidharma. The original root texts of Buddhist psychology, written down five to ten centuries after the Buddha's death. They contain a very thorough and detailed analysis of states of mind and levels of consciousness.

Aikido [Japanese]. A Japanese martial art, developed by Ueshiba, Morihei based on principles of nonviolence, by which the practitioner blends with the energy of an attack and throws the attacker off-balance.

Basic goodness. A term translated from a Tibetan phrase referring to a fundamental, unconditional quality of presence, wakefulness, receptivity, and sensitivity that all human beings share, beyond conditioned ideas of good and bad. This term is not meant to deny or ignore the existence of greed and aggression, or evil and suffering in the world, but it points to a more basic human quality underneath these phenomena.

Basic intelligence. This term translated from Buddhist psychology refers to a universal quality of wakeful awareness that all human beings share, underneath the many forms of ignorance, delusion, and self-deception that exist. This intelligence operating in us is considered to be a direct expression of the universal life tendency to move toward balance and greater wholeness.

Buddha nature. Literally, "buddha" means awakened one. In Buddhist psychology, all humans are considered to have this awakened quality operating in them.

Dharma. Literally, the way: the way the universe works, the universal laws of reality. This can be experienced, but never fully conceptualized, because concepts exist within the law of Dharma.

Ego. The meaning of this term in Eastern psychologies is different from that in Western psychology (see Welwood and Wilber, 1979). In this book, the term generally refers to the activity of grasping, holding onto ideas and images of oneself, and trying to defend a separate territory for oneself apart from the whole of life.

Egolessness. This term from Buddhist psychology implies that all self-images and attempts to create a fixed identity are not primary or ultimate. Just as we cannot tighten our hand into a fist unless the basic condition of the hand is open, so a more fundamental openness of mind is considered to underlie the grasping attempt to forge a separate, solid self-concept.

Emptiness. *(Sunyata).* The basic, open nature of mind which is more primary than all concepts and interpretations. This quality of emptiness can be directly experienced through meditation practice. It is not mental blankness or a tranquilized state of mind. Rather, it is a liberation from the interpretations of discursive thought, allowing us to perceive the world more clearly and fully.

Enlightenment. Realizing the true nature of what is, apart from all conditioned beliefs and concepts about what is. This alignment with the nature of reality is said to result in a radical shift in how one lives one's life.

Karma. The chain of cause and effect, conditioned responses and habitual patterns.

Ki [Japanese]. Universal life energy, which is thought to animate the body as it circulates through certain channels or meridians in exchange with the environment.

Kleshas. In Eastern psychology, certain emotional patterns that accompany the activity of ego-grasping: jealousy, pride, ignorance, greed, and aggression.

Koan [Japanese]. A meditative device used in the Zen Buddhist tradition, in which the meditator must contemplate and answer a question that cannot be solved by discursive, rational thinking.

Maitri. Unconditional friendliness, loving kindness, self-acceptance. Mindfulness. Clear attention to what is happening, both inside oneself and in the environment. This would include noticing thoughts and feelings, without, however, becoming totally absorbed or caught up in them. Mindfulness practice is a form of meditation in which this kind of attention is practiced.

Open ground. The fundamentally open nature of awareness underlying all conditioned states of mind. It may be glimpsed in the spaces or gaps between any two moments when the mind is fixated on a content of consciousness. Meditation allows one to discover these gaps which point to this larger freedom of mind.

Samadhi. A stillness of mind arrived at through meditation. This does not necessarily mean that thoughts do not arise, but in *samadhi* the mind is not distracted or disturbed by them.

Samsara. The state of suffering and confusion that results from not being in touch with our true nature as human beings.

Satori [Japanese]. In the Zen tradition, a moment of sudden enlightenment.

Vajrayana Buddhism. Tantric Buddhism, which developed primarily in Northern India and Tibet. While based on mindfulness practice and the development of compassion, its orientation is toward working with the energies of the phenomenal world and transmuting negative forces and emotions into qualities of awakened mind.

Vipassana. Panoramic awareness, which develops out of mindfulness practice. This larger awareness is not imprisoned in an egocentric perspective, but rather can see the interactions of self-and-world as one whole event. *Vipassana* practice is the meditation which develops this kind of awareness.

Zazen [Japanese]. A Zen Buddhist term for the practice of meditation.

Zen Buddhism. The most influential form of Buddhism in Japan, based on the simple realization of awakened mind through *zazen* and *koan* practice.

Bibliography

Benoit, H. *The Supreme Doctrine*. New York: Viking, 1955.

Blyth, R. H. *Zen in English Literature and Oriental Classics*. New York: Dutton, 1960.

Castaneda, C. *Tales of Power*. New York: Simon & Schuster, 1974.

Cox, H. *Turning East*. New York: Simon & Schuster, 1977.

Freud, S. *New Introductory Lectures on Psychoanalysis*. New York: Norton, 1933.

Gendlin, E. T. "A Theory of Personality Change." In *Personality Change*, edited by P. Worchel and D. Byrne. New York: Wiley, 1964.

Gendlin, E. T. *Focusing*. New York: Everest House, 1979.

Gendlin, E. T.; Beebe, J.; Cassens, J.; Klein, M.; and Oberlander, M. "Focusing Ability in Psychotherapy, Personality, and Creativity." In *Research in Psychotherapy*, Vol. III, edited by J. Schlien. Washington, D.C.: American Psychological Association, 1968.

Guenther, H., and Trungpa, C. *The Dawn of Tantra*. Boulder, Colo.: Shambhala Publications, 1975.

Hillman, J. *Emotion*. Evanston, Ill.: Northwestern University Press, 1961.

Hisamatsu, S. "The Characteristics of Oriental Nothingness." In *Philosophical Studies of Japan*, Vol. 2, translated by R. DeMartino. Tokyo: Maruzen, 1960.

Hume, D. *A Treatise on Human Nature.* Oxford: Clarendon Press, 1888.

James, W. *The Principles of Psychology.* New York: Henry Holt, 1890.

James, W. *The Writings of . . .* New York: Random House, 1967.

Lasch, C. *The Culture of Narcissism.* New York: Norton, 1978.

Maslow, A. *The Farther Reaches of Human Nature.* New York: Viking, 1971.

Needleman, J., ed. *Speaking of My Life: The Art of Living in the Cultural Revolution.* San Francisco: Harper & Row, 1979.

Ornstein, R. *The Psychology of Consciousness.* San Francisco: W. H. Freeman, 1972.

Reps, P. *Zen Flesh, Zen Bones.* New York: Penguin, 1971.

Sartre, J. P. *Being and Nothingness.* New York: Philosophical Library, 1953.

Sartre, J. P. *The Transcendence of the Ego.* New York: Noonday Press, 1957.

Satprem. *Sri Aurobindo or the Adventure of Consciousness.* New York: Harper & Row, 1968.

Searles, H. *Countertransference and Related Subjects.* New York: International Universities Press, 1979.

Shapiro, D., and Walsh, R. *Beyond Health and Normality: Explorations in Exceptional Psychological Well-being.* New York: Van Nostrand, 1982.

Suzuki, D. T. *Introduction to Zen Buddhism.* London: Rider, 1949.

Suzuki, D. T. *Zen and Japanese Culture.* Princeton, N.J.: Princeton University Press, 1959.

Tarthang Tulku. "On Thoughts." *Crystal Mirror* 3 (1974): 7–20.

Tarthang Tulku. *Openness Mind.* Emeryville, Ca.: Dharma Press, 1978.

Tomlinson, T., and Hart, J. "A Validation of the Process Scale." *Journal of Consulting Psychology* 26 (1962): 74–78.

Trungpa, C. *Meditation in Action.* Boulder, Colo.: Shambhala Publications, 1969.

Trungpa, C. *Cutting through Spiritual Materialism.* Boulder, Colo.: Shambhala Publications, 1973.

Trungpa, C. *The Myth of Freedom.* Boulder, Colo.: Shambhala Publications, 1976.

van Kaam, A. *Spirituality and the Gentle Life.* Denville, N.J.: Dimension Books, 1974.

Walker, A.; Rablen, R.; and Rogers, C.R. "Development of a Scale to Measure Process Change in Psychotherapy." *Journal of Clinical Psychology* 16 (1959): 79–85.

Welwood, J. "On Psychological Space." *Journal of Transpersonal Psychology* 9 (1977): 97–118.

Welwood, J., ed. *The Meeting of the Ways: Explorations in East/West Psychology.* New York: Schocken, 1979.

Welwood, J. "The Unfolding of Experience: Psychotherapy and Beyond." *Journal of Humanistic Psychology* 22 (1982): 91–104.

Welwood, J., and Wilber, K. "On Ego Strength and Egolessness." In *The Meeting of the Ways: Explorations in East/West Psychology,* edited by J. Welwood. New York: Schocken, 1979.

Acknowledgments

I would like to extend my appreciation to the authors and publishers who granted permission to reprint copyrighted material in this volume. I would also like to thank Barbara Green, Joanne Martin, and Mary Goodell for their help and feedback with some of my own contributions to this book.

Chapters 1 and 2 are condensed from chapters which appeared in *On the Way to Self Knowledge* (Knopf, 1976), edited by Jacob Needleman and Dennis Lewis and reprinted by permission of the authors.

Chapters 3 and 6 are excerpted from *Zero*, Volume II, 1979, by permission of Zero Press.

Chapter 4 is a revised version of an article, "Reflections on Psychotherapy, Focusing, and Meditation," which appeared in the *Journal of Transpersonal Psychology*, Volume 12, 1980, pp. 127–42.

Chapter 5 is an excerpt from "Psychoanalysis and Zen Buddhism" in *Zen Buddhism and Psychoanalysis* by D. T. Suzuki, Erich Fromm, and Richard DeMartino. Copyright© 1960 by Erich Fromm. Reprinted by permission of Harper & Row Publishers, Inc.

Chapter 7 is reprinted from Karl Sperber, "Psychotherapeutic Materialism," *Journal of Humanistic Psychology*, Vol. 19, pp. 65–69. Copyright © 1979 by the Association of Humanistic Psychology, with permission of Sage Publications, Inc.

Chapter 8 is revised and adapted from an article, "Befriending Emotion: Self-Knowledge and Transformation," which appeared in the *Journal of Transpersonal Psychology,* Volume 11, 1979, pp. 141–60.

Chapter 9 is excerpted from *Humanitas,* Volume 12, 1976, pp. 256–76, by permission of the author.

Chapter 10 is reprinted in a condensed form by permission of the author.

Chapter 11 is adapted from a lecture given by Chögyam Trungpa at the Naropa Institute Psychology Symposium in the summer of 1978. It originally appeared in slightly different form in the *Naropa Institute Journal of Psychology,* Volume 1, Number 1, 1980, pp. 4–20. Copyright 1980 by Chögyam Trungpa. Reprinted by permission of the author.

Chapter 12 comprises excerpts from various chapters of the book *Existential Metapsychiatry* by Thomas Hora. Copyright © 1977 by the Seabury Press, Inc. Used by permission.

Chapter 13 is condensed from a chapter in *Zen in the Art of Helping* by David Brandon. Copyright © 1976 by David Brandon. Reprinted by permission of Routledge & Kegan Paul Ltd.

Chapter 14 is adapted by permission from an article, "Vulnerability and Power in the Therapeutic Process: Existential and Buddhist Perspectives," which appeared in the *Journal of Transpersonal Psychology,* Vol. 14, pp. 125–40.

Chapter 15 is reprinted from "Nondeterministic Supervision," by Diane Shainberg, which appeared in *Studies in Nondeterministic Psychology,* edited by Gerald Epstein. Copyright © 1980 by Human Sciences Press, Inc. Used by permission.

Chapter 16 is printed by permission of the author.

Chapter 17 is condensed from an article, "The History of Sanity in Contemplative Psychotherapy," which appeared in the *Naropa Institute Journal of Psychology,* Volume 2, 1983. By permission of Nalanda Press.

Chapter 18 is reprinted from the *Naropa Institute Journal of Psychology,* Volume 1, 1980, pp. 58–69. By permission of Nalanda Press.

Index